KD

KIDDERMINSTER

19. FEB. 10.

11 APR 11

14. 05. 11
09. AUG 11.
27. 6. 16

Please return/renew this item by the last date shown

worcestershire
countycouncil
Libraries & Learning

7000305891?X

D0487704

WAKING UP IN TOYTOWN

By the same author

FICTION

The Dumb House
The Mercy Boys
Burning Elvis
The Locust Room
Living Nowhere
The Devil's Footprints
Glister

POETRY

The hoop
Common Knowledge
Feast Days
The Myth of the Twin
Swimming in the Flood
A Normal Skin
The Asylum Dance
The Light Trap
The Good Neighbour
Selected Poems
Gift Songs
The Hunt in the Forest

NON-FICTION

A Lie About My Father

WAKING UP IN TOYTOWN

John Burnside

JONATHAN CAPE
LONDON

Published by Jonathan Cape 2010

2 4 6 8 10 9 7 5 3 1

Copyright © John Burnside 2010

John Burnside has asserted his right under the Copyright, Designs
and Patents Act 1988 to be identified as the author of this work

This book is substantially a work of non-fiction based on the life, experiences and recollections
of the author. In some cases names of people, places, dates, sequences or the detail of events
have been changed solely to protect the privacy of others. The author has stated to the
publishers that, except in such minor respects, the contents of this book are true.

This book is sold subject to the condition that it shall not,
by way of trade or otherwise, be lent, resold, hired out,
or otherwise circulated without the publisher's prior
consent in any form of binding or cover other than that
in which it is published and without a similar condition,
including this condition, being imposed
on the subsequent purchaser.

First published in Great Britain in 2010 by
Jonathan Cape
Random House, 20 Vauxhall Bridge Road,
London SW1V 2SA

www.rbooks.co.uk

Addresses for companies within The Random House Group Limited can be found at:
www.randomhouse.co.uk/offices.htm

The Random House Group Limited Reg. No. 954009

A CIP catalogue record for this book
is available from the British Library

ISBN 9780224080736

The Random House Group Limited supports The Forest Stewardship
Council (FSC), the leading international forest certification organisation. All our titles that are
printed on Greenpeace approved FSC certified paper carry the FSC logo. Our paper procure-
ment policy can be found at www.rbooks.co.uk/environment

Mixed Sources
Product group from well-managed
forests and other controlled sources
www.fsc.org Cert no. TT-COC-2139
© 1996 Forest Stewardship Council
FSC

Typeset in Adobe Garamond by Palimpsest Book Production Limited,
Grangemouth, Stirlingshire
Printed and bound in Great Britain by
CPI Mackays, Chatham, Kent ME5 8TD

My heart passionately cried out against all my phantoms, and with this one blow I sought to beat away from the eye of my mind all that unclean troop which buzzed around it.

Augustine of Hippo

But the worst consequence is the romance conferred on doubtful actions; until the child grows to think nothing more glorious than to be struck dead in the act of some surprising wickedness. I can never again take so much interest in anything, as I took, in childhood, in doing for its own sake what I believed to be sinful.

Robert Louis Stevenson

Flight is intolerable contradiction.

Muriel Rukeyser

This book is as factually accurate as memory allows. Some of the characters, especially the homicidally inclined, have been camouflaged for their own protection.

CONTENTS

THE EPILOGUE

Not so long ago, when I was still mad, I found myself in the strangest lunatic asylum that I had ever seen. The atmosphere in *any* lunatic asylum is strange, of course, but the room in which I found myself on that occasion put me in mind of a certain type of church, one of those places where you stand waiting for God, or one of His minions, to arrive at any moment with Good News, or a foretaste of Armageddon, or both. Most of the other patients were middle-aged men, but there was one ancient soul in a wheelchair by the garden window, his face sallow, the skin on his head stretched too tight, his straggling grey beard spotted with egg yolk. There were no women present, which meant I was on a ward, but I wasn't in or near a bed, and it felt like the middle of the afternoon, when the majority of the patients should have been in a day room somewhere, filtering Bible verses and alien invasions from a daytime soap, or walking up and down the corridors reciting the seven times table to the fire extinguishers and the specially commissioned acrylics.

Something wasn't right. I must have sat in that room for three or four hours, wondering how I got there and waiting hopefully for someone to realise that a mistake had been made, but nothing happened. Nobody came, nothing was corrected. I wasn't even offered medication. Something definitely wasn't right. Those patients should have been doing something active, something that occupied their hands, maybe practising therapeutic craft skills in an art room somewhere, but here they were in this strange antechamber, sitting in stacking chairs and mumbling into their dressing gowns. And I was there with them, talking to the dead – which, I realised, was what I had been doing moments before I looked up and saw where I was – talking to a ghost who had been sitting opposite, just then, just there, her head slightly averted, her eyes avoiding mine. Who was she? I *had* been talking to her a moment before, and she had been listening, nodding slightly from time to time, but not speaking, and not looking at me either, her head turned away, looking off towards the outside. We had been there like that for some time and, now, suddenly, she was gone and I was in this room with all these men, and something definitely wasn't right.

I sat up straight in my chair then, and looked about. The others shifted slightly, adjusting their positions to mine, which is what always happens in places like that: one person moves and everyone else shifts accordingly, maintaining the balance of the room. I waited while everything slid back into place, then I turned my head slightly and saw that there was a nurse close by, sitting in a chair near the door, just eight or ten feet away. It was a male nurse, quite a young man, in a dark blue sweatshirt and black jeans. He looked as if he'd just come in from outside; he had that greenish, slightly cool quality to him. Perhaps he *had* just come in from outside, which was why I hadn't noticed him earlier, and now he was sitting in a plastic chair, craning forwards slightly, his elbows resting on his knees. He was reading a book: it was the old Penguin Classics edition of *Notes from Underground*.

2

'Hello?' I said.

He gave me a look of what appeared to be good-humoured recognition, but he didn't answer.

I shifted slightly in my seat and the room shifted too, but he seemed not to notice. 'I think I missed my medication,' I said.

He smiled wryly and shook his head. 'I know,' he said. 'You told me already.'

'What?'

'You missed your meds,' he said. 'You told me already.' He wasn't smiling now, though he seemed at ease. He looked at his watch. 'That was about ten minutes ago,' he said.

I shook my head. 'No,' I said.

'Yes.'

'That wasn't me,' I said. 'It must have been –'

'Well, never mind,' he said. 'It doesn't matter. You didn't miss your medication. OK?'

I nodded. He was right, of course, I hadn't missed my medication. It was just that I *felt* as if I had. Which meant, of course – and this came as a sudden revelation, which made the place seem even more like a church than ever – that there was no point in my being there. Because why would I be there if the meds weren't working? Why would I be sitting in this room with all these middle-aged men and this sarcastic young man with his Penguin Classics *Notes from Underground* and that terribly old man with the egg-yolk beard, when I could be somewhere else? Of course, I wasn't at all clear where that somewhere else might be, but I did know that a somewhere else existed. So why not go there, now?

I looked at myself. I was dressed in clothes I recognised. I wasn't covered in grime or vomit or blood, I was wearing a shirt and jeans and a pair of Caterpillar-style work boots.

3

I could have been out for the day, waiting at a country station for the train to arrive. I wasn't *normal*, but then, there was nothing obviously abnormal about me. If I had been sitting in a waiting room at some branch-line station and somebody had come in to wait for the same train I was waiting for, would he have known that I was a lunatic? Probably not.

I stood up.

The nurse lifted his head, but he didn't put down his book. I gave him a quick, no-problem-just-off-to-the-loo glance and he returned to Dostoevsky. My mind was utterly clear now: I hadn't been sectioned, so I could do what I liked, but to avoid any kind of fuss, I would just leave, because if I *mentioned* I was leaving they would make me wait to see a doctor before discharging myself, and then they would go through the necessary steps of telling me that I had only just been admitted – I was fairly sure I had only just been admitted – and that I was therefore acting against medical advice and so on and so on, and I didn't want to go through all that. And there was no reason to believe that this lunatic asylum was any different from the others I had attended, which meant I was free to go out and walk about in the grounds, which in turn meant nobody would take much notice as I headed towards the door – though, of course, if I really *had* been admitted very recently they would be keeping an eye on me because I was a new patient and they did that, when they didn't just put you out altogether for that first therapeutic sleep which does so much to set common or garden lunatics like me on their way to a gradual, but full, recovery. And so on.

By this time, I was walking down the corridor. It was a long corridor with a wood-panelled wall on one side and full-length windows on the other, through which I could see a mass of the shrubby Victorian ground cover typical of such

4

institutions, dark-hearted and damp and speckled with watery sunlight. And then, out of nowhere, a voice came.

'All right, John?'

It was a woman's voice and it sounded friendly. Not even concerned, just passing the time of day, making sure I wasn't lost or troubled in my mind. I turned and smiled. The woman was standing in a doorway I had just passed: petite, early-middle-aged, she wore thick-soled tennis shoes, greyish slacks and a white blouse. Something about her seemed familiar, but I couldn't work out what it was.

'I thought I'd take a walk,' I said. 'While it's sunny.'

She nodded. 'All right,' she said. 'Don't go *too* far.'

My hand flickered upwards, as if to allow itself an autonomous mad wave, but I managed to regain control. 'I won't,' I said, still smiling as I turned round and continued, in no hurry whatsoever, just a man going for a walk, for no particular reason, on a warm summer's afternoon.

Where I live now there's a road that runs past the front of the house and away, over the brow of the hill, towards the village and the sea beyond. It's a narrow road, with trees on one side and fields on the other and, since I can't see over the hill, it's like the road in the dream I've had ever since I was a child, the road that leads to the afterlife – but sometimes, in a certain light, it reminds me of the road I walked back then, on the day I left my last lunatic asylum, certain that someone would come after me and try to take me back. I walked a long time and, I have to say, it did me the world of good. Walking usually does.

When I *was* a full-scale lunatic, I suffered from a condition called apophenia. This condition, this unease, was described by Klaus Conrad, the schizophrenia specialist who coined the term, as *the unmotivated seeing of connections,* coupled with the *specific experience of an abnormal meaning-fulness.* In other words, seeing things that weren't there. Hearing voices in the background static. Finding God or the Devil in the last scrapings of Pot Noodle. For normal folk, this connective faculty allows them to make sense of the world, to find a modest, local and hopefully *shared* order by which to live. For the apophenic, it means a wild and unrelenting search for the one vast order that transcends all others, a hypernarrative, an *afterlife* – though what he ends up with is usually a tidal wave of incomprehensible and overwhelming detail: the whole world at once, jabbering constantly in a mind that can only find rest in oblivion. I still suffer from this condition, though only very occasionally. It's far milder than it was, but I can't quite put my hand on my heart and say that I am one of those people who mistakes the Holy Ghost for a gust of wind. I also continue to suffer from occasional bouts of insomnia and, when I do, my favourite remedy is to go out in the dark and stand in the road, as if about to walk off somewhere. Mostly, I sleep better than I once did, but there are times when I lapse back into the old insomniac pattern and, when I do, this road is my remedy. There's never any traffic here at night, and I can stand out under the moon, listening to the quiet – and, if there *were* such a thing as a transcendent order, if the afterlife really did exist, the way to get there would look something like this: a road, a meadow, dusk at the fence line, maybe a fox on its early-morning rounds in the whitening grass.

And, as it happens, I still believe there *is* an afterlife. This morning, in the first sunshine, I caught a glimpse of it again as I was walking home through the frosted woods, the rose hips turning to slush in an unexpected thaw and all around me a silence that I could feel, sudden and considered, like the caught breath of the choir before they sing the Kyrie. I had risen in the dark and walked off down that paradise road while my wife and children slept, the first time I'd been out and about by myself for what felt like weeks, and I was happier than I remembered being in a long time, thinking about the coal towns of my childhood and my lunatic-asylum days and watching them quietly dwindle into a past that no longer seemed mine, a past of history books, or television documentaries. A past of memoir, orderly and contained, almost annotated and no longer subject to the flow of time. I remembered the close where I played as a child, and the woods full of rubble and clinker as if they were something I had invented to pass the time on a long bus ride, and I saw the people I had sat with on Sunday afternoons, watching their eyes and fingers as they considered the corned beef sandwiches, or poured tea into bone-china cups that, to the child I once was, seemed both eternal and impossibly fine. *Bone china.* They liked to repeat those words, all the aunts and grown-up cousins and neighbours: *bone china*, a rare instance of something delicate and beautiful in their lives, the interior of every cup, the painted roses on the rim of every saucer impeccably clean and strangely reassuring, though we were all of us terrified, for as long as they were set out, that an accident might happen and one of the set – almost certainly a wedding gift, or what passed for an heirloom in those parts – might be broken or damaged. I knew those people the way I knew the labels on the corned beef tins and the pink and leaf-green patterns on the cups and saucers; they were just as familiar to me, and just as perishable. Sometimes, when Auntie Sall or my cousin Madeleine offered me a slice of cake and, after glancing off to one side for my mother's approval, I lifted a plate and held it trembling

7

in mid-air to accept that dense slab of fruit and marzipan and
snowy icing studded with hundreds and thousands, I was struck
by the terrible idea that all of them – my mother, my aunts,
my cousins – would soon be dead, and that I didn't know
where death would take them. Though I was still deeply religious then, a Catholic boy thinking of the priesthood, I had
abandoned the promise of heaven, partly because it seemed so
obviously contrived for comfort's sake, but mostly because,
when I thought about what it might be like, I always pictured
the communal washrooms behind my Aunt Margaret's house,
off-white, low-ceilinged and dull, the air heavy with the smell
of laundry powder and starch. I remember, once, I was with
my mother, out on one of our walks, when it occurred to me
that the dead go back into the land, not just their bodies, but
their souls too, the ineffable fabric of memories and knowledge that I knew was there, in each one of them, and I thought I
could see, in my mother's face, the greenish shadow of what was
to come, an old, dark gravity to it like the rainwater that
gathered in the stone cisterns out by the water houses, and yet
there was a sweetness there too, a hint of lily of the valley and
cut grass. That impression only lasted a moment, yet it stayed
with me – has stayed with me, in fact, till now – and I have
never quite given it up because, however ridiculous it seems
to talk about an afterlife, it is part of the story I have to tell,
when I am telling myself who I am. It is not an afterlife in
the usual sense, but it is a story that I can tolerate, because at
its heart is the knowledge that the dead do not stay with us,
watching over our adult lives as they watched over us in childhood, they do not even continue in any recognisable form,
though the world continues and something of what they were
continues with it. Sometimes my son asks me what I think
about all this, and I remember that waterish green shadow on

my mother's face, but I never talk about that. I talk about ideas and notions, myths and memories, but I cannot tell him what I truly believe – which is that both the dead who were once our own and the lunatic *I* once was disappear into a narrative that, year by year, seems more and more like a story – and I can't find the words to say the one other thing I know in this matter, which is that the dead we once knew, but who were never ours, the dead who never belonged to anyone, not even themselves, will go on forever, or some element of them will, folding endlessly into rain and leaves and new animals hunting in the first grey of dawn. I will not call that heaven, or an afterlife, because it wouldn't be right to give it a name, just as it wouldn't be right for me to tell my son that I will never leave him, yet it is something I know, on mornings like this, as the dead I remember dwindle to nothing, and the lunatic memories I thought were mine become part of an anonymous fabric of events. There is a technical term for this, a term for the state in which all memories – my own, those I have borrowed, those I have invented, those that have been implanted, with or without my consent – are equally valid, equally real or unreal. Some people call it *post-memory*, a phenomenon we could easily rationalise by talking about the ocean of information and imagery and narrative that surrounds us, but I don't think that this is the whole explanation. The known dead recede into stories and mingle with those we never knew so that the world can continue and they can move on, into the world to come – and this morning, as I walked back up the hill I could feel them all around me, shifting aside, making space for the future, just as I finally sensed that old lunatic self, who had stayed with me, like a faint shadow, was beginning to flake away and vanish into the air.

* * *

In the early days of television, there was a programme they showed late at night, called *The Epilogue*. I think I remember a man, a clergyman perhaps, talking directly to the viewer, offering words of comfort and inspiration, words that suggested an inherent and utterly dependable order to the world. This was what order meant, at that time – and *The Epilogue* was a quaint and faintly touching advertisement for this order. It said that, if you placed yourself in the hands of someone – or something – wiser and more established than yourself, then order would come into your life, the way Christmas and bank holidays came, with nothing required from you, the customer, beyond a quiet and perfectly understandable acceptance. It was a programme my mother liked to watch, not so much for the religious sentiments expressed as for the presenter's air of gentle conviction, a faith that was neither strident nor complacent, neither Presbyterian nor Catholic, a matter more of ginger biscuits and Ceylon tea than actual theology. I have no doubt that there is more to ginger biscuits and tea than there is to theology, especially if bone china is involved, but this morning, as I came up through the woods, everything white and still around me, I felt an odd nostalgia for the God of my childhood – or if not God, then the Holy Ghost, the one who looked like a bird, when He bothered to look like anything at all. The late-night clergy didn't usually talk about him, which was a stroke of luck, all things considered. Instead, they concerned themselves with the day-to-day problems of being in the world, with having to deal with other people, and marriage and such, which meant I had the Holy Ghost all to myself, a private mystery to carry out into the fields and the woods, a subtlety in the shadows of the water houses or the unroofed barn at the far end of the Old Perth Road – and I suppose, as I climbed the hill this morning, He or maybe

It was with me still, going along with me through the frozen world, a slightly animal presence in spite of His or Its catechismal invisibility, my one dogged companion, on the way to the afterlife of here and now.

SURBITON

'Hi. My name is John and I am an alcoholic.'

So there it was. I had said it. I had been planning to say it for weeks, and now I had. Nothing original, and nothing fancy, just the standard wording, the prescribed formula that I had heard from those who preceded me, spoken aloud and duly acknowledged. Only, now that I had said it, I could see that something was wrong. Something was not as it should be. There was no weight to what I was saying, no gravitas, and no one in that high, brown, rather melancholy room was entirely convinced – least of all me. I could see it in their faces: I wasn't there yet, I was faking, *faking it to make it*, or maybe just faking it, because I was supposed to have reached this point already, wasn't I? I was supposed to have achieved some kind of perspective, I was supposed to have looked at myself in a new light and been humbled by what I saw, humbled and shamed enough to speak out and maybe accept a higher power into my life, because I couldn't do it all by myself, that was obvious enough. But I hadn't spoken out and I hadn't accepted anything into my life and, over the last several weeks, over the last several months, in fact, my silence had been deafening.

Not that I hadn't shown willing. I'd gone to the meetings, day after day: Mondays and Thursdays in this place,

Wednesdays and Sundays in another high brown room supplied by the Quakers, Tuesdays, Fridays and Saturdays at a mousy-smelling church building in Guildford. I liked these brown rooms, and I liked the people who came to the meetings to tell their stories and dole out coffee and biscuits to the newer arrivals. They were graceful and kindly and they were capable of speaking of that 'higher power' without embarrassment, and I was fond of them in any number of ways, but I knew I didn't belong *with* them, and I knew they knew it too. I was faking. Everybody knew that – and everybody knew that *I* knew it. I had said the words, but that was all I had done. What I had said may well have been the truth, but the way I said it turned those words into a lie.

'Hi, John.'

And there it was. The stock response. Twelve, maybe fifteen voices in unison, responding in the set manner, according to the book. They knew I didn't believe, but they carried on undaunted, willing me towards recovery – and, as soon as the words were out, I felt sad, not for myself, but for them. Because what I had said was wrong –

Hi. My name is John and –

What was it? Where was the flaw? Where was the lie? Was it the informality of *Hi?* Should it have been something else? *Hello? Good evening? Sorry to trouble you but . . . ?*

Or was it maybe that I didn't feel comfortable with such an unqualified admission? Because as soon as I got to the end of that bald statement –

My name is John and I am an alcoholic –

I realised that I'd been hoping all along for the small, but significant grace note of a *but –*

Hi. My name is John and I'm an alcoholic, but then again –

Or maybe –

14

Hi. My name is John and I'm an alcoholic, sort of. A bit of a dope fiend, too, at the end of the day. Any port in a storm, when it comes down to it –

No.

I had said the words and I had stopped in the right place, but I'd been thinking of something else – and I hadn't quite made it. I hadn't done anything, in fact, that I hadn't done all my life, repeating the memorised text demanded by the occasion in which I happened to find myself –

Credo in unum Deum.

Sorry. I won't do it again.

Of course I love you –

So there we were, in that longish room, woody and a little too dry, like an oversized Scout Hall. The windows were high and narrow, the walls were painted a soft oatmeal colour, the furniture was old and covered with dents and bruises. Nothing was *terribly* brown in this room, yet the overall sense was *of* brownness, the sad brown of the presbytery and of hospital corridors, the brown of public spaces where people come and go, doing what they do for love or self-improvement. In one corner, a large urn simmered: after an hour, we would all get up and drink instant coffee from chipped mugs, while the older men, the ones with eight or ten or even twenty years of sobriety, dispensed sugar and biscuits and inspirational litera-ture. At the end of the formal meeting, I found myself alone, silent, and slightly shamefaced; then a big, horsy-looking man called Harry came to where I was and sat down next to me. For a long moment, he just sat there, his face and hands soft and totally at rest, the way they might have been for a lost child or a bird trapped in a conservatory.

'Give it time,' he said.

15

I didn't look at him to begin with, then I did. I was thinking of something, a memory, half formed at the back of my mind. A memory from long ago. I nodded, but I didn't speak.

'You wouldn't believe me if I told you that it gets easier,' he said. 'But it does get better.'

I nodded again. I had found the memory, and I was following the line of it into another brown room, a room from long ago, but not unlike the one where we were all sitting, with our coffee and biscuits and roll-ups. It was in the days of tuberculosis, when I had to have a chest X-ray, and everyone was scared, because people remembered TB and what it could do. I didn't know why I was having this *check-up*; I couldn't recall what my supposed symptoms were, but there I was, in the memory, standing in a brown room, waiting to be attended to. And I remembered being happy. I remembered being fond of that brown room. I remembered liking the smell of it, that stale dust and liniment smell, and I remembered being totally unconcerned about the outcome. I think I was hoping to die, not necessarily in a beautiful way, like some Romantic hero out of a book, but with a modicum of colour and satisfaction. I was fifteen, I think. I liked Mussorgsky and foreign books and the colour brown and I wasn't very good company.

Finally, I was summoned into the presence of a lady doctor. She studied me closely, presumably trying to assess my frame of mind, or maybe this was just one final check that I wasn't at death's door after all – then she asked me questions, none of which seemed relevant to the TB scare, or to anything else for that matter. I think she sensed trouble in me and, out of curiosity, or concern, or both, she was trying to put her finger on something and I was suddenly aware of my bad clothes, my poverty, my profound immaturity. She was rather beautiful, this doctor, and it bothered me that she was beautiful, because she was so remote, so much a part of a faraway, privileged world.

'So, you like books?' she said.

I looked at her. I was puzzled by the question. 'Yes,' I said. 'I like books. Why do you ask?'

She smiled and pointed at the fat hardback in my anorak pocket. I had forgotten about that. It was a library book I had brought along, in case I had to sit for hours in a queue. D. H. Lawrence. A volume from that old edition with the dark green covers, though I've forgotten which one. 'I'm curious,' she said, with the tiniest stress on the *curious*. 'Is Lawrence a favourite of yours?'

I looked at her. I was fifteen years old, and I didn't know anybody I liked, but I wanted to go back to her world and do with her whatever people did there: have a gin and tonic and talk about the cinema, go out to a French restaurant for dinner, come home early and make love for hours in an upstairs room in the suburbs, the curtains half drawn and everything – the furniture, the bed, the pictures on the walls – transformed to a dusky gold by the orange street lights. I looked at her and I wanted to say, yes, sure, *Sons and Lovers*, it's a classic, after all; but I didn't, because the truth was, I hadn't been enjoying this book at all, and I was more than a little disappointed by D. H. Lawrence in general. I suppose part of me knew that I was too young and inexperienced to get it, or, at least, to get it *right*, in all its psychological and sexual subtlety – but I also felt entitled to my disappointment. It was mine and, even if I didn't know why, I knew that there was something *just* about it. I shook my head. 'I don't know,' I said. 'I think I was expecting more.'

She gave an odd little laugh at that. It was a kindly laugh, an indulgent laugh, but it didn't stop me feeling slightly angry with her, because she had seen through me, of course she had, but even there she had missed the point, because I wasn't the precocious working-class boy that she thought I was. I wasn't *quite* the naive autodidact that she fancied me to be, and I was far from being as innocent or bookish as I seemed. In fact, I was something from another kind of novel altogether, a more desperate and empty novel, with my solemn indifference to death and my dreams of blood and linen. I didn't want to be educated enough to understand the ins and outs of D. H. Lawrence, I wanted a room at the end of a brown corridor, with a view of street trees and crimson road lights. I wanted time to stop, I wanted to linger forever over some small and local act of destruction, a wounding, say, or a slow, drawn-out torture, my own, or another's, it didn't matter. My own, or hers. I mean: what was my disappointment with D. H. Lawrence compared to that?

And, all of a sudden, I had it. *That* was the qualification I had been looking for, earlier, when I had said my piece. I had wanted to say, *Good evening, my name is John and I know alcohol is not a pleasure, I know drinking is not something to be enjoyed, like tea, or flirting. Alcohol is a substitute for something else, but I can't give it up because, if I do, I'll remember that something else, and that something else is an unbearable, and at the same time, impossible desire, and the only thing that stops me from remembering that desire, that brown room with the crimson lights at the end of that dark corridor, is a drink, and no matter what happens, no matter what idiocies I inflict upon myself, nothing is as bad, or as beguiling, as that room –*

But I didn't say any of this. I kept on going to the meetings and I kept on trying to convince myself that I was going to make it, because making it was the first step on the path to a normal life, and that was what I wanted, more than anything. A normal life. Sober. Drug-free. Dreamless. In gainful employment. A householder. A taxpayer. A name on the electoral roll. A regular, everyday sort of guy. The next-door neighbour whose name you can never remember, the one who keeps himself to himself, but is basically OK. I wanted, in short, to be comfortably numb. It was the early eighties: prime-time Conservative backlash era. The big picture was suddenly painfully grey, all tomorrow's parties had come to an end and *I* had pretty well run out of options. The only hope I had left was to disappear into normality and hope nobody from the old world followed me down the tunnel.

So I went to the suburbs.

I went to the suburbs because I wished to live deliberately, to front only the essential facts of life, and see if I could not learn what they had to teach, and not when I came to die, discover that I had not lived. I wanted the order that other people seemed to have, the non-apophenic order of a normal life. A normal life, as a normal person – in Surbiton, or some-where like it.

It was a ridiculous idea, but I didn't really have much of a choice. Six months before that AA meeting, I had been rescued from my own private bedlam and, to keep myself from sliding right back into it, I had decided to disappear, like some disgraced character in a Victorian novel who vanishes into the fog at Chatham Docks and surfaces years later in the Far East, or the penal colonies. Unlike my fictional ancestors, however, I didn't take myself away to Siam, or to the engine room of some ocean-going vessel. I went to Surrey. What I had in mind was office work, tea, hedge clippings, crosswords, Ovaltine. What I had in mind, in other words, was Surbiton. No more good times, and no more wandering from place to place, living in squats and bedsits, subsisting on kitchen porter's wages, always on the edge of a drift that might take me to some mental facility in the green belt, or the anonymous powder blue of casualty, always on the lookout for the happy deal that would end in a fog of sweet wine and barbiturates, or the fleeting good luck of pharmacy-grade narcotics.

It wasn't the life my mother would have chosen for me; it wasn't even the life I had chosen for myself. I had simply drifted into it, out of weakness and indifference and, to begin with, it had been oddly satisfying, even rather wonderful. Over the last two or three years of that wasted decade, however, I had begun to see that my life had taken a very wrong turn indeed and, by the time I came up with the idea of Surbiton, I was oscillating between *Schadenfreude* and terror, between the momentary joy of self-erasure and the dread of ending up in some cramped, squalid place with the wrong kind of people and no way out. And all the while, I had been telling myself to *stop*. Ever since I had started going off the rails in my mid-teens, there had been a voice in my head repeating, over and over, that I needed to pull myself together, a sensible voice that, as luck would have it, sounded just like everyone I'd ever mistrusted – all those nuns and teachers and professional helpers whose thankless task it is to deal with people like me. That voice kept talking at me, but the good advice fell on deaf ears and for a while I didn't think I'd ever change – but then, towards the end of that long drift, I found myself suspended between what I had come to think of as my own special brand of hyperlucidity and a delusive, paranoid state of grace that could only be properly managed in a psych ward, and I knew that the only way to avoid an eternity of picture windows and Largactil and tasteless breakfasts laced with bran was to get away from everything I knew and start again as somebody different. Somebody normal.

So I made my plan – though plan is rather a grand name for a series of events in which I played such a small part. For as every down-and-out knows, a time comes when nothing can be decided, when everything depends on *grace* – and, though I hadn't seen it yet, I had reached that point. Or I think I had. My memory of that time is more than a little confused, and I can't fully account for how I got clear. What I do recall is a room that I can picture so precisely, it doesn't feel like a memory at all. It's more like the film I saw last night, or a photograph from a magazine where the central figure is strangely familiar, even if he isn't *quite* the person whose name first comes to mind. This central character – the one vague spot in a memory that is otherwise extremely vivid – is familiar in the way that an actor in an old black-and-white film noir would be familiar if I saw him out of context, crossing the road in my home town, maybe, or paying his bill at the cafe on the high street. Farley Granger, say, or John Garfield, or the snivelly would-be blackmailer that Humphrey Bogart has to slap around for a while in some old Howard Hawks movie. Now that this is a story I am telling – and it's *me* telling it, not *him* – I can accept that the central figure in this scene is a version of myself, or at least someone I used to be; but when I say as much, it seems wrong, because what I recall is so obviously an actor or an impostor playing a role, and even that role, even the character he is *pretending* to be, is not the person I think of now when I try to summon up the image of *myself then*.

In fact, everything in this scene has an aura of fiction to it, even though I know that it actually happened, more or less as I recall. In the grubby room that I see in my mind's eye, the person who looks like me is sitting on an unmade bed, gazing at himself in the plain, almost full-length mirror that, to

21

create an illusion of space, has been fixed to the wall adjacent to the one window. The room is small, with few furnishings and no ornaments: just the bed, the mirror and, in the far corner, a laminate wardrobe which, in this atypical instance, is crammed with clear glass bottles – clear, not green, not brown, and all of them full almost to the brim with the same sweet-smelling dark gold liquid that can also be found in the dozen or so bottles that have been placed at precise intervals around the bed. This liquid is a mixture of blood, honey, alcohol, olive oil and urine; the bottles are open, there are no screw-top caps or lids, just a single feather, balanced precariously on each rim. If one feather falls, then the spell fails – so it is important that every last one of them stays balanced, for this spell has been carefully devised to protect the man on the bed, who is naked and, though he is not frightened now, has recently witnessed an event that, even if it only happened in the private screening room of his own demented imagination, was terrifying enough to pin him to this spot, in a tangle of damp, grimy bedlinen, for the past two days. Now, looking back, I do not know exactly what it is that he has seen. Even though I am, or once was, *him*, I have no memory of that particular nightmare. Yet I am certain, from those I do recall, that he would have been awake throughout. Awake, to all appearances rational and, at the same time, entirely persuaded that everything he has witnessed is *real.*

At the point where I remember him, he is calm, in spite of the nightmare; calm, though not at peace. He has simply come to the end of every possible train of thought and has finally fallen quiet. He is waiting, that is all. Waiting; resigned; ready to surrender. His nightmare vision has faded and now he is suspended in its aftermath. He no longer sees demons and beasts flaring out of the dark around his bed; he no longer feels worms boring holes in his flesh or embroidering his skin with a filigree of decay. He no longer hears someone screaming in the street below, a faraway sound that he has strained to make out for hours at a time, even though what he wants more than anything is for it to stop. Now, finally, he and the world are quiet; now, though he is incapable of sleep, incapable even of closing his eyes, he is exhausted. He knows that the end of the world is coming – yet in spite, or perhaps because of his exhaustion, he is surprised by the realisation that it will be a slow, even gentle end, not the cataclysm he would have expected, no *après moi le déluge*, just a gradual withering away – a slow, physical dissolution, over weeks, or months, or even years, till nothing is left. He knows this because he has seen it, as if in a vision.

Today, looking back, it's hard to know what preceded this moment, or what peculiar logic governed this character's actions in the hours leading up to his abandonment. I think, when he began the project of the bottles, his intention was to cast a spell that would stop the world from disintegrating: he wanted to bind everything together, to make it hold. Later, though, having accepted the inevitability of disaster, he probably saw what he had done as a way of protecting himself, not from the coming dissolution – which would, by definition, be all-consuming – but from having to witness it. Because what he has come to expect is not the violent end portrayed in some nineteenth-century painting of the Apocalypse, where the earth shatters at God's command and the whole of nature cascades into the void. No: what he sees is a slow rot, a quiet, yet agonising fade into nothingness. A man wakes and goes from room to room, searching for the children he put to bed the night before, or for the wife who might be taking a shower, or having an early breakfast in the sunlit kitchen. A cinema audience emerges blinking into the daylight from a matinee and the town they knew has almost completely disappeared, with just a few scrubby trees and a street lamp, or a scatter of bedlinen and broken crockery to show that it was ever there. This is the way the world ends, not with a bang but with a series of almost imperceptible whimpers – and this is what appals him: not the fact that everything is about to end, but that the collapse will happen piecemeal, first here, then somewhere else, one thing disintegrating, then another, while the rest of the machinery continues to function. This is the worst, this vision of slow, but total decay. For the world was bound to end – he knew that – but he hadn't expected the cruelty of a drawn-out horror in which the victims would be so vividly aware of what was happening to them. He hadn't imagined that they would be singled out, one after another, for such a slow and painful corruption, not just mental and spiritual, but *physical*: fat and muscle and bone collapsing in on itself over hours or even days, till all that remains is a last howl of pain and rage and the horror of those who are left, knowing that, sooner or later, they too are destined to suffer that long and apparently futile disintegration, a disintegration so total that it will eliminate, not just this world, but the world to come. The afterlife. And this, I think, is what troubles him most, that person who used to be me: that the afterlife will be discontinued, along with everything else, and he will never see the light of a new morning, where the dead wait to welcome us like ushers at a wedding, guiding us to our appointed places as the organist takes his seat and the congregation falls silent for all eternity.

Though as it happened, the world didn't end. By sheer chance, someone came looking for me – someone I had fought with, a few days before – and, by sheer chance, one of the other tenants of that anonymous bedsit house had skipped work that day. The weather was fine, as I recall: a warm, sunny morning in the middle of an unseasonably hot springtime but, perhaps because the pubs weren't open yet, this truant neighbour was still around when my unexpected visitor came to the door. She had never been to that house until then: I didn't like my few remaining friends to see me in that grubby, half-derelict maze of bedsit rooms, redolent with the mixed scents of takeaway food and three-day-old milk cartons left out to curdle on upstairs windowsills. In fact, under normal circumstances, I would have been annoyed, but on that day, I wasn't quite up to my usual petulance and, unable to offer any explanation of my circumstances, I let myself be gathered together and driven away. I never saw that room again. My friend – a rational, if unusually stubborn professional woman in her mid-forties – called around to other friends I had used and abandoned along the way and, with a generosity that I have always found puzzling, they got together to drag me out of the hole I had managed to dig for myself. A fortnight later, temporarily housed in a clean, well-lighted place full of books and pictures, I was sitting at an upstairs window, looking out over a long suburban garden full of roses and apple trees and making a plan that had something to do with Surbiton.

Surbiton. Shorthand for a place that almost existed, a simplified world of autumn leaves and buses and a house in a side street where a man could live clean and true – and alone, of course, with his books and music and not even a Siamese cat for company. I could see that house in my mind's eye, and I could see myself as that man – and on that warm spring afternoon, as I sat by the window staring at my friend's garden, I had a sudden vision of the rest of my life. It was perfectly clear: *I* would become one of those isolates who make clock-work of their existence in suburbs and market towns all over the country, my life mapped out in a perfect, banal – by which I mean to say, *normal* – routine: get up, go to work, come home, read a book, watch TV, go to bed, get up. I would do the same thing every weekday; then, on Saturdays, I would stay at home, cooking and cleaning, or I would go to the cinema – not to the giant multi-screen in the high street, but to some old fleapit in a not-yet-gentrified quarter near the railway station, an old Ritz or Alhambra that some gay couple had taken over and done up so they could show Fassbinder or Kurosawa films for six or seven hours on a Sunday after-noon, marathon viewings of underrated greats with occasional, bitter-sweet intermissions for tea and home-made gingerbread. I would live in the heightened state that Andy Warhol talks about when he advises his readers to do the same things every day, in exactly the same way and in precisely the same order. I would even have a routine for food, just like Andy. And all the time, I would be aware of myself going from one room to another, lighting a lamp, or picking up a wooden spoon and using it to stir the soup I was heating on the stove. Campbell's Cream of Chicken, say.

It was a perfect plan. Ridiculous, yes; but perfect. I would become someone else and so be cured of my indelible shame. Cured of my obvious insanity. All I needed was to be contained, to be delimited, in a routine that was so set as to be unbreak-able. I wanted a job where I could work in isolation, solving minor problems or processing data. I would arrive at exactly nine o'clock every morning and, at exactly five o'clock, I would go home and watch old movies on late-night television. To be rid of my dishonour, I would live simply, alone and undis-turbed. Gradually, by trial and error, I would create the perfect routine and then I would follow it, day to day, week to week, year to year, decade to decade. Then, when the appointed time arrived, I would die, halfway through a rerun of *Danger Man* if I was lucky. Maybe I would collect something – stamps, say, or old records from the sixties – and I would live for years in silence, like the philosophy student whom Wittgenstein ordered to give up his studies and work for the rest of his days in a factory. My pleasures would be simple and, to others, almost negligible: marble cake for afternoon tea, a pot plant on a windowsill, Grace Slick's surprised laugh at the end of 'Sally Go 'Round the Roses'. It wouldn't be much of a life, perhaps, but it was the most elegant acknowledgement of honourable failure that I could imagine.

The owners of the clean, well-lighted house were a couple I had known for several years. I had met them in the early days, when my dissolution was still wonderful from time to time, and what they saw when they looked at me was the potential I must have shown back then. Maybe they also remembered how blessed I had seemed when everything was going well and the glamour of a wild night, or a long, tipsy afternoon, hadn't quite dissipated, so that I went about with a slight gleam to me, five parts neurasthenia no doubt, but maybe one or two parts aura. It was a borrowed light, I can't pretend it wasn't, but at times those good people managed to convince themselves that it was something else, something good and honest and worth preserving – and, even as that light faded, they had kept faith with the original illusion. Looking back, it comes as a shock to remember how often they intervened in the mess I was making of my life, putting me up when I had nowhere else to go, lending me money, feeding me when I was hungry, listening to my wild imaginings when I was having one of my 'episodes', visiting me in the mental hospital when I was incarcerated there for my own protection. On the day a young policeman turned up on their doorstep to question me about a burglary that had been committed at a shop in the town, they supplied me with an alibi and so got me off the hook, though they had no way of knowing if I was innocent or not. On another occasion, they enlisted a friend of their daughter's to hoik me out of the Lion Yard, where I was dug in over a fistful of pills and some industrial-grade alcohol with a company of winos and ne'er-do-wells. Now, as I contemplated my very few options, they were the ones who encouraged me in my plan to head south and start again, and they went out of their way to set me up in that new life, lending more money, pulling in favours, providing moral support when I woke with a start from the reverie and asked myself what the hell I thought I was playing at. Of course, they knew enough to see that my Surbiton was a Surbiton of the mind, a dreamscape that I was constructing around a *soi-disant* outsider's confusion of the normal and the banal, but they also knew enough to see that I would sink like a stone if I didn't grab on to *something*. Maybe that something was a fantasy, but it was better than nothing. So they put me on the train and waved me off, in the hope that, even though the Surbiton I was headed for didn't actually exist, I might still end up somewhere safe.

A BAR ON MERROW DOWN

By the time I reached Surrey, it was summer. The perfect season to go in search of the normal world, or so I thought. A week later, with a little help from my friends, I was living in a shared flat at the Worplesdon end of Guildford. Not quite Surbiton, in geographical terms, but it doesn't take much of an imagination to see that Surbiton is where you find it. The flat belonged to another in the chain of unlikely friends, and it bore no resemblance whatsoever to the terraced house in the backstreets that I had pictured for myself, but after a while, it was as close as I had ever come to home. Late at night, or in the wee small hours when I lay awake, listening to the quiet, I could see that I'd have to move on eventually, but for the moment I'd been granted a fresh start, and I knew I had to make the best of it. The hallucinations and delusions were on pause, I had been prescribed medication that would keep me out of hospital. After a while, I had meetings to go to and, for a short time, a counsellor to help me with my Addictive Personality. I'd even found something that passed for a job. Now I had somewhere to stay and, though I didn't like to admit as much, I knew that there was a backup system to catch me if I stumbled. In short, I was being given the opportunity – an opportunity that I didn't really deserve – to live a normal life.

And yet.

And yet – deep down, in spite of my Surbiton fantasy, I wasn't altogether convinced that I was *ready* to be normal. *Theoretically*, I wanted a normal life, *theoretically*, I wanted to vanish into my own private world and take up stamp collecting in the suburbs, because I knew I needed a *cure*. That was why I had signed up, voluntarily, for an official, twelve-step recovery programme, so I could confess my drug- and drink-fuelled disasters to a group of like-minded souls and so find the humility to hand over my life to the proverbial higher power. I kept up with that for a long time, too, even though I didn't *like* instant coffee and Rich Tea biscuits, but I knew from the word go that I just wasn't that eager to accept a higher power into my life. As it happened, I didn't necessarily doubt that there was something out there that equated to a higher power, but I was by no means convinced that He, She or It was in any way interested in guiding *me* through the minor and fairly seedy problems I had created for myself. It went without saying that I was glad to have been rescued from my predicament, and I was full of good intentions, but when night fell, and I lay down, sober and drug-free, in my clean bed, or when I sat through a long, genial meeting with nothing but Hobnobs and Nescafé for comfort and the first day of the rest of my life hovering ominously on the morrow, it was hard to see the attractions of my suddenly normalised existence.

I say *existence*, because that was what it was over the first year or so: no excitement, no upsets, nothing out of the ordinary. No acid, no dope, no barbiturates, no methedrine and, most of the time, no alcohol – which meant being self-aware, and avoiding the kind of situations that might plunge me back into the party life – and I really didn't want to go back to the world I had just left, or not consciously, at least.

Consciously, I wanted to be cured. Consciously, I was glad to have left my old self behind. The only problem was that, on Friday evenings, the whole world seemed to be heading out into the long night, suddenly alive after a week of data entry or customer relations, girls in white dresses and too much lipstick crossing my path on the way back from the takeaway, boys in their good shirts waiting at the bus stop to go out, feel the heat, be an adventure. Or I would turn a corner on a Saturday afternoon and see them coming from some pub on the backstreets, ordinary children made beautiful by whatever was running through their veins for an hour or two, making their way to some secret place along the riverside to sit out in the sunlight all afternoon, smoking and flirting and dropping pills till the pubs opened again. At night, I would lie awake in the dark and hear them coming home along Worplesdon Road, calling out to one another and laughing, just twenty yards away. Or I would stand at the kitchen window in the small hours and watch as a taxi pulled up and dropped a girl off right outside the flats – and it would be the pretty dark-haired girl who worked at the newsagent's, the one who always smiled when I went in for the Sunday papers. She would be on her way home from a party, a pale, silvery glow to her as she crossed the road and let herself into her parents' house opposite and, knowing that I wouldn't be able to sleep after this vision, I would fix myself another pot of not-instant coffee and sit up till morning, running through the good old days.

So there it was: the usual struggle. Jolly red devil on one shoulder, anaemic white angel on the other. I really *was* full of good intentions, but even I knew how dangerous good intentions could be and, when I weighed up the odds, this supposed return to the fold looked like a particularly long shot. Besides, I was hopelessly ill-equipped for my new life. Especially for Surrey. I was twenty-eight years old and I didn't have a car, or a mortgage. I didn't even have a fridge, or a vacuum cleaner, or a compact stereo system. What I did have were two sweaters, a bagful of Army & Navy shirts, a couple of pairs of blue jeans and a drawer's worth of assorted underwear. Three or four books, one snapshot, a notepad full of scribbles that even I couldn't decipher. Everything else had either been lost or given away. Meanwhile, getting what I needed to make the next steps in what my fellow self-helpers coyly referred to as my *sobriety* would take time, and everything depended on me behaving myself – on staying clean, sober, out of debt and more or less sane – which meant, of course, that whatever progress I had made on the road to normality could be cancelled out in the twinkling of an eye, leaving me right back where I started, with nothing but the furtive consolation of knowing that I had repaid my friends for all their kindness by failing them completely.

For the first couple of months, I worked maintenance – tidying the gardens, painting and doing minor repairs – at a retirement village just outside Cranleigh. To get there, I had to cycle five miles cross-country in the morning dusk, then wait on a back road for a man called Frank, who gave me a lift the rest of the way. On the return, I had the same journey and, as much as I enjoyed the daily round of raking and mowing and sanding, I found it hard to deal with the people in charge. According to the site manager, I had a problem with authority. For some reason I didn't take to being ordered around by a man who struggled to finish the *Mirror* cross-word – but then, I wasn't alone in *that*. There were four maintenance workers permanently on site, and they all had the same problem. The only difference between me and them was that they didn't get sacked after nine weeks.

My next job was at a garden centre in a desirable commuter village a few miles along the A3 from where I lived. The garden centre was a joint venture between two local businessmen with money to spare and a bored aristocrat who happened to own a large walled space that he wasn't using. It was run by one of the wives, who needed something to do, and it could have been a huge success, but somehow it wasn't. Working there was fun, though: the village was straight out of central casting, a rustic melting pot of forelock-tugging locals with too much facial hair and their better-off *Country Life* neighbours, all green wellies and sporty saloons and motley children from previous marriages squirrelled away at minor public schools. Sometimes, when the slow day was done and we had ruefully shut up shop, I'd wander into the village and have a pint of orange squash, no ice please, at the Ram's Bollocks, before the bracing cycle ride home along the A3. Eventually, unsurprisingly, I succumbed to temptation and downed a pint or two of Dead Badger with one of the locals. After all, I would tell myself, there was no point living like a monk. A glass of wine with dinner, a pint after work: there was no harm in that. It would do me good to learn how to drink in moderation. I had to learn to adjust. I couldn't keep going to those AA meetings forever. I had to remember, on the booze front, that I should never drink alone. That was one of the more important laws, maybe the *most* important: NEVER DRINK ALONE. If you drink by yourself, the conventional wisdom said, you were bound to come to grief, and with my Addictive Personality, I had to be doubly careful. But then, as my friend Paul liked to say, in the months leading up to his untimely death from pancreatitis, the true drinker *always* drinks alone, no matter who else is around.

Paul was a dangerous friend to have made, because he really was as true a drinker as any I had ever met. He worked in London, but he lived in a village on a Surrey branch line, just a few minutes' walk from the station. This was fortunate, because it meant he didn't have a car and I'd hate to think what kind of a driver Paul would have made. I'm not sure what he did, some kind of office job, but two or three times a week, he would go out drinking in town after work with colleagues or clients or whoever else happened to be around. He'd sit in the wine bar or the pub till the company drifted off for a meal or to catch their trains home, then he would head down to Waterloo, stopping off at the South Bank or the station bar for a couple, before heading back to dormitory land. If there was a bar on the train, he'd have a couple for the road; if not, he'd bring his own supplies and sit gazing out into the darkness, as the inner suburbs flashed by. After that, things would be hazy. Sometimes he would get home, sometimes he would end up in a waiting room, cursing himself for having stayed too long at the pub, or for having fallen asleep and missed his station, but secretly happy that there were no more trains and he was stuck there till morning. He had options, of course, depending on how far from home he was, but he never considered them: he preferred to sit in the dull, coppery light of a waiting room, his suit crumpled, his hair a mess, his watch ticking slowly through the minutes and hours till daylight. He might only have slept for an hour or so on the train, but that didn't matter – he couldn't sleep again, he was fully awake now and he had an odd compulsion to *stay* awake, now that he was alone, and stranded. That kind of thing happened to him all the time: he fell asleep,

34

missed his stop and ended up at the far end of the line, or he'd wake up suddenly and jump off the train at some tiny rural station and he wouldn't realise his mistake till it was too late. To begin with, he'd make some effort to get home, but after a while he went through this routine almost wittingly, even going to the lengths of supplying himself with a half-bottle of brandy for the long sleepless hours. After the first few occasions, he'd just stop where he ended up and sit sipping the brandy, the dark fields gathered around him, or maybe the lights of a dormitory town winking just beyond the line of trees that screened the station. At times like that, he would feel utterly bereft, but he wasn't so unaware of his true nature that he didn't recognise the satisfaction that ran under the surface of that loneliness – satisfaction, really, because he was totally free. For an hour or five, his drink problem wasn't an illness, or a character flaw, or a consequence of his difficult upbringing. It was a spiritual exercise, a ritual observation of the self in its purest form and, more than anything else, it was a variety of prayer. By the time he was diagnosed with pancreatitis, he was too far gone to take the doctors' advice and straighten himself out. He'd been drinking alone for years – and he knew that, when the time came, he'd have one more for the road then slide into an agonising and unseemly death. He wasn't *choosing* to die, it wasn't like that at all – he just couldn't choose to live, if it meant not drinking.

Afterwards, I discovered he had a wife. No children, but a wife who had stuck with him for fifteen years, then left when things got out of hand, probably in an attempt to scare him into self-preservation. It hadn't worked. At the funeral, she surprised us all – a few drinking cronies, a couple of dismayed colleagues – by turning up and standing by the grave in an elaborate black outfit, complete with hat and gloves, her face

35

set in a determined-not-to-cry expression that only exaggerated what I think of now as an appalling and somehow inappropriate beauty. Her name, I discovered later, was Maria. She was obviously younger than her husband – and, though it was almost beyond belief, I could tell, just by looking at her, that she had loved him to the end, even when he was killing himself on a daily diet of Chardonnay and vodka tonics. I only knew Paul for a few months – I met him around the same time that I started backsliding into days-of-wine-and-roses mode – but I thought of him as a friend and his death should have been a warning to me. It wasn't, though. In fact, quite the contrary. Secretly, as I fought to hang on to my hard-won *sobriety*, I envied him those last weeks, when he'd thrown his life away and given himself over to the cool of the night in a dingy waiting room, somewhere between Waterloo and Portsmouth. As messy as the end might have been, that last, long binge had been decisive and, in its own way, rather honourable. I found nothing perverse in the desire to which I sometimes succumbed, a pathetic, yet oddly logical impulse to follow in his footsteps and devote myself, once and for all, to the long and solitary ceremony of self-erasure.

I kept trying, though. I tried *very hard* – which is usually the wrong way to do anything. For a year or more, I went to meetings and stayed more or less clean, and I was on the cusp of being a reformed character, doing what I needed to do, and avoiding what I'd pledged to avoid. Eventually, though, the garden centre palled, and I started looking around for something else – which was how I came to be sitting in an office in Whitehall on a wet afternoon in 1985, convincing three very bored interviewers that I would make a *great* civil servant. I had no work history to speak of, but it was heartening to think that, during a decade of chaos and borderline madness, I had managed to acquire a degree and, apparently, an air of credibility. If the interviewers had been paying attention, they would have spotted that there were huge gaps in my cv and, had they looked me in the eye and held that gaze for more than a few seconds, they would have seen that I was a total fake, an out-and-out chancer, winging my way through a process I barely understood. I was interviewing for an EO programmer job in the Ministry of Agriculture, Fisheries and Food, but the only computer knowledge I possessed was a hobbyist's slender and very recent grasp of BASIC coupled with a confirmed autodidact's childish passion for logic problems. What I didn't know, at the start of play, was that the Civil Service was as desperate for credible recruits as I was for a proper job, but that fact quickly sank in as the panel went wearily through the motions of scrutinising me for serious character flaws – is this the kind of person you'd want working for the government? – before (or maybe it was after, my memory of the entire event is hazy) tucking me away in a tiny room with the easiest aptitude test ever devised by humankind.

I passed the test, which didn't surprise me, but I also got through the interview, which did. Before I could quite take it all in, I had gone through the required training course and I was working at MAFF, writing programs to retrieve information about stubble burning or intervention payments, so that the minister – the very aptly named Mr MacGregor – would have the necessary answers at his fingertips when he stood up in the House. It was ridiculous. I was an executive officer, the lowest of the technical grades, working on ancient equipment – at MAFF, we still had to punch cards to run overnight jobs, and I would spend hours cursing and redoing

37

them on the ancient card-punch in the Census office – and I was only a few months out of training, but once or twice there was only one degree of separation between me and the minister and, since nobody ever checked my work – there was never time, everything was always done in a rush at the last minute – I could have said anything. Which was exactly the point, of course: my reports weren't really being used to inform Parliament, they were simply the raw material from which someone higher up the food chain extracted what he *wanted* to extract. It struck me, once, that I could as well send forty pages of randomly generated numbers instead of my carefully parameterised reports and the outcome would be the same. When the minister spoke, he said what he needed to say; it had nothing to do with the program a humble EO had spent four or five hours writing and compiling and running earlier that same day.

Still, none of this troubled me in the least. On the contrary, I found it heartening. The work I did was entirely abstract, a series of problems that had to be solved in a given time, like doing a crossword puzzle over lunch. It had no purpose and so was done for its own sake, like art, or flirting. This was probably the only interesting job I had ever done, and it didn't mean a thing, it was just going through the motions. And I didn't mind. To be irrelevant in that way was, I had to admit, rather satisfying, almost like being invisible, or like honourably disappearing from the face of the earth, disappearing without a trace, like the Cheshire Cat, leaving only the hint of a smile behind, to show that you had always known how ridiculous life was.

And, for at least eight hours every day, life *was* ridiculous – not because the job was irrelevant, and not because, this being computer work, we kept flip-flopping between sudden panics and days of having nothing to do. When the work did arrive, it was occasionally rather interesting and, in between, there was the tea trolley, office-level flirting and an endless round of marginally work-related periodicals – *Farmers Weekly*, *New Scientist*, even the *Ecologist*, in its old non-glossy format – that appeared in my in-tray as if by magic. In summer, we could play croquet on the MAFF lawn during long, flexi-timed lunch breaks, or wander off to Merrow Down for the sunshine and butterflies. The more adventurous might sneak out for furtive, though mostly theoretical, liaisons on the Down, just a street away from the office, or they would clock out early and head for the Silent Pool, five miles along the road towards Shere, to practise full-blown adultery in the surrounding woodland. None of *this* was ridiculous. On the contrary: it was the rest of the time, the official time, the *job*, that was ridiculous, because the job was constantly being organised and then reorganised by people who had just come back off a management training course and wanted to try out the new techniques they had learned. They wanted, in other words, to prove that they were Managers, and to be a Manager you had to be fully qualified in a wide range of meddlesome practices that prevented others from doing what they were good at. Perhaps this was a form of revenge – managers being drawn, on the whole, from the ranks of people who aren't good at computing, or systems design, or anything else that takes a certain level of intelligence and a soupçon of imagination. There were exceptions, of course, but I only ever saw them from a distance: most of the time, my daily round was planned out and delimited by somebody called Brian or Simon who didn't quite know his arse from his elbow, and rather resented anyone who did.

Finally, to ice the cake, the powers that be put me in an

office with a guy called Tim, a tall, ruddy-cheeked HEO of seven years' standing whose main ambition was to appear on *Mastermind*. Tim was involved in several quiz teams and spent a good deal of time, both in and out of the office, memorising pages from the *Guinness Book of Records*, or looking up film details in *Halliwell's*. He could tell you what was number one in the charts on any given day since the charts were started; he could tell you, not only who won the Best Supporting Actor Oscar in 1962, but who else was on the list of nominations; he knew the state flowers of Mississippi and Minnesota and the currencies and former capital cities of every country that had ever existed. His specialist subject was pop music, and he had memorised the names of all the members of every girl group who ever recorded with Tamla Motown, and the life histories of every acid rocker who ever lived, from Darby Slick to Gary Duncan. Because he was an HEO and I was a lowly EO, he was effectively my boss, which suited him perfectly. Until I arrived, he had been on his own – there were various rumours as to why other long-term employees didn't want to work with him – and he'd had to interrupt his studies in *Wisden* and the *Encyclopædia Britannica* to write the odd program, or file some unnecessary report. Now he had an underling again, which meant that he could *delegate*. Delegating was good, delegating was encouraged: by delegating the line manager freed himself up for other tasks, while the less experienced worker gained in confidence by taking on and solving new problems. Best of all, for Tim, was the intangible, the immeasurable benefit of increased study time. With a new EO to train and supervise, his workload was bound to increase, so he put in for overtime and spent his Sundays in the office, alone and undisturbed, so he could gen up on League Cup winners and current affairs. Often, I would come in on a Monday morning and find the bins in our office stuffed full of newspapers and beer cans, but nobody else ever seemed to notice. After all, the work was getting done, and done better than it had ever been – mostly, because Tim wasn't doing any of it, for Tim was busy. Tim was on a mission. The year before I moved to his department, Tim's quiz team had made the Regionals, but had got knocked out in the quarter-final. Now, with a new lackey to keep the office running smoothly, he could concentrate on his true calling. I would see it in his eyes as he sat at his desk, memorising Wimbledon champions. Today: the Nationals. Tomorrow: the Black Chair.

So there it was. Normality. Which only goes to show that, when it comes to the crunch, normal life is boring. Office life, in particular. Which, in turn, probably explains why MAFF, in its wisdom, installed a *bar* at the very centre of its Epsom Road site, just by Merrow Down. A real bar, with *subsidised* drinks. How could I have resisted, me with my Addictive Personality and all. That bar called to me every day and it wasn't long before I gave in to the call.

KAFKALAND

The bar called, and I answered that call but, even then, I did quite well to begin with. I had a beer or two over lunch, and sometimes I had a couple at the end of a long day, but I was still going to work and, for a long time, I didn't see anybody or anything that wasn't actually there. And I still wasn't drinking alone.

After a while, though, I might as well have been. Within months, I was out every night, heading off to the bar around six, then moving on to one of the hotels on Epsom Road before drifting into town. The intention was always to have a quiet drink and, sometimes, that was exactly what I did. Occasionally, however, things didn't go according to schedule. I might start innocently enough, sipping on a mediocre Chardonnay and studying the menu in some polite country-style pub, thinking that I'd have a bite to eat then head for home, but it was only a matter of time before I ended up in some dive. Or I'd find myself in the kitchen of a shared house in Worplesdon, swigging bourbon from a plastic cup with a gang of new-found friends from the agricultural college. The next thing I knew, I would be waking up on the floor of a room full of snoring tree surgeons, face to face with some whiskery bloke I'd never seen before, or hauling myself out of a skip behind a pet shop on an anonymous estate. Or I'd be crashed out alongside a woman to whom I'd never been properly introduced, wondering how far we had gone before we drifted into oblivion. Every time I left the office, the plan was white wine and conversation, French food, maybe a mild flirtation with someone glimpsed across a crowded room. All the beautiful clichés. Two hours later, it was vodka wasters and handfuls of Bennies, or beer and whisky at some over-priced late-night drinking hole masquerading as a disco.

Still, I always started out with high hopes that things would be different this time and, for a good while, I pinned those hopes on the bar of a hotel not far from work. It was one of those places that might or might not liven up around nine but, until then, it belonged to the quiet men who drink for drinking's sake, slow and steady, supping on pints and chasers or gin and tonics, a newspaper folded open on the bar in front of them, usually at the crossword, to discourage idle conver-sation. There were two regular bar staff: a bespectacled, puffy, overly formal man in late-middle age called George, and a very pretty girl who, when she wasn't serving, stood at the far end of the bar and stared out across the garden, as if she was waiting for someone. Maybe she was, but in all the time I drank there, nobody came. Her name was Linda. George didn't say much, but Linda would pass the time of day. She lived close by and she knew the extreme regulars by name, though she was a good deal younger than any of them. Most likely, they were friends of her father's, which was probably why nobody tried to hit on her – or almost nobody. As I recall, there was a brief period when things were interestingly ambiguous between us, which was about the same time that I met Greg. I suppose, if I hadn't met him, Linda and I might have progressed from the interestingly ambiguous to the briefly tragic, but I'll never know that now.

I'm calling him Greg, but that wasn't his real name. He came in with Chris, a short, rather seedy-looking character with a blot of a face, all wet-looking beard and smudged glasses. Chris worked at MAFF, though not in the computing section. I'd encountered him in the bar from time to time and I remembered him as one of those cheery souls whose self-appointed vocation was to entertain everyone he met, whether they wanted to be entertained or not. Chris told jokes, indulged in repartee about film stars and politicians, invented seamy gossip about colleagues and extravagant lies about himself, but his real speciality was games. Darts, snooker, pub quizzes, skittles, croquet, even cricket with his local on Sunday afternoons. All the usual boys' pursuits. Chris was podgy, gauche, and far from athletic, but he was a self-certified expert on every outdoor pursuit from netball to cross-country skiing and he talked about leading tennis players and footballers with the ungrudging approval another man might reserve for a talented sibling.

His chief fondness, however, was for the tricks that people learn late at night in the bar on residential training courses. How to push a whisky tumbler through the handle of a pint mug without breaking it. How to stand an egg on its pointy end. All the infantile word games and practical jokes that would gratify a nine-year-old.

'Repeat after me,' he'd say, coughing. 'Mary had a little lamb, its fleece was white as snow.'

Someone would repeat the rhyme, and he'd grin triumphantly, then make a noise like a buzzer. 'Naaah. Thanks for playing,' he'd say. 'OK. Who's next?' He would put his hand to his mouth and give a little cough. 'Mary had a little lamb . . .'

Meanwhile, when he wasn't doing tricks, he would dispense

44

wisdom. According to Chris, everything could be broken down into categories, and he knew them all. 'There are three kinds of people in the world,' he'd say. There were two kinds of women. Five types of song. Seven basic stories. He had a theory about everything.

That night, he came in with a group of folk, including Tim and a couple of attractive women who worked in IBAP. All but one of this group were MAFF employees and I knew their faces, if not their names and positions, mostly from the bar or the canteen. The one exception was Greg. He was someone I hadn't seen before, which was probably why I noticed how out of place he looked. A tall, angular man a couple of years older than me, with sparse, ash-coloured hair and dark-rimmed, slightly tinted glasses, he had an ex-hippie air to him, but what was striking was how different he looked, how out of place among that gang of jovial, besuited clerks. That night, he was wearing a green sweater reminiscent of army fatigues and black drainpipe jeans over faded Converse trainers, which only served to emphasise the odd geometry of his body, a geometry part construction kit and part exoskeleton. A geometry that suggested that he wasn't quite human – and there really was a certain insect-like quality to his face and neck that suggested a praying mantis, or a locust. If he had been an actor, he would have been perfect for the part of Gregor Samsa in an experimental staging of Kafka's *Metamorphosis*.

If Linda hadn't been on duty that night, I would have been long gone, but she was, and I wasn't – which meant that, being MAFF myself, and officially on my own, I couldn't avoid being sucked into the revelry. I didn't like the idea: none of those people meant anything to me – and yet, much as I preferred to deny it, I *did* belong to this bitter fellowship of naysayers and nihilists. What I had in common with them

45

was exactly what held them together as a group for, like them, I was defined almost entirely in negatives. What they hated was what I hated, what they despised was what I despised: modern life, popular taste, social success, common sense, good-natured acceptance. As soon as they settled in, an odd hysteria took over, as the conversation drifted from the day's business to wider issues, and they vied with one another to give voice to the simmering, gut-deep disgust that possessed them all. Some of this was a pose, of course, and none of them was quite as contemptuous of everything as he pretended, but it was ugly nevertheless. Nothing was good, nothing was beyond suspicion and nothing was beneath contempt. There had been occasions in the past when, purely for sport, I had fanned the flames of such conversations by dropping in a guarded, but essentially kind word for something that had succeeded, some film that the critics had raved about, some song that had gone to the top of the charts, some book that had made the best-seller lists, then waited for the reaction. That night, though, I wasn't in the mood.

We were sitting around two tables, in a sea of glasses and ashtrays. I was wedged between the girls from IBAP, directly opposite Tim, whose plump reddish face now partly obscured my view of the bar, where Linda stood wiping glasses and listening in, bemused and, I thought, mildly repelled by it all. Off to one side, Greg sat on his own, his chair pulled away from the table, as if he wanted to say that he was *with* the group, but not quite *of* it. For a while, he only watched, occasionally smiling at some more than usually moronic expression of distaste – Tim's claim that George Harrison wasn't that much of a guitarist, say – but he offered no input to the conversation. Now and again, he looked across and caught my eye, and I could see that he was wondering about me, the only other person at the table who had nothing to say. Most of the time, though, he sat with his head down, rolling stick-thin cigarettes and lighting them up with a tiny flourish intended only for himself. Finally, as the conversation lost its impetus and people started talking about moving on, he stood up and nodded to the table in general.

'I'd better get going,' he said. He looked over at me and nodded. 'See you later.'

Chris looked up from the trick he was demonstrating for the IBAP girls. 'Don't go now,' he said. 'We're just getting started.'

This was patently untrue, but Greg didn't argue the point. 'Nah,' he said. 'I'd better get home to the Millstone.' He smiled ruefully. 'See if she's still in one piece.'

He waved one hand vaguely, but he wasn't looking at anyone in particular. 'Have a good one,' he said.

With that, he was gone – and, though he hadn't said a word all night, the evening went flat as a pancake. Twenty minutes later, the group dispersed, the talk of going on to some late-night place in town more for show than anything else, and I was back at the bar having one for the road, while Linda collected our dead glasses and emptied the ashtrays in silence, like someone who is waiting for the other person to talk, but doesn't much care if they do or not.

My flatmate had moved out by then, so I spent the weekend alone, watching old movies on TV. That was how I passed the time, when I knew I was going to be by myself for a while: I would stock up on milk and Carr's Water Biscuits, borrow a heap of videos from the local rental store, lock myself away in a celluloid dream and try not to go to the pub. It reminded me of the times I'd spent in the Arts Cinema in Cambridge, when things were more than usually difficult – the world outside might be full of demons and angels, but for an hour or two, I could live in this other place, in the perfect snow-fall of *The Magnificent Ambersons*, or the hushed stairwells and spectral gardens of *The Innocents*. Usually, I watched the same films over and over: *Ashes and Diamonds*, say, or *Throne of Blood*. Renoir, Welles, Kurosawa, Bergman, Pasolini, Jack Clayton, Wajda – these were the people I knew, these were the people I trusted. I would rent two or three films and watch one for a day or so, winding it back to the beginning as soon as it ended, replaying over and over the moment when Zbigniew Cybulski lights the vodka glasses, or when the angel of the Lord appears to Joseph in *The Gospel According to Matthew*. That weekend, I locked myself away with two of my all-time favourites, but for some reason my mind kept returning to Greg. There was something about him that I didn't necessarily like, but he was interesting, and that was more than could be said for the other men I knew.

Maybe I was just curious. Maybe I was bored and needed a mystery to invest in. I asked Tim about Greg when I got back to work the following Monday, not that I thought I could trust anything he might say.

'God,' he muttered, shaking his head. 'Somebody should figure out what planet that guy comes from, so we can send him back there.'

'How do you mean?'

Tim grinned, then assumed a wild-eyed look. 'Space: the final frontier . . .' he said, in a fairly accurate Captain Kirk voice. I wondered how long he'd practised.

'That bad, huh?' I said.

He shook his head again. He'd done his party piece and he was already losing interest. 'Oh, he's all right, I suppose,' he said.

48

'He's not dangerous or anything. It's just . . . I don't know. I wouldn't let him go out with my sister, put it that way.'

'Do you *have* a sister?' I asked.

Tim gave me a tight smile. 'Figure of speech, old boy,' he said.

'Oh.'

'Anyhow, he's got a wife,' Tim said. 'Never seen her, but I've heard tell she's a bit of a dragon.'

I remembered that closing remark, then, about going home to *the millstone*. 'Really?' I said. Greg hadn't struck me as the henpecked type. 'How so?'

Tim did a sitcom double take as if it had just come into fashion. This line of questioning annoyed him. 'Search me,' he said. 'It's just what people say.'

'Ah.'

'Anyway,' he said, 'haven't you got something better to do than sit here and chat? I know *I* have.' He smiled. Tim's secret weapon was that he was totally barefaced. Everybody knew what he was up to, and he *knew* that they knew, and he just didn't give a toss. He'd probably risen as far as he could go, given his history, but he wouldn't get fired no matter what he did, so he could do what he liked, really. 'The Regionals are next Tuesday,' he said. 'Got to work on my sports knowledge.'

I nodded. 'I'll get on then,' I said. 'Leave you to it.'

He nodded too, but he was already preoccupied. What if something odd came up, something about lacrosse or college basketball? Sport wasn't his strongest suit. He could just about get by on football and cricket, but the guy who usually covered the more esoteric stuff had transferred to Alnwick or someplace, and it was down to Tim, as team captain, to be prepared. I lingered a moment. 'So. Who won the Stanley Cup in 1964?' I said.

'What?' Tim looked up in alarm.

'Who won the Stanley Cup in 1964?' I said. 'And who scored the winning goal in the final game of the series? *And* –' I put on my best Magnus Magnusson this-is-a-hard-one-so-I'll-really-be-impressed-if-you-get-it voice – 'what was *special* about him?'

Tim stared at me. He hadn't a clue. '*You* don't know that, do you?' he said.

I deadpanned. 'Of course I do,' I said.

'So who was it?'

'You mean you *don't* know?'

'No. Tell me.'

I turned away. 'Sorry,' I said. 'Can't stand around gassing. I've got work to do.' I opened my drawer and pulled out a fresh pad of coding paper. '*Your* work,' I said.

I met Greg a few nights later, in the same place. George was on the bar, and there weren't many punters – just a couple of old-timers who lived locally, settled in over their half-pints and just one step away, it seemed, from a deep slumber of one sort or another. I don't know, now, if Greg came there looking for me, but at the time it seemed innocent enough: he lived just a few streets away and, though I'd not seen him there before, that hotel bar would have been a convenient hiding place when he needed to get out of the house. And, for reasons that soon became obvious, he got out of the house quite a bit. 'You got time for a drink?' I asked.

'All the time in the world,' he said.

I ordered a couple of pints, and we stood silent while George ambled back and forth, fetching glasses, carrying them to the pumps, sighing softly for his own edification as the beer flowed, then peering over the top of his half-rimmed spectacles when it neared the top, as if he were engaged in some delicate high-precision experiment. I turned to Greg. 'Have you known Chris long?' I asked.

He looked at me. 'Chris?' He pondered this for a moment, as if it were a word in a foreign language, or a cryptic clue in a crossword puzzle. Then he worked it out. 'Ah!' he said. '*Chris.*' He paused ceremonially while our host set the beers down on the bar with an air of immense solemnity and, whether out of secrecy or respect, didn't say anything more until George had been paid and had retreated to the far end of the bar, where the locals were. 'No,' he said. 'Not long.' He took a sip of the beer, then set it back down on the counter. 'Actually, I don't really know him at all.'

'Ah.' I nodded. I could see the logic of his disavowal. 'It's just – well, I saw you coming in with him and I thought –'

'I didn't come in *with* him,' he said. 'I just came in at the same time.' He shook his head. 'We met at the door,' he added, with a tight smile, to show that he wasn't being deliberately rude.

I laughed. 'I take it you're not a big fan, then,' I said.

'Of Chris's?' He shrugged. 'He's all right.' He lifted the beer again and, this time, he took a long swallow, so the glass was more than half empty.

'Christ,' I said. 'You're thirsty.'

'Oh, *yes*,' he said, allowing himself a faint sigh which I took to indicate satisfaction. 'Another?'

I took a long pull on my own glass. 'Don't mind if I do,' I said.

Three hours later, we were still there, on shorts now, and sitting at a table in the far corner of the almost empty bar. The locals had drifted away and, though a few punters had passed through, it was mostly just us. We had been drinking steadily throughout, but neither of us was what you would call drunk. Or what *we* would have called drunk, at least. We had talked about work, the town, cautiously given out a few titbits of personal history, then moved on to more comfortable subjects. Music. Film. Sport. Men's stuff. Only it wasn't the *usual* men's stuff. And it wasn't the nasty, naysaying talk you got with Chris and Tim and their crowd. It was better than that, funnier, slightly more paranoid, self-consciously absurd and, at the same time, utterly passionate about the most ridiculous things. I could see right away why Tim didn't like him. It was jealousy. Greg was a mine of pointless information and random memories, a walking encyclopedia of curious facts and supertrivia, and his mind was both fantastical and stuck in some weird groove where everything he touched upon was caught up and included in a pointless, unending narrative with no plot, no purpose and characters straight out of some paranoid daydream – but, for me, the geography of that dream was extremely familiar. It was like meeting my taste-clone. Fifties noir. *Eyes Without a Face*. James Ensor. The Grateful Dead.

'The only time I ever saw Pigpen,' he said, 'would have been at Bickershaw, in 1972 –'

'*Right*,' I said. 'I remember.'

'You were there?'

I nodded. 'Oceans of mud. Hell's Angels. Country Joe trying to get those people off the scaffolding.'

He pursed his lips. 'Yeah,' he said. 'Country Joe.' He put on a laconic, West Coast, fixin'-to-die-rag voice. '*That structure was built for four people, and there's about four hundred of you up there. And if you don't come down off that fucking structure, you're going to fall and crush the shit out of everybody below.*'

'And that guy started screaming, the one who was having a bad trip,' I said. 'Right under the big lights . . .'

Once again, we took a moment to reminisce. I didn't know what he was thinking, but I was remembering the heavy rains on the Sunday morning, and how I had taken shelter in one of the big tents, already soaked to the bone and standing face to face with a skinny biker in a German World War II helmet. He had a black swastika painted on his gaunt, terribly white face so that, in my hallucinogenic haze, I thought he was already dead. From somewhere outside, Brinsley Schwarz was playing. Or was I just imagining that? It's not true what they say about how, if you can remember that time, you weren't really there. The truth is, you remember plenty, only it's all the wrong stuff.

'And there was *Pigpen*,' Greg said. 'Still alive. He died not long after that, and I suppose, if we had looked closer we might have seen the signs of death in his face, but he was too far away.' He glanced over at me, and I offered up a solemn, valedictory nod. 'I couldn't believe it,' he said. 'He was still young.'

'Yeah,' I said. 'I remember playing "Turn On Your Love Light" for about three days solid after I read the news. The way he keeps saying *huh* all the way through. All that arrogance and joy.' Maybe I *was* drunk.

Greg smiled sadly. It was like a personal loss – and there we had it, the one thing that binds men in bars together. Shared nerdhood. The simple fact of talking about such things as if they mattered, because they did matter, and all the stuff that other people talked about as if it mattered didn't count for shit. Because we *knew*. We had *values*. We didn't buy the crap they advertised on TV and we didn't belong to any in-crowd. *Shared nerdhood*: the true bedrock of every masculine

53

friendship. How could we have avoided becoming friends? Shared nerdhood, common memories, too much beer in a half-empty bar on a weekday night? And then, add to that the fact that we were both doggedly blue collar, no matter where we happened to work – which meant that, our out-of-the-way taste in films and books notwithstanding, all we really *wanted* from life was to go out on a warm summer evening and stand in the corner of a field, drinking beer out of a can and smoking dope, the Allman Brothers on a tape deck somewhere and a vast gloaming just beyond the hedge, where the night begins. We were callow, sentimental, defiant, unsophisticated, paranoid and totally unapologetic about it – and because of all this, I decided that very night that I was going to like Greg. I was going to like him because he was fanatical about all the things that supposedly didn't matter, and completely indifferent to everything that supposedly did – and over the weeks to come, everything he said reinforced that sense I had of him. He judged people in a wholly arbitrary way, coming to swift and irrevocable decisions based on their taste in music, or on some tiny detail of dress or grooming. He disliked bearded men in suits; to him, they couldn't make their minds up about selling out. Anyone wearing a striped tie was treated with open contempt. Every new male acquaintance would be presented with a casual, but for Greg, utterly vital test in pop music trivia, but it had nothing in common with Tim's quiz team mentality. It was a test of values. What make of bike was Duane Allman riding when he was killed? Who wrote the song, 'Death Don't Have No Mercy'? Who made the original, superior recording of the Moody Blues hit 'Go Now'? Women weren't expected to know any of this stuff, of course. They were just supposed to avoid liking the wrong things – and Greg believed that, in most instances, they chose well, more or less instinctively. Exceptions – Simon and Garfunkel fans, girls who liked Rod Stewart – simply proved the rule. I never quite figured out why someone so deeply misogynistic should feel that way – perhaps it was the MCP equivalent of the racist's belief in the instinctive rhythm of black people – but he was quite convinced that any real woman worth her salt had a native, though entirely unschooled feeling for good music – and his contempt for the Millstone, when it inevitably emerged, could be summed up in the fact that, according to Greg at least, she spent a good deal of her time lying around on the sofa listening to 'Bridge Over Troubled Water', or *Tapestry*.

Greg hated *Tapestry*.

'How could Carole King do it?' he wailed, when the subject came up. 'She betrayed *everything* she ever stood for with that pseudo-hippie shit-bag of an album.' His anger was genuine. 'She wrote all those great songs for the Chiffons and the Shirelles. 'One Fine Day'. 'Will You Still Love Me Tomorrow'. Amazing stuff. 'Going Back', for God's sake! What did she have to go and do *Tapestry* for?' He gazed at me dolefully, and I shook my head. He was pushing the point way too far, and we both knew it, just as we both knew that any sane person would have just shrugged and wandered away – but we also knew that neither of us could have been described as a sane person. I wasn't crazy the way *he* was crazy, but all craziness is kin. The mad prefer the company of the mad to the company of the sane; it's less irritating, even though it can sometimes be catastrophic.

So we proceeded over the next several weeks, meeting every few days and drinking steadily through an evening, talking rubbish, constructing a whole other world from old songs and movie trivia. We never met anywhere but in a pub; whatever connection we had, it only worked in bars – and we knew it. Or I did, at least; but then I didn't have an agenda, I just thought I'd run into a kindred spirit, someone as pathetic and crumpled as I was. Someone not quite as dull as the others, because he wasn't dull like them, he was dull like me.

There are laws to drinking, just as there are laws to everything else, and one of the most important is that, eventually, under the right circumstances, every true drunk comes to recognise that human beings are inherently dull, especially himself. The one thing that rescues us from complete tedium is our gift for perversity and anybody who is even remotely perverse is at least temporarily interesting. In most cases, though, that perversity is compromised: people are perverse for a reason, they want to prove something, they have motives for being contrary that make their contrariness seem petty and inelegant. Greg's perversity, however, was as pure as the driven snow. His contrariness was always gratuitous and informed by a twisted logic that, on his part, was a matter of principle. That was what I thought then, at least, and my grudging admiration for this pose carried us a long way. If I'd only known what he had at the back of his mind, I would have gone back to drinking by myself, like a proper barfly. I reckon, when they made that rule on the old twelve-step way, they only printed half of it. It should have said, there's only one thing worse than drinking by yourself, and that's drinking with other people.

I can't recall how long I knew Greg, before our conversation got round to the subject of his wife. *The Millstone.* I never did find out her real name. He volunteered a number of possibilities, but none struck me as particularly convincing and,

56

even at the last, when I was standing over her in their neat little sitting room, being invited to take her life, I didn't know her for sure as anything other than this: The Millstone. The one Greg had hanging around his neck. It had been hanging there for some time when I arrived, and I only ever got Greg's side of the story. Looking back, I try to find a pattern, even an intent, in the way he talked about his marriage, a series of conversations that seemed to lead up quite naturally to his proposing that I kill the woman he so obviously hated – and I think there *was* a pattern, though not an intent, or not a conscious one at least. It came from somewhere further down, from some dream world that he was only half aware of, a world where Hitchcock movies are translated into reality at the drop of a hat, and the only governing principle is desperation. It came, in other words, from the back of his mind.

The happy couple had met six years earlier at an office party. They were drunk, and he had been taken with her, and one thing had led to another. That should have been that, but it wasn't. Quite *why* it wasn't, he never made clear. Together, they seem to have drifted into a marriage that, according to Greg, they both repented within the year. Or he did, anyway. Sex hadn't lasted long and, by the time I met him, they were barely talking.

'We live in separate worlds,' he said. 'I have no idea what's happening in hers, and she couldn't care less what goes on in mine.' He was quite matter-of-fact about this, perhaps because he'd had so long to get used to the situation. Besides, it wasn't as if he could look about him and find examples of marriages that worked very much better than his own. As far as he could see, every marriage was a war of one kind or another; the only good thing about his was that a lackadaisical, but more or less functioning peace had been declared, silently, and in a spirit

57

of wholehearted indifference or, in the Millstone's case, a consuming passion for vodka and long naps in front of the TV. Or so he said – though I couldn't quite bring myself to believe it was as bad as he described. Once upon a time, she'd had a job; now, she just stayed at home all day, sleeping, or talking on the phone, till it was late enough to justify opening another bottle of Smirnoff.

'Well,' I said, 'she can't do that *all* the time. She must do *something* else.'

Greg pondered. 'She knits, sometimes,' he said. He seemed surprised by this.

'That's all?'

He nodded. 'Pretty much.'

'What does she knit?'

'Baby clothes.'

'Oh.'

He smiled ruefully. 'She gives them to her friends,' he said.

'You don't have kids of your own, though,' I said. I didn't know what else to say.

Greg made an odd, guttural noise, but he failed to elaborate further.

'That would be a no, then,' I said.

He grimaced. 'That would be a *never*,' he said.

'Ah.' And now I thought I understood. *They couldn't have kids* – and maybe that was the trouble. Maybe the Millstone was depressed. Women always want children eventually. That's why they get married in the first place and, if they can't have children, they get depressed. Case solved.

'So – what's her name again?' I asked. I had asked before, and he had dodged the question.

'Zelda,' he said.

'Zelda?'

58

'Yes.'

'Is that her real name?'

'Yes.' He looked bewildered. 'What's wrong with Zelda?'

'As in Zelda Fitzgerald?'

'Her dad was a big *Gatsby* fan,' he said.

I didn't believe him. 'Come on,' I said. 'What's her *real* name?'

'I'm telling you,' he said, all butter-wouldn't-melt. 'It's Zelda. Scout's honour.' He pondered for a moment. 'Or is it Lois?' A dark look crossed his face. 'I do believe I've forgotten,' he said. 'It's been a hell of a long time.'

'Well,' I said, 'maybe you should try to remember. And maybe you should talk to her about all this. Tell her how unhappy you are. Maybe she's unhappy too. Maybe she's depressed. You won't know what's wrong unless you talk about it.' I came to an abrupt halt, feeling slightly breathless. I hadn't meant to say any of this, and I looked at him for a reaction.

He didn't seem offended, just a little surprised. Finally, he shook his head. 'Thanks for the advice,' he said. 'But if I want to talk to myself, I'll go down to the chapel.'

All this time, I was living alone in the flat. It was still owned by someone else, but by then she had moved jobs and was renting another place, somewhere near Reading. She popped back from time to time, just for the odd weekend, but mostly I was alone, wandering about the place like some half-wild creature trapped in an abandoned building.

Or maybe not trapped. Maybe this animal was just injured, or scared of something – hunters, say, or a gang of bored kids with a borrowed airgun. I could go out; I could function; but my days were empty, utterly procedural and as rudimentary as a Primary 4 exercise book – and, all the time, no matter how long I stayed away, the flat was waiting, not in the least rudimentary, not in the least procedural. There was no logic there: time did strange things in the small hours and, as every insomniac knows, there is nothing small about the small hours. They are vast and slow and beyond all cartography, like an ocean, or the surface of Jupiter. Sometimes, I would wander back and forth all night, seeing things, sensing other bodies in the hallway or in the next room, hearing sounds in the walls, sounds that were there and, presumably, sounds that were not, sounds that made no sense and so became susceptible to an infinity of possible interpretation. Looking back, I can describe those nights in terms of a known set of symptoms, a pathology laid out in textbooks and identified in certain types of mental patient, but that would be as procedural and rudimentary as my fallow and stepwise days at the office or the surface glide through Guildford market on a Saturday morning where, every week, I went to the same stalls and had more or less the same conversation with the pretty blonde woman who sold flowers at the foot of the town, or with the man who had the best aubergines, halfway up. I was looking for order, the way everyone does – and sometimes I found it, or something like it. And sometimes I found the cosy nooks and crannies of my own private purgatory.

Yet, as unsettling as they were, and they certainly could be very unsettling, these rambles in the small hours were only part of the problem, and not the worst part. To be frank, there was even a certain beauty to some of those long nights, a beauty of possibility, whether it be the possibility that time would actually stop altogether, or that, in the rinsed gloaming of the wolf hour, when the light from the street was like the light from the projector in an old-time cinema, I might slip into the hypernarrative forever and stay where nothing matters except the details: the coffee cup on the dining-room table, the vase of irises by the bed, the open door to the hall through which, at any moment, someone might enter. There was a beauty to that, and there was a beauty to the way things continued as they were, to how the doorway remained empty, to how the walls fell silent after a time and, more than anything, to the moments when, having sat for hours, gazing into the half-dark, I suddenly woke and realised that I had been asleep and dreaming, the dream miraculous and logical and, even as it melted away, genuinely significant – apophenia be damned – like the dream Dmitri dreams, after the long hours of inter-rogation in *The Brothers Karamazov*.

Those nights held their share of terror, I will not deny it. Terror, and sometimes dread, which is not beautiful, but empty and sickening – but there was a worse time, a daylight time in the late afternoon, when I would come back to the flat and find it different, slightly changed, subtly altered from how I had left it that morning. I would get home and, even as I was turning the key in the lock, I would know that someone had been there while I was out, and, slowly, walking through from the hallway to the kitchen, I would search for clues, for the tiny, almost imperceptible evidences of intrusion, afraid to find what I was looking for but, at the same time, desperate to know, one way or another, who or what was haunting me. And there was always something. I always *knew*. Things had been disturbed, things had been handled and used – and what-ever that presence was, it was still there, inherent in the objects it had touched, like a stain, or a virus. I'm not talking about ghosts or bogeymen, here. I'm not even talking about demons or angels or Maupassant's Horla. I'm not talking about the doppelgänger or pixies, either. I'm talking about *presence*. Something had been present in those neat, beige rooms while

61

I was gone – and I had so wanted an absence to come home to. I had so wanted there to be nothing. More than anything else, I wanted my life to be normal – but it wasn't. Something was present in those objects and in those rooms and, whenever it showed itself, I couldn't stay in the flat for long. I had to be out, away, anywhere but there.

It was a Saturday lunchtime. Greg and I had met up, more or less on purpose, for a drink at the Three Pigeons. In those days, the pubs still closed between lunch and six, so when last orders came, we had to think of something to do for the afternoon. For me, that usually meant the bookies, or a cafe, or maybe a bottle of wine in the park, up behind the castle. That day was different, though. I had known Greg for several weeks by then, and he had never been to the flat, and I had never been to his house off the Epsom Road. That was a tacit agreement we all had, in those bars: drinking was one thing, and the sad wreckage of home was something else entirely, and we kept the two strictly apart. So I was quite surprised when he invited me back to his for the afternoon.

'It's all right. The Millstone's away.' He seemed pleasantly surprised by the fact. 'She's gone to her mother's,' he said. 'She does that, from time to time.'

If I'd been stone-cold sober, I might have thought twice about the invitation. If I'd been drunk, I almost certainly would have gone off somewhere else. Halfway between the two, however, in that limbo state where nothing really matters as long as there's another drink in sight and a quiet-afternoon-place and some music, I went along for the ride. I think I even suspected him of something, at that very moment, but I didn't know what and, in my state of alcoholic suspension, I didn't really care. So we got four bottles of wine and some cider and headed up to his place. I had to admit, I was curious to see what it was like.

He lived in a semi-detached house on a quiet, even leafy street, behind a red-painted door and a pyracantha bush that badly needed pruning. True Surbiton country, in fact. Inside, though, the house was very much smaller than I had imagined, and it was a dump. There was a smell in the hallway, somewhere between curry and malt, and the stair carpet had bald patches all the way up. In the living room, which seemed to double as a dining area, dirty plates with dried-on pasta sauce and curry stains were stacked high on the table, and there were empty bottles everywhere. On the sofa, in a pile of magazines and newspapers, a pool of what looked like brandy was slowly evaporating in a soggy pit of newsprint, flecks of dust and tobacco floating on the surface. Cigarette papers littered the floor. On top of the TV set, in the furthest corner of the room, a row of empty beer bottles stood brown and solemn and oddly meaningful, like some sinister message, in the near-gloom. Greg looked around and shrugged.

'Sorry about the mess,' he said. He gathered up the brandy and newsprint and carted it out to the kitchen, then he busied himself with opening a bottle and fetching glasses. I was still standing in the middle of the room, wondering where to sit.

'Grab a pew,' he said, as he laboured with the corkscrew. 'Make yourself at home.'

I sat down on a chair by the fireplace and he gave me a half-pint glass full of red wine. Then, when he'd poured for himself, he put on a record. I didn't know what it was, but it sounded a bit like Brinsley Schwarz. Before I could ask him, though, he was back on his feet, heading for the kitchen. I'd had it in mind that we'd just sit a while, listen to the music, keep the blood alcohol level topped up – but he couldn't seem to settle.

'Come on,' he said. 'I've got something I want to show you.' He walked through, glass in hand, and I followed. But when we got there, he just stood, with a reverent look on his face, by the fridge. It was a big, old-fashioned model, of the kind that used to be called 'American-style'. Greg smiled wistfully. 'We didn't have a fridge when I was a kid,' he said. 'Not to begin with.' He opened the door, and a bluish light came on. 'Then, one day, it was summer, really hot, and the delivery van arrived. My dad had just changed jobs, they had more money, so they bought this massive fridge, a beautiful – appliance.' He reached into the light and pulled out two bottles of Carlsberg. 'I loved that fridge,' he said. 'I used to get up at night and go into the kitchen. I'd open the door, look inside. Feel the cold on my hands and face. Stand there in the cool of it. It made everything seem –' He broke off and went over to the window by the sink and stared out into the back garden. 'I do the same thing now. I've had this fridge for twelve years and it still runs perfectly. It's the same model, more or less, as the one we had back then.' He put his glass down on the draining board. 'I love this fridge more than anything. When we first got married, I used to come in here and sit for hours, listening to it hum. I'd stare out of that window at the night, or I'd watch the dawn come up. It was like a *companion*.' He looked at me, to see if I was following – and I could see he was playing me, because he had somehow figured out that I felt the same way about it all, about the fridge and the night and being in a house where someone else, some stranger, lay sleeping upstairs. 'And no matter what happens,' he said, 'I can't let her take this fridge away from me.'

'Well,' I said, 'I don't imagine she would fight you for custody of the fridge.'

'No,' he said. 'She wouldn't. But she'd take half of everything. I'd have to sell this house. I would be losing everything.'

We were back on familiar territory. For some time now, he had been talking about the consequences of a divorce. How he would lose the house. How he would have to support her. How he couldn't live with himself if he let that happen. I had tried reasoning with him, but he had already worked it all out in his head and, by now, I was a little bored.

'She would only get half,' I said. 'Surely you can manage, somehow.'

'And then I'd have to pay alimony. I'd be working all hours, just to keep her in vodka and *Hello!* magazine.'

I didn't know anything about how divorce worked and every time this line of conversation came up, I wished I had checked it out, just so I could shoot him down. 'I don't think you can make that assumption,' I said. 'I mean, you don't have kids or anything –'

'She'll say she gave up work to get married. She'll get some top-end barrister to say she had a promising career before she met me. Then I'll have to go out and pay through the nose for somebody too, and we'd just piss it all away on lawyers. Not that there's that much to piss away . . .'

And so on, and so on. It was all getting hopelessly repetitive.

Finally, we went back to the living room, leaving the precious fridge humming in its warm corner. We opened more wine, then we opened the cider. Greg put on the first Steven Stills album, and then some ridiculous compilation from the early seventies and we sat quiet for a while, listening to Nick Drake or somebody. He couldn't leave it alone, though. When that

65

record was finished, he didn't move, he just sat on the sofa, looking a little bleary and smiling an odd smile.

'Well?' I said. 'Are you going to put something else on or what?'

He didn't move. 'You remember that film,' he said, at last, '*Strangers on a Train*?'

I nodded. 'Yeah,' I said. 'Farley Granger. Robert Walker. 1953, I think –'

'1951.'

'OK. If you say so. What about it?' I knew, of course, that I shouldn't be asking, because I knew, just by looking at him, that he was off somewhere on his own.

'Well,' he said, 'you know the plan. How Robert Walker asks Farley Granger to kill his father, and in return he'll kill Farley's wife –'

'Is it his wife?'

'Of course it is. She's been unfaithful to him, so now he's got this other woman, only she won't let him go –'

'I don't remember.'

'Trust me.'

'Oh, I'm sure you're right.'

'Only Farley Granger doesn't keep his end of the bargain.'

'I don't think –'

'Which is why it all goes wrong –'

'That's not . . .' I was trying to think. I remembered a tennis game, and something about a lighter, but I wasn't sure what happened at the end. All I knew was that it wasn't Farley Granger's fault, he was just trying to save himself and set it up so the police could catch Robert Walker, or something like that. One of *those* deals. But I couldn't remember. I was getting mixed up with the Leopold and Loeb film, with colour in my head for some of the memories and black and white for others.

66

Only I couldn't think what that Leopold and Loeb film was called. 'I don't remember,' I said.

'Sure you do,' Greg said. He sounded far away, as if he were talking in a dream. 'Robert Walker comes to him with this *perfect* plan, only it goes wrong, because Granger has second thoughts –'

'Well, I'm not sure –'

'It's a good plan, though,' he said. 'It *could* work –'

'Doesn't Granger reject him right from the start? Or is that –'

'Well, yes, but that's just a plot device. What's interesting is that the plan could work, if Granger could just use his imagination. Anyhow, it's not Granger you're with, it's Walker.'

His voice rose a little and I could see that he felt strongly about this – and that was when I realised something was up. 'What are you *saying*?' I said, not wanting to hear what the answer was going to be.

'What I'm saying is – what if you and I were the men on that train. What if I was Robert Walker and you were Farley Granger?'

'What of it?'

'Well, we're just like them. There's no real connection between us –'

'No –'

'And, you said it yourself, it could work –'

'All right, Greg,' I said. 'Stop right there. It's not even remotely funny.'

'I'm not trying to be funny,' he said. 'I'm telling you – there's nothing to connect us, not really. We've had a couple of drinks together, but this is the first time you've been to this house –'

'Shut up, Greg.'

'I'm telling you,' he said, 'we could do it. It would be easy. You've never even met her. She's a stranger to you. I'd make it easy, set it all up. Give you a key. Slip something in her drink. Not that she needs it. You'd just let yourself in while I'm out, do the business and – gone. Like a ghost.' He caught his breath and made a low, soft noise, a kind of muted whistle, as if to say, look how easy it is, it's almost a sin that it should be so easy. 'In return,' he continued, 'I'll kill anybody you tell me to kill. No questions.'

I stared at him. I couldn't believe what I was hearing. He was serious. He'd thought about this, and he'd worked it all out. All he had to do was convince me. I felt empty-headed, almost sick with dismay, not because he wanted his wife dead, but because it was me he was asking to kill her. Why did he think I was capable of that? Why did he think *I* was a killer? 'You're not kidding, are you?' I said, at last.

'Not even for a second,' he said.

'But what makes you think –'

'Quid pro quo. You do this for me, and I'll do something for you –'

I let out a dismayed laugh. 'I don't have anybody I want to *kill*,' I said.

'Are you sure?' He looked puzzled. 'What? Nobody at all?'

'Well, no,' I said – and at that moment I decided that this was a game after all, because he couldn't have been serious. It was too ridiculous. 'God,' I said, 'you had me there.'

'Hm?' He had gone quiet now, thinking, as if my not having anybody I wanted dead really was a surprise to him, and maybe a failing on my part, but I just decided this was part of the bad joke, part of his stupid, drunken game.

'For Christ's sake,' I said. 'Put another record on.'

He looked up. 'You're right,' he said. 'I *had* you there.' He laughed.

I didn't say anything. I'd been convinced it was all going to be fine, until he said that. It wasn't the words, it was his expression. He realised he had gone too far, too fast, but I could see that the thought was still at the back of his mind. He'd just let it out too soon.

I should have walked away then, but I didn't. I have no idea why. Maybe I thought I had to stick around and keep an eye on him. Make sure he had dropped the idea for good. Make sure what was happening at the back of his mind didn't end up seeing the light of day. The following Monday, I was sitting at my desk, with Tim's Sunday-afternoon detritus all around me, running through it all again. Why *had* Greg chosen me as his assassin? We had talked about murder several times, in the context of old movies, working out how to commit that old cliché, the perfect crime, and we'd talked about methods and timing, and about how to avoid getting caught, but then I'd always imagined we were talking in the abstract. Now, it seemed, those conversations were a basis for something. Greg had been impressed, in some way, by my familiarity with the subject and he'd decided I was his Farley Granger.

All the time, I was trying to get my head down and work, instead of running through all this nonsense over and over again – and after a while, from exhaustion more than anything, I got started on one of those routine maintenance jobs that so often came my way. Agricultural Census had this ancient validation program that was so huge and badly documented that nobody really knew what it did any more, only that it more or less worked, if you tweaked it occasionally. And, occasionally, it was my job to do the tweaking. Not the most interesting work but, that day, it was all I had to hand and, eventually, I got mired in the code, falling deeper and deeper into the creaking machinery of it all. I barely noticed when Tim came in and sat down at his desk, and I forgot him as soon as he was settled. Not that he minded. The quiz team were coming up for some kind of quarter-final thing, and he was revising. The day before, he'd probably spent five or six hours of precious overtime drinking warm beer, reading the Sunday supplements and revising Oscar winners in all categories between 1950 and 1975, which accounted for all the mess. I didn't care, though. Usually, I had to suppress a tiny frisson of irritation whenever he clapped his book shut and muttered something like 'Goldie Hawn? I don't believe it!' Or '"Behind the Painted Smile". What an idiot!' Eventually, however, I realised he had put his book aside and was staring at me.

I looked at him. 'What?' I said.

'I'm trying to read,' he said.

'So, read,' I said.

'I can't.'

'Why not?

'Because you're talking to yourself.'

'No I'm not.'

'Yes you are.'

'Am I?'

'Yes.'

'What am I saying? Is it interesting?'

'I have no idea. But would you please stop it?'

I didn't respond. Tim had no brain, but he was officially my line manager, so even though I could have pointed out that it didn't matter whether I was talking to myself or not, because he was only revising for a fucking quiz anyway, I didn't. Better he revise for a quiz than actually do something,

70

because whenever he did have a crisis of conscience and made an effort to help out, he would mess up so badly that it would take me ages to sort it out. I was far better off doing everything myself in the first place. Better if he just kept out of the way with the *Guinness Book of Records* or *Brewer's Phrase & Fable*.

'Didn't mean to disturb,' I said, after a moment, keen to move on. The truth was, I believed him. I probably *had* been talking to myself – which didn't bother me terribly, but there was something obscene about his having overheard. 'So – what are you on now?'

'What?'

'What are you *on*?'

He shook his head. 'It's what *you're* on that worries me,' he said, then he smiled to himself, and went back to his book. It was some kind of sporting encyclopedia, the kind of book that could tell you who won the Stanley Cup in any given year, and how many games it went to, and which of the players scored the winning goal.

It was after dawn, but not by much. I rose slowly to a roomful of sparkle and glitter – sparkle and glitter and then shadow, further away. A large room, with a huge bay window at the far end, facing the bed where I was lying, naked and half tangled in a white cotton sheet. Outside that window, everything was still – no traffic, no passers-by – but I knew there was a city out there, and I tried to remember what had happened, where I had been the night before, who I had been with, and how I had come to be there, in that roomful of glitter and deep marble shadows. Then, all of a sudden, I heard a series of bright, hard knocks through the wall behind me: a series of knocks, then silence, then more knocking and

71

then, slow, deep, somehow rubbery and, at the same time, as if strained through muslin, a quiet, low scraping sound, like someone working the meat off a bone. I had no idea where I was. I searched my memory again, but all that came to mind was a huge mirror in an elaborate gold frame over a limestone fireplace, and I looked round to see if that mirror was there, part of the furniture of this room where I had come to be, without knowing why or how. It wasn't. And then, the noise came again, a slow, painful flensing sound, followed by a loud, wet splash, as if someone had spilled a huge bucket of liquid – liquid, but not water, it was thicker than water – over a tiled floor. After that, silence for several minutes and time to think again, time to remember. Only I couldn't remember, so I started to get out of bed – only when my feet touched the floor, there was this thick, warm film of something wet, some-thing thicker than water, and I fell back on myself, hearing my own voice call out, only it wasn't my voice really, because I was asleep, wasn't I? And then I woke, and I was on the floor, in my own flat, which wasn't mine at all, but was the closest thing I had to home.

I didn't seek Greg out for a while, and I really don't think he was looking for me. Inevitably, though, we ran into each other and, because some time had elapsed, I managed to convince myself that I'd simply got the wrong end of the stick the last time we'd talked. And though it seems odd, now, to think that I fell back in with him so readily, it isn't really, not if I take into account the sheer inertia, the utter indifference, with which I dealt with the world outside my front door. At home, in the flat, sane or otherwise, I was, or felt to myself, *real.* The rest of the time, though, I might as well not have both-ered to turn up. Whatever happened, I went along with it, in a wandering, blind drift: work, pub, occasional opportunistic bouts of sex with strangers, it was all the same. From time to time, I would go up on to Merrow Down and walk about by myself, or I would lie down in the grass in my office clothes and stare up at the sky, listening to the insects in the long grass and the birds in the trees around the rim of the open down. I knew I had to change my life, I knew I had to pull myself out of this new fall or I would end up in yet another mental hospital, but I didn't know how. Or maybe I just didn't care – and besides, once you've sampled the medication, there is nothing quite so comforting as being carried away to the loony bin.

So maybe I had no good reason to start meeting Greg for our nerdy little drinks parties in the stale corners of various Guildford pubs and hotels, but I couldn't find a very good reason not to. He was entertaining, most of the time, and, for the moment, at least, he wasn't talking about his wife. He even seemed happy. So happy, for a while, that I thought the Millstone had gone back to her mother's for good, leaving him in full custody of the fridge and its contents. In fact, he seemed so content, in those last days of our friendship, that I began to assume that he was now living on his own – which was why I was so utterly wrong-footed, about a month later, when he suggested we go back to his after the pub.

I stalled. 'I don't know,' I said.

'Come on,' he said. 'It'll be like old times.'

That struck me as funny. It was as if we'd grown up together in some backwater somewhere, watching Paul Newman movies and fishing on a Saturday afternoon, blood brothers who, through no fault of their own, had been parted by time and circumstance, only to meet again by sheer chance, older, but not that much wiser, for a last drink before fate carried us away again. 'Oh, yes,' I said. 'Old times. I remember them well.'

'Oh, well,' he said. 'Don't bother then.' He seemed hurt.

And of course, I immediately relented. Because there had been old times. When you drink, there are always old times, no matter who it is. There's something in us that constructs them, rewriting everything so it's all a long evening at the edge of the woods, sitting on a car bonnet and drinking beer, while the traffic rushes by just yards away. The dumb old world going about its pointless business. All that fuss and noise – and there we are, in the old times, exempt from it all, wise fools, holy reprobates.

We'd had a few by then, which is probably the main reason I went. That, or the voices back in the flat. There was a crate of wine back at his, Greg said, but we got a bottle of vodka anyway and hit the road in a taxi, even though our last worthless evening was just four streets away, in a dark little house that I was stupid enough to imagine was empty.

The Millstone was asleep on the sofa, an odd, troubled look on her face. I knew it was her right away. She was plump, pallid, utterly inert; a woman in her mid-thirties, I would have said, with dirty blonde hair and large white hands that looked like they had been blown up with a bicycle pump. As soon as we came into the living room, Greg went and stood over her, staring down at the sleeping woman as if he were trying to read her dreaming mind. Finally, he turned to me. 'She's sleeping,' he said. 'Best we don't wake her.'

I was annoyed, but not as annoyed as I wanted to be. 'You didn't say *she*'d be here,' I said.

He gave me a puzzled look. 'She lives here,' he said. 'Where else would she be?' He went into the kitchen and brought back two half-pint glasses. When he was at home, Greg drank everything in half-pint glasses, it seemed: vodka, wine, cider, it didn't matter, it was always the same half-pint, near-brimming measure that he poured. 'Besides,' he said, passing me my glass, which I accepted in spite of myself, 'she's not really *here*, is she? Not really *with* us.' He sat down on one arm of the sofa, so that I could sit on the armchair by the fireplace. 'Have a seat,' he said. 'Make yourself at home.'

I sat down. 'All right,' I said. 'But I don't want to hear any bullshit. All right?'

'What bullshit?'

'You know what I mean.'

He didn't reply, but turned back to the sleeping woman. 'She's probably been drinking all day,' he said. 'She does that sometimes.' He drank half of his vodka in one go. '*She* likes vodka too,' he said, with an odd softness to his voice, as if he were speaking of someone he still cared for. Someone he had loved once, then stopped loving, but still cared for, for old times' sake. 'Vodka – and baby food,' he said.

'Sorry?'

'*That's* what she likes,' he said. 'Vodka and baby food. Baby food and vodka –'

'Maybe she's broody,' I said.

Greg shuddered. Then he smiled knowingly. 'Luckily, she can't be,' he said. He leaned over and looked carefully into the Millstone's face, as if he thought she might be listening. 'She's been eating baby food for years,' he said. 'She just *likes* it, I suppose.'

My wanting-a-baby theory came back to me, then, and I wondered if this was just some elaborate game they played, the two of them together maybe, or maybe just singly, taking

75

it in turns to probe the wound, like George and Martha in *Who's Afraid of Virginia Woolf?*. 'That must be difficult,' I said.

He turned to me sharply. 'What?' he said.

'It must be *difficult*,' I said. 'That she can't have children –'

Greg laughed out loud, to show how wildly amused he was by this remark, completely ignoring the sleeping woman. 'Oh, God,' he said. 'That's a good one.' He gave me a big-hearted, appreciative look, as if I'd just cracked a great joke. 'No, no,' he said. 'That's not it. *She* can have children.' He broke off and thought for a moment. 'Well – I suppose she can.'

'So what did you mean then?' I was starting to get annoyed again. I took a swig of vodka and decided that, as soon as I'd finished this one drink, I'd leave. 'You said she can't –'

'I had a vasectomy,' he said. He grinned, then turned back to the woman on the sofa and gazed into her face. 'Not that we ever fuck. I mean, look at her. Have you ever seen anyone so – unattractive?'

I looked at his wife. She wasn't beautiful, nobody could have accused her of that, but she wasn't hideous either. And he must have wanted her, in the beginning at least, or presumably he wouldn't have ended up here. 'She's all right,' I said.

He smiled at an irony I hadn't intended. 'OK,' he said. 'She's not *ugly*. Well, not very.' He gave me an enquiring look, as if he cared about my answer. 'Do you think she's ugly?'

'Not at all.'

'You're *right*,' he said cheerily, as if I'd paid her some extravagant compliment. 'It's *not* that she's ugly. It's worse than that.' He turned back to the unconscious woman and studied her face. I had the impression that he'd done this often, watching her while she slept, thinking about what he had got himself into. 'I had every opportunity to get away from her,' he said. 'Nobody forced me to marry her. I did it of my own free will.'

'Well,' I said. I didn't know what to say. 'That's something.'

He gave me an odd, surprised look, then he turned back to the Millstone. 'It's so easy to get married,' he said. 'Much easier than getting divorced, right?'

I gave him a warning look. I didn't mind this soft, elegiac strain, with the vodka and all, but I had no desire to go back to the divorce rant.

He moved on quickly. 'And then it turns out to be a mistake. So what do you do?' He straightened up and finished off his vodka. 'You freeze up. You feel guilty for getting yourself into such a ridiculous situation. And then you start punishing your-self. Punishing yourself for something that happened totally by accident. Punishing yourself for somebody else's failings.' He took my glass, which was still half full, and retreated to the kitchen, talking as he went. 'I mean, it's one thing to look back and say you made a mess of your life, but how do you think it feels to look forward and know you are about to waste what's left of your pathetic existence on some pointless charade . . . ?' He disappeared into the dark and I heard the vodka being poured – and, too late, I remembered that I'd been planning to leave after one drink. A moment later, he reappeared with the freshened glasses, full to brimming once more.

'We've been through all this,' I said. 'And I can't see why you don't just leave, if you're so unhappy. Surely that would be –'

'I *told* you,' he said. His voice was quiet, but I detected a hint of exasperation. 'She would *take* everything –'

'And *I* told *you*,' I said. 'No more of this bullshit –'

'It's not bullshit,' he said. 'You know it's not. She'd want *everything*. And that's exactly what she'd get.' He looked at me and I felt sure that he believed what he was saying enough to take some kind of action. He believed that he had worked for what he had, and he wasn't going to allow anybody to take that away from him. Whether it was true or not was beside the point. He believed it, and it was a matter of principle, not to let that happen – and he was prepared to take steps, whatever they might be, before he relinquished that ground.

'You need a *lawyer*,' I said. 'That's what you have to do. Find yourself a lawyer.'

'And then the fucking lawyer would take his chunk, and her lawyer would take his, and –' He seemed close to tears – and the odd thing was, at that moment, I actually felt sorry for him. I knew what was coming – there was no avoiding it – and I still felt sorry for him. He shook his head softly and looked at me and I could see that he was desperate – but I could also see that he wanted me to see that he was desperate. 'You could do it now,' he said. 'Nobody would know.'

'Stop,' I said.

'You could do it. She'd be better off –'

'Oh. It's for her own good now, is it?'

'You know what I mean –'

'But why *would* I?' I said.

'I'll kill somebody for you,' he said. 'Fair exchange.'

'I don't want you to kill anybody,' I said. 'I told you that already.'

'There must be *some*body.'

'No.' I put down my glass. 'You have to *stop* this. You really have to let this go and get a lawyer and –' I didn't know what else to say. I was there, in this man's living room, standing over his unconscious wife – who, for all I knew, could have been drugged hours ago, just so that we could have this conversation – and he was trying to get me to kill her. I wasn't going to do that, but I was starting to wonder if maybe her life wasn't in my hands, anyway. If I put down my glass and walked out, as I'd been planning to do for the last twenty minutes, he might do the deed himself, and maybe then he'd try to pin it on me. Or he would just do it, and to hell with the consequences. He'd had enough to drink by now, and he was definitely not thinking straight. But then, he'd had enough to drink any number of times, and the woman was still lying there, on that sofa, and she would no doubt wake sooner or later, none the wiser. So maybe it was me who wasn't thinking straight. Maybe it really *was* a game – a serious game, a fantasy that kept him going because one day, not now, but later, there was a chance that somebody would come to this house and accept his offer, and he would be free, without really having done anything other than play out this ridiculous scene. And so it all went around in my head: murder, a game, a game, murder, and wasn't it all the same anyhow? I was heart-sick and exhausted and I'd had enough. 'I'm tired of this,' I said, at last.

His voice dropped again. For a man who had drunk as much as he had, he sounded remarkably sober. 'Nobody would suspect you,' he said. 'It's perfect. Just wait till I'm gone, give me half an hour say, an hour maybe, to be on the safe side. Then you can do it.'

That made me laugh. 'Well, that's just stupid,' I said. 'Half an hour isn't enough. An hour isn't enough. And where are you going to go, around here? The pubs are shut.' I shook my head. I should have been on my way out the door, and instead there I was debating it with him. 'Christ,' I said, 'if that's your plan, I would give up now.' I was talking too loudly now, and I was speaking for the hidden microphone, for the unseen witness. 'And I don't know why you thought I would ever agree to this.' I got up and started for the door.

Greg jumped up and grabbed at my arm. 'All right, all right,' he said. 'Take it easy.' He stood thinking for a moment, as if we were stuck in some shared dilemma, and it was up to him to work out a solution. Then he sat down again, took a swig of his drink and sat for a while in silence.

I waited. I wanted to leave, but I didn't want to leave him there alone with his possible victim. 'Tell you what,' I said. 'Let's head back into town. Take a look around till the pubs open.'

Greg looked up at me, but he didn't say anything. He seemed to be thinking and that worried me. Finally, he shook his head. 'This may come as a surprise to you,' he said, 'but I've always really *liked* Petula Clark.' He looked at me to see if I shared his opinion of the great songstress, but I was a step behind, still thinking about the threat to his wife. She had started to snore all of a sudden, a very gentle burr, punctuated by odd little grinding sounds, and I thought this meant she would wake up soon. *Because she was sleeping now,* I thought, *not unconscious.* He had drugged her, earlier, and now the drug was wearing off. In a moment, she would be waking up, all groggy and confused, but probably out of harm's way. I wasn't sure about that, though. 'What a pity she had to stop singing,' Greg continued, as if nothing out of the ordinary had happened.

I looked at him. 'What's *this*, now?' I said.

'Petula *Clark*,' he said. 'Don't you remember? She contracted that rare disease. Who knows what she might have achieved, if she'd been able to realise her full potential –'

'What in Christ's name are you *talking* about?' I said. I felt indignant now, for Petula Clark's sake as much as my own. I had loitered all that time, while he plotted his wife's murder, but I was annoyed now by this minor lie about one of my mother's favourite singers. I could see Petula Clark in my mind's eye, singing 'Downtown' on some sixties television programme. 'Petula Clark never contracted any rare disease,' I said. 'She didn't have to give up singing. In fact –' I heard my voice rising, loud enough to wake the Millstone, but I couldn't help myself – 'she's still singing to this day. She *did* realise her full potential. That was it. End of story.'

Greg seemed shocked. 'I don't know how you can say that,' he said, genuinely wounded. 'How can you say Petula Clark achieved her full potential when –'

'*What the fuck difference does it make?*' I shouted. The Millstone stirred, sighed, then shifted a little, before falling back into the land of nod, but I didn't care, now, if she woke up or not. '*What does it bloody well matter about Petula Bloody Clark?*'

Greg smiled sadly. 'Well, *I* think it matters,' he said quietly.

I shook my head. 'It doesn't, Greg,' I said. 'It doesn't make a blind bit of difference. Get a fucking lawyer, don't get a lawyer, do what you like but I'm going now, all right?'

He didn't move and I took the last few steps to the door and opened it – but I didn't leave. I couldn't. I still didn't know what he was going to do. So I stood, waiting, hoping that he would say something, or that his wife would wake up, or maybe Petula Clark would walk through the door and start singing 'Downtown' and everything would be OK. Finally he spoke. 'Are you sure?' he asked, with something like dismay in his voice. I wondered if we were still talking about Petula Clark.

'I'm positive,' I said quietly.

There was a silence, during which I struggled absurdly to remember the words. *When you're alone, and life is making you lonely, you can always go – Downtown* . . . What was next? What came after that?

81

Greg jerked to his feet. 'OK,' he said. 'You stay. I'm going out now.'

I looked at him in alarm – and then I realised that Greg's going was the best thing that could happen now. With him out of the house, I could wake his wife, warn her of what he was planning, maybe even get her to safety. I didn't know if that was possible but, for the moment, the Millstone was safer with me than she was with him. 'Where are you going?' I asked.

'*Downtown,*' he said. 'You wait here. If she wakes up, no problem, just get out before she sees you and we'll do it some other time. But if she's still asleep after an hour – you should just do it.' He fixed me with his eyes to let me know he was serious, but I was too tired to say anything. 'Any method you like,' he said. 'You choose. Just give me an hour.' Then he walked through to the hall, without another word. Leaving me with the snoring woman, the one I was supposed to kill. I could have gone with him, I could probably have stopped him, but I didn't. The front door opened and, just as he left the house, I realised he had started to whistle. I knew the song – not 'Downtown', something else – but I couldn't place it. After a moment, the front door clapped shut and it was quiet again.

I waited a long time, but he didn't come back, and the Millstone didn't wake up. I had no idea how long she had been asleep, maybe all day. If he had drugged her, he must have done it just before he went out, at the very latest. She could wake up in the next few minutes, or she could sleep till noon the next day, I had no way of knowing – and the truth was, I didn't care. I didn't care, now, if Greg came back, or if she woke up, or what the bastard was planning to do, or had done. A cold quiet had fallen on me, and all I could think of was Petula Clark. She'd had other hits, back in her heyday, and I was trying to recollect what they were, but I couldn't, or not to begin with. Then I remembered 'Don't Sleep on the Subway, Baby', and I felt a little better – and then I realised I was feeling bad about Petula Clark, because I hadn't realised she'd been ill, and I hoped she was OK. I sat a long time thinking about Petula and listening to Zelda snore, as she slept off whatever was in her blood, oblivious to the danger she could so easily have been in. For the moment, though, she was safe. For as long as I stayed, she would be all right – only I *couldn't* stay, or not forever, anyhow. I put it off for as long as I could, then I decided it was OK to leave. Greg might be outside somewhere, under a tree, or in some-body's darkened doorway, waiting for me to go, but there was nothing I could do about that. I couldn't keep him at bay forever. I did my best to stay, I even poured another drink and went through Greg's records, to occupy myself for a while longer. I didn't come across Petula Clark, but I did find *Tapestry* and I read the titles silently to myself, like someone mem-orising a spell, before I finally left.

VALIUM AND LULLABIES

April, 2008. My eldest son wakes me to say that it's snowing.
I have been up half the night and I've only slept for a couple
of hours at most but, as I surface just enough to see him there,
in the greyish light of very early morning, I realise that I have
been dreaming about Gina – or not really about Gina, but
about one of the parties she used to have in her little house
on the north side of Guildford, not so much a party, even, as
a kind of sad orgy, the participants flabby and slightly desperate,
a bad sex film flickering silently in the corner, broken glass
in the fireplace, a child's toy half concealed in the gap between
the sofa and the wall. I'm surprised by this – I haven't thought
about Gina since the last time I saw her, and I didn't give her
that much thought back then – but the dream is so vivid,
even as I'm falling out of it, that I imagine my son can see
what I'm seeing, or rather, what's still evaporating around me
as I open my eyes. He's not long up, I can see it in his face:
a faint blear, a tousled quality.

'It's snowing, Dad,' he says. I nod and try to go back to
sleep. He persists. 'Can I go out and make a snowman?'

I half sit. 'Not in your pyjamas,' I say.

He laughs. 'No,' he says. 'I'll get dressed first –'

I look towards the window: drawn curtains, just barely
touched with grey. 'What time is it?' I ask him.

'It's getting-up time,' he says.

I shake my head. 'It's Sunday,' I say. Now I know what the dream was about. It was a Saturday-night dream and Saturday night is party night, even when it isn't. A disheartening notion – like some virus your body never quite recovers from, something that's always there, waiting to flare up, like herpes simplex. That Saturday-night ache, part miracle, part affliction.

'I'll be very quiet,' he says – and I realise that, as usual, he's the first one awake. This child is a carbon copy of me, same face, same eyes, same imagination, same insomnia.

I nod. 'Wait till I get up,' I say. 'I'll not be long –'

– and then I'm asleep again, and this time I'm in a city that looks like Prague, but with a touch of Amsterdam about it, a city full of trams and narrow bridges and wide gaps between the house fronts and the river, Amsterdam and Prague and a hint of Bruges, but it's not any one of them, it's the city that always appears in my dreams: a corner from one place, a street from another, a bird singing on a balcony, the smell of coffee, snow and steam and a lamplit bridge in the first grey of the morning and a huge crowd of people crossing a black river to – where? An avenue of blackened trees, an icy park, a museum of some kind, or maybe a government building, where my son is standing in a doorway in his crew cap and padded jacket, his face still bleary from the night, his voice insistent now.

'Dad,' he says. 'Dad!'

I look at him. I'm awake again, and I'm still dreaming, both at once and so neither, quite. He looks like me, same face, same eyes, and I am afraid for him, suddenly. Afraid that my history might be his future, afraid that what I have left might behind might be waiting for him somewhere along the road, across a narrow bridge in some smoky suburb at the end of the tramway: same restlessness, same insomnia. Same imagination.

After that last night at Greg's house, I decided to lay low for a while. At work, I stopped going to the trolley, because I was afraid I might hear something in passing that I didn't want to hear. Or not like that, at least. I considered going round to Greg's house, or finding him in a bar and explaining to him, patiently and in no uncertain terms, that if anything ever happened to Zelda, or Lois, or whatever her name was, I would either turn him in to the police or break every bone in his body. But I didn't. That was a fantasy, nothing more. I had no proof of anything – all Greg needed to say was that I had misunderstood him, that he'd just been talking about a movie. Alfred Hitchcock's 1951 classic, *Strangers on a Train*, with Farley Granger and Robert Walker. You've probably seen it, officer; everybody knows that one. *I beg your pardon, but aren't you Guy Haines?* We'd talked about it several times, he would say, when we'd had a bit too much to drink, but it was only a film. Who in his right mind could imagine that, even if he did want his wife eliminated (which, of course, was not the case), he would be foolish enough to go to someone like me, of all people, to arrange the hit. But then – I wasn't in my right mind, was I? All they needed to do was check the official records.

So I did nothing. I stopped going to the pubs on the Epsom Road and, even though I checked the papers for weeks, I tried to stop thinking about Greg and his millstone wife, and the fridge he loved so much. The initial plan, in fact, was to stay home: to go to work early, then key out at four in the afternoon, so I could cycle back across town before the pubs opened and immerse myself in an old film, or a book, and so avoid temptation. But then, there were pubs at my end of town, too: seedy, ugly places full of petty criminals and squaddies that might, on occasion, suddenly erupt into pointless brutality at the end of an evening – but pubs nonetheless. Nothing I wasn't familiar with from growing up in Corby. Or so I thought.

Weeks passed. Then months. Season gave way to season and that was the only change I noticed: a leaf turning here, a wet flurry of snow there. Wintersweet in a public garden. Crocuses. Forsythia. I cycled back and forth to work and I locked myself away with old movies and there were times when I came close to living in the Surbiton I'd had in mind when I sought refuge in these slightly dismal not-quite-suburbs. My flatmate would drop in from time to time, to check on me, and I must have *seemed* fine. I wasn't though. I was suspended. I even knew that I was suspended. I was waiting for something – an excuse, a reason, an accident, a curse. It didn't matter which. All that mattered was for the back of my mind to find some way to overturn the front-of-mind logic that kept me there, sober and, to the outside world, border-line normal. And all the time, I told myself that I was going to get through this time. I was going to stay sober. Things would get better. Every day, in every way, tomorrow was going to be the first day of the rest of my –

I did try. I did my absolute best and I hung on for almost a year, but I was still alone in the flat most of the time, and I was still suffering from bouts of apophenia, so – after a long struggle – I ended up in one of those pubs at my end of town, a particularly vile and notorious hole that I might as well call the Pig and Bucket, for want of a less descriptive name, and in tribute to its vaguely porcine regulars. I didn't want anything to do with those regulars, of course; I just wanted to go somewhere and drink for a while before facing the voices in the wall and those specific experiences of abnormal meaningfulness. After eight beers and a couple of rums, those voices began to seem quite friendly, especially when you compared them to the boys in the Pig and Bucket, for whom, quite obviously, experiences of abnormal meaningfulness were not an issue.

This was ugly terrain, nevertheless, a low-ceilinged bar with what passed for a dance floor at the back, and a soured pool room off to one side, where ex-squaddies and small-time crooks drank whisky and Coke with their lager and did secret deals for bad drugs and electronic goods in the car park. I had no real business being there, but I couldn't help myself; the truth was that, at that point, it felt more like home than anything else I knew. It felt more like home than the flat, or the office. It certainly felt more like home than those hotel bars on the Epsom Road, with their pub grub and roasted peanuts set out in Swedish-style whiteware around the bar. I didn't mix with the squaddies and crooks, of course; my fellow drinkers came from the agricultural college or the industrial estates near the A3, but everyone here was much of a muchness. The only difference between one man and another wasn't so much *how far* he was prepared to go as *how soon* he was prepared to get there. One or two got there in seconds.

But I wasn't of *that* company, at least. I was just along for the ride: an observer, a tourist. I especially liked going into the Pig and Bucket of a Saturday night. It reminded me of something I couldn't quite put my finger on – something I didn't want any more, but still couldn't do without. There was a calm there, an equilibrium, and it was always the same. The regulars were, for the most part, men in their twenties: natural scavengers, they ran in packs of six or seven, standing around the bar with straight glasses – always a straight glass, never a mug – in their freshly scrubbed hands, laughing and trying it on with the barmaid until closing time, when they congregated outside to scrap playfully among themselves or abuse passers-by, most of them only half drunk because, of course, the night was still young. This was the most dangerous part of the outing: none of these boys amounted to very much on his own, but in a gang, all excited and getting ready for the rut, they could sometimes lose control. Occasionally, things turned really ugly – like the time when a gang poured out of the Pig and some innocent who managed to get caught up in the fun was thrown into the path of a passing vehicle and bounced a few times before he came to a halt, yards away, all quiet and limp like the proverbial rag doll. Everything stopped for a second, and the night returned in its darkest form, cold and silent and timeless before somebody laughed and the gang hurried away, taking off in twos and threes down the side streets, their feet slapping away in the darkness. Blooded and happy again, and heading off to *the rut*.

The rut usually meant a nightclub in the centre of town called Cinderella's. I went there once or twice, when there was nothing else to do. Under the mirrorballs, the boys tried to come on all smooth and sensitive, but it didn't really work. They were still the same scavengers, even when they broke away from the pack and applied what passed for charm in that place, still boys who thought a designer shirt, a souped-up car and a nodding acquaintance with the letters page of *Forum* made them interesting to women. It was sad to watch, and I avoided it most nights. Now and again, though, when I was in a particularly masochistic frame of mind, I'd go in and sit at the bar, pretending it was worth the price of entry to get a late drink and enjoy the floor show.

The floor show. More *Survival Special* than cabaret, I suppose, but it was still something to behold. The women ranged from dolly to plain, but there was something interesting about every one of them. Even the ones who confused sexy with vulgar were worth the price of admission. The men, however, were a different story. The men were so alike, and so repellent, it was as if some evil genius had cloned them all from one dastardly original, some brickie's mate who'd been steeped for ten years in Brut, then let loose to prowl the night in a tailored shirt and loafers. His name was Mick, or James, or Darren, and he was always clean, always neatly presented. He could talk a little, and he could smile; if he thought things were going well, he could pick up the tab and pay for the taxi, but he was only ever one step away from rapist and the borderline assault he perpetrated at the end of a good evening on whoever he'd conned back to his was the only thing he ever did without his crew around him. The rest of the time, he was one of the boys, first among equals and out for a good time, pillage and plunder, search and destroy.

It was at Cinderella's that I met Gina. By that time, I'd been off the wagon for a couple of months and I'd given up pretending otherwise. It was a sixties night, as I recall, or Golden Oldies – something like that. I hadn't intended to be there, but the flat had felt particularly oppressive that evening, and I didn't want to go back until it was completely unavoidable. Besides, who could have resisted a sixties night? The Troggs. The Hollies. Tamla Motown. Better than standing around with a bunch of wan E-heads listening to the same tape loop for forty minutes on the trot. Better than going to one of those trendy places further up the high street where the bouncers were polite rather than surly, and the drinks were

90

seven fifty a pop. Better than staying at home and listening to the voices in the plasterwork.

I saw Gina on the way in, and she smiled at me, so I smiled back. I wasn't looking for a date, I was just being polite and, besides, she didn't seem my type. She was attractive, in a women's magazine way, or like one of the women in a TV soap, but she was a little too ripe, not quite overblown, but heading that way. A bit luscious. By that time, I could hardly have claimed to be very discriminating in matters of the heart, but I'd never done luscious. I had pretty much assumed that luscious was not in my ballpark.

I headed for the bar. Once I'd stocked up – always buy at least four drinks in a place like that, it saves queuing again for a while – I found myself a shadowy place to hide, my array of tumblers perched on one of those high tables they put next to pillars and walls in such establishments. No chairs, just a place to put a handbag or a drink. Or, in my case, four drinks. I didn't mind about the chairs, though. I preferred to stand. It's not a good idea to sit down at these late-night places – you could get trapped in any number of ways. Harder to get out quick, too, if getting out quick becomes an issue.

Then again, even standing up and minding your own business doesn't guarantee a quiet night's inebriation. On this occasion, the guy who started things was a complete stranger – or if he wasn't, I had no memory of ever setting eyes on him – and no particular threat, at least to begin with. He was dressed in a greenish, slightly shiny lounge suit, with a silvery open-necked shirt – no tie – and he was fairly drunk, but not slurring yet. If I'd been obliged to hazard a guess, I would have said he was around twenty-five, the younger brother of somebody more substantial, slightly chippy, ready to start trouble but not really equipped to see it through,

91

and engaged to someone called Cheryl. He himself was probably a Kevin, or maybe a Keith – it was written all over him. And he *knew* me. He and I had crossed paths before, and I had done something to upset him. That was written all over him too.

What made it funny was that I couldn't hear a word he was saying. He was talking in a normal voice, but the music was too loud and all I could hear was an odd, gutteral striving. He was most definitely annoyed to see me; though if he was explaining why – and doubtless he was framing his objections to my presence in the most eloquent prose – his words were falling on deafened ears. I shook my head. 'I can't hear you,' I said.

His face beamed interrogation at me, but he didn't swing a punch or try to grab me, so I was fairly certain he was going to be all talk. Talk which I couldn't hear over 'What Becomes of the Broken-Hearted'. I didn't want to be impolite, though, so I offered him my own interrogative face, and waited to see what he would do next. I assumed that this would involve a loud noise of some description.

It didn't. He was trying to communicate something, I could see his mouth moving, but I still couldn't hear a word. If anything, his voice was a little quieter than before, and what I did hear was hoarse, like he had a sore throat, maybe, or was still recovering from his mother's entirely understandable attempts to strangle him at birth. And then the music stopped, all of a sudden, in mid song.

'– you fucking cunt.' That was all I caught, a snippet from a Derek and Clive session. And he was still just standing there, looking at me. Unfortunately, so were the ten or fifteen people in our immediate vicinity, including an ugly gaggle of Bruts, who all turned in unison, like a team of synchronised straight-glass bearers at some alternative trooping the colours. And this made things a little more serious, because if it came to taking sides, they would go with the green shiny suit – a few of them probably even knew the green shiny suit by name – rather than with the guy in the God-what's-that-he's-wearing button-down shirt. What I needed, at that very moment, was the cavalry – and, at that very moment, the cavalry arrived.

'Graham!' she said, in a perfect headmistress voice. 'What's all this shouting about?'

She was prettier close up. Certainly very pretty for cavalry. Her lipstick was the reddest and shiniest I had ever seen, and her dress was a size too small, but she had beautiful, tanning-salon skin and tiny freckles all over her shoulders. Her hair was thick and dark and she was doused in a perfume that I could smell from where I was standing, but couldn't identify, other than to say that it was most definitely not Nina Ricci's L'Air du Temps. It was, of course, Gina – though at that moment I only knew her as the smiling woman I had seen coming in – and she had company, in the form of a large, very buxom, obviously martial-arts-trained blonde in an absurdly red dress and probably no knickers.

Graham tried to stay fixed on me, the fucking cunt in question. He seemed surprised that I hadn't said anything, but there are very few suitable ripostes in such circumstances, other than to continue the Derek and Clive skit a little further, and I didn't think that was advisable. Besides, the blonde, obviously aware of the straight-glass carriers lowering on the horizon, was moving in to help defuse the situation. 'You want to watch your language, Graham,' she said.

At this, the music started up again so, whatever Graham said to her, I couldn't make it out and the two women weren't interested in anything he had to say anyway. The straight-glass boys had turned away now, the tension had gone, I still wasn't saying anything, and the women were obviously immovable – so Graham, bristling slightly but obviously defeated, shrank back into his shiny green suit and, having mouthed what looked like *see you later, mate* at me, wandered off into the crowd of revellers.

Gina turned to me and leaned in. 'All right?' she said. Oddly enough, I could hear her quite clearly. I nodded – and she smiled. 'We were just about to head off,' she said. 'Do you want to share a cab?'

I nodded again. 'That would be nice,' I said.

In the cab, we got acquainted. I was John, *Hi, John, nice to meet you*, the cavalry was Gina, *Hi, Gina*, and the blonde was Maggie, *Hi, Maggie* – though I didn't get much of a chance to chat with Maggie, because we dropped her off first, her house being closest and everything, and then there were two and the two decided to go to just one address for a nightcap. Which made absolute sense to me, though Graham and the straight-glass gang would have been completely bewildered by it all. That night, I discovered that Gina was happily divorced, but still got on great with her ex, had three kids who were staying at their gran's for the weekend and worked in customer services at a high-street building society. I hadn't planned to get that familiar, but Gina was the easiest person to like that I had met in a very long time, and she was, as she confessed, extremely sensual. So I stayed over. I stayed over till breakfast the next morning, and then I stayed over until her ex-husband – a very pleasant, dark-haired man who worked at a sports centre – brought the kids round. His name was Rich. I hadn't been expecting to meet Rich, but since I was fully clothed when he arrived, Gina introduced us, and

I got to hear about his working weekend, teaching karate classes at another sports centre, not the one where he worked, but another one, off some side road in some town I'd never heard of. And I also got to meet his children. There were two boys, aged nine and seven – I'll call them Jack and Tom – and a three-year-old girl called Petra, pretty like her mother and cute as a button and all those other clichés, only she really was, and she did the one thing a kid can do that nobody who doesn't have kids of their own can resist. She *chose* me. She waited till her dad had said it was nice to meet me but he had to dash, and then she chose me, and I stayed to play while Gina cooked. By the time I dragged myself away that first time, Petra had adopted me, and I was in love, if not with Gina, then with her immediate environment. The house, the nice ex-husband who had chosen *not* to break both my arms, the kitchen full of gooey and crackling foodstuffs that I hadn't seen in years and had more or less forgotten, the neat but very sensual bedroom and, most of all, the children. I fell in love with the children. I had never been so surprised in my life.

For the next several months, I had something close to the normal life I had been looking for. I went to work, I came home, I drank moderately, I stayed over at Gina's on the weekend. I would go over on Saturday afternoons and play with the kids for a while, then Gina would take them to their grandma's, or Rich would pick them up. Sometimes Maggie would babysit, which the kids loved, because Maggie always turned up with a vast bag full of sweets and ice cream and ready salted crisps. Maggie had an interesting theory about snack foods, which was in itself fairly complex, but more or less boiled down to the notion that crisps were good for you, as long as they were plain ready salted and not cheese and onion, or smoky bacon or, in fact, anything with flavouring added. 'Stick to plain,' she would say, 'and you won't go wrong.' The same went for crackers and peanuts. Maggie attributed her own robust good health to eating plain food, not putting mixers in her drinks and never drinking red wine. 'It's full of tannins,' she would say. 'Like tea. Why do you think British people are so bloody sickly? Tea, that's why. Continental people don't drink tea, they drink coffee, which is why they are so much healthier.'

The kids loved Maggie. The odd thing was, they loved me too. And, though I knew I was only borrowing them for a while, I wanted them to be happy – and that was why I lost them. I wanted them to be happy, and to go on just the way they were, laughing and watching TV and having little kid fights and playing football in the garden. Normal kids: happy, confident, safe.

Things started to come apart one Saturday night, a couple of months into what Gina would no doubt have called 'our relationship'. I had been meaning to take her somewhere special, instead of just going to the pub like we always did, and I had booked a table at a fancy new restaurant that had opened in town. Gina was excited: I had guessed that she would like that kind of thing. She pretended to be one of the girls – down to earth, no airs and graces, what you see is what you get – but really her dream was to get all dressed up and go to places where you had to think about which cutlery to use and the waiter came and told you the specials for tonight were truffles or quails' kidneys in aspic or something. I liked that about her. I liked her happiness – and because she was happy, she looked quite beautiful that night, simple and under-stated in very light make-up and a plain, cream-coloured dress that I'd never seen before. She must have bought it specially and it suited her so well that when she came downstairs and did a twirl for me and the kids, I suddenly couldn't wait for our special evening out to be over so I could get her home again.

We were almost ready to leave when the phone rang. Gina hurried out to answer it. The kids had been watching a cartoon but, as usual, they had drifted away, leaving the video on at close to full volume. I put it to mute, and Gina smiled at me as she picked up the receiver: dark, sweet-mouthed, her usual dogged cheer softened a little by an awkward tenderness for me, and for the occasion. If I say she was basically a simple person, I don't mean to be unkind or to belittle her. She was someone who knew what she liked and what she didn't like, and she managed her life accordingly. Good things, she kept; the bad she cut away, without a second thought. I even envied her that, sometimes.

'Oh, hiya.' She was still smiling for a moment; then her face went dark. 'Oh no,' she said. She listened. 'Oh, no. Oh, Maggie. I'm so sorry –' She listened again. For a long time. Then she put the phone down and came through to the living room.

'Where are the kids,' she said. She was obviously upset.

'Upstairs,' I said. 'What –'

'Maggie's had an accident,' she said.

'What?'

'Maggie's in hospital. She's got a broken leg and a couple of broken ribs and – I don't know. She banged her head –'

'What happened?'

'She fell down some steps.' Gina sat down on the chair by the mute TV, some cartoon about a dog and a penguin running silently behind her. 'No,' she said. 'I tell a lie, she didn't *fall*.

97

She was pushed.' She stood up again. 'I knew this would happen. I fucking knew it.' She looked at me. 'Pardon my French,' she said.

When she finally got it together to explain, she told me that Maggie had been seeing some guy called Peter for a while about six months earlier. The guy had seemed fine to begin with, or so Maggie thought, but Gina had never trusted him and when he and Maggie broke up, he turned weird on her and started sending her scary letters and making nasty, late-night phone calls saying what he was going to do to her, one night, when she was on her own. Because he was watching, he said, and he knew when she was alone, and he would get her, when the time was right, and he would make her suffer, and it would last a long, long time. He'd also sent her porno magazines, really nasty stuff with animals and torture. That kind of stuff. Maggie had gone to the police, and they'd told her she could get a restraining order or something, but they couldn't do anything about the guy because he hadn't actually committed a crime.

'What about the magazines? Surely –'

She shook her head. 'She threw them away. Anyway, can you imagine a *woman* walking into a police station with a pile of porn and saying, look what my ex-boyfriend sent me?'

'So now what?' I said.

'Now what what?'

'They'll have to do something now –'

She laughed, a bitter, very small laugh that surprised me – and I wondered if something like this had happened to *her* at some point. 'It's Maggie's word against his,' she said. 'No witnesses. And she didn't see him. She was just coming down the steps and somebody pushed her.' She came and sat down next to me. 'We'll go and see her tomorrow, OK?'

I nodded. 'We can go and see her now, if you want,' I said.

She shook her head. 'Let's leave her in peace for tonight,' she said. 'Let her get her rest.' She smiled sadly, then she gave me a friendly hug. Like she wanted me to know that *she* knew that I wasn't the kind of guy who would push somebody down a flight of steps. When she let go of me, she was back to her usual self. 'Anyway, we're going *out*,' she said.

'We can't –'

'Oh, it's all right. Maggie would want us to.'

'No,' I said. 'I mean, what about the kids?'

'Oh.' She laughed. 'That's OK. I'll give them some medicine. They'll be fine.'

It is one of life's great mysteries that almost every woman I have ever met has had a secret supply of barbiturates stashed away somewhere. A woman I know went to see her doctor complaining of a severe pain in her head and neck and he gave her diazepam. An old lady who rented me a room in her house for a few weeks had a bathroom cabinet full of all kinds of goodies that had been prescribed for her over the years, including several bottles of Seconal. If *I'd* had that many Seccies in my room, I'd have been banged up for life. I'd tried faking symptoms that would get me this kind of stuff a few times, and I'd been sent away with some harmless placebo or other, but this old lady couldn't even remember what hers were for.

'You know,' I said, 'you really ought to get rid of those things. They're dangerous.'

She gave me a big, innocent, wide-eyed look. '*Are* they?' she said.

'Oh, yes.'

'Better throw them in the bin, then,' she said.

I nodded. 'You're really supposed to take them to the chemist's,' I said. 'So they can be safely disposed of.' I paused for a moment's thought, then moved along. 'I'll do it, if you like, though,' I said. 'I've got to go into town tomorrow anyway. Save you the trouble.'

I had never seen Gina take a pill of any kind and then, suddenly, there she was, Valium in hand, and there were the kids, lining up to take their medicine. Not that they minded. They were obviously familiar with this medicine and what it would do to them. And I stood watching, appalled, hypocrite that I was.

'Gina?'

She smiled. Radiantly. Nice nursey, making everybody well. 'Ye-es?'

'Are you sure this is safe?'

'Absolutely,' she said. She popped Tom's pill into his mouth, then gave him a glass of orange squash. 'Drink it up, now,' she said.

'Gina?'

She tensed a little, but the smile did not slip. Jack came up for his dose. 'They love it,' she said. 'Don't you, Jack?'

Jack nodded and took his glass of orange. 'Wash it down nicely,' she said.

'Yes,' I said. 'But that's not the point, is it?'

Gina laughed, but the tension was growing. 'I know what I'm doing,' she said. 'Besides, everybody does it. Tina lets her lot have a vodka and orange every Saturday night.'

'You're kidding!' I wasn't pretending, I really was shocked – and that amused Gina even more.

'Wait till you're a parent,' she said.

'I don't think so.'

Gina studied my face. She'd made no attempt to conceal what she was doing, so she presumably hadn't expected me to be shocked by the medicine routine. She'd probably done the same thing in front of other men, and got no reaction. Now, seeing that I really was concerned about *her* kids – concerned in a way that she wasn't, which meant I was being presumptuous – she considered being offended. I could see it in her face, that she was about to give me a ticking-off for being so self-bloody-righteous, but then she changed her mind. It was Saturday night, after all, and we had a table booked at Casa Something Or Other, and she didn't want to spoil things. 'It doesn't do them any harm,' she said, going for concilia-tion. 'Honestly. And besides, what's better for them? A good, long sleep and a nice mum who's had a chance to relax and let off steam, or a weekend in front of the telly stuffing them-selves full of crisps and chocolates with some miserable old bitch who can't be bothered because she's dog-tired and bored and frustrated?' She put on her best sexy barmaid, nudge-nudge wink-wink grin, then modulated beautifully into the picture of innocence. 'You don't want me getting frustrated, do you?' she said.

I didn't want to spoil things either, but I didn't say anything. Petra was waiting for her turn.

'Want some medicine, sweetie?' Gina said, dropping down to eye level.

'Yes, please,' Petra said.

Gina gave her the pill and then her plastic cup full of orange. 'Wash it down nicely,' she said.

Petra took her medicine, then had a big slurp from the cup. Orange ran down her chin. 'Yummy,' she said, breathless for a moment.

Gina glanced up at me, beaming. 'See what I mean?' she said. 'Can't get enough.'

I didn't know what to say. I wasn't happy, but I hadn't done anything to try and stop her, and it was too late now. The kids seemed fine and I didn't want to think about what might happen if we went out and left them wide awake all night, with the electricity and gas and carving knives to play with. Unconscious, they would be incapable of doing themselves any great harm. But then, didn't harm come of its own accord? It wasn't like the old vampire films, where somebody had to get up and open a window to let Dracula in. In real life, the vampire comes of its own accord, and it slips in under the door before you even notice it's there. No: but the truth was that it didn't matter what I said, or thought, unless I was prepared to do something – and I couldn't think of anything to do to save little Petra from all this, other than going to the authorities, who would probably take her into care and put her and her brothers into some cold, bleak care home run by sadists and paedophiles. It was obvious to me that these kids loved Gina and, as long as she had what she would have called *some kind of a life*, she was a pretty good mother, all things considered.

So I did nothing. After the medicine had been dispensed, the kids ran off back to the TV and Gina turned to me, a putative smile on her face – though there was a warning behind it that I couldn't miss.

'All right?' she said. 'Give them a little while, and we'll be off.' She let the warning look slide and brightened. 'Unless, of course, you want to stick around and sing them a lullaby,' she said.

I had no right, of course. That was what she would have told me, if I'd pressed her on it, and she would have been justified. I had no right to tell her how to bring up her kids. And even if I *was* right, I had no right to be right, because I hadn't been there on all the occasions when things had gone wrong.

She had. She had been there to see that these kids were fed and clothed and kissed better when they needed it; she had borne them and brought them up and gone through a divorce and come out in one piece and she had kept the peace with Rich after he left, which wasn't easy, which was, in fact, *bloody hard*, because he had been the one to leave and she was the one who held it all together. She was the one who had put these kids to bed every night, then sat down with a bottle of wine and cried in front of the TV, while they slept warm and safe in their beds – little Petra was only seven months old when her father left – and their dad ran around town with his new girlfriend. Then, when she was all cried out, she would force herself to go to bed for a couple of hours, so she would have the energy to get up the next morning and start all over again. Gradually things had got easier: that phase had ended, and she'd started going out and enjoying herself and seeing her friends again, but even there she had to be strong, because Rich was fine, and all that, but he was pretty much a fair-weather dad, all sweeties and outings, and Maggie was constantly getting herself into weird situations – this thing with Peter was just the latest of them – and it was Gina she always turned to when she needed someone to say that things would be all right. Which is what friends do. They make you laugh and they cry with you and they bring you a big pile of magazines and some chocolates when some fucker pushes you down a flight of steps, or puts you down on the floor of your own kitchen and kicks you till you bleed inside.

The next day, we took a big pile of magazines to Maggie and she was pleased to see us, but you could see in her eyes that she was scared. When we were coming away, Gina took my arm, and huggled up to me. The kids – having come through their drugged night unscathed – were running ahead of us, looking for the shop they remembered from the last time they had been there and I wondered what the last time had been about.

'Thanks for coming,' Gina said.

I felt sad. She wasn't really saying what she was saying, she was saying something else. Testing the water. The night before, we'd had a subdued dinner, and then we'd come back to the house in a cab and tumbled around determinedly all night, but it hadn't been sensual at all, and I couldn't stop thinking about the kids, wanting to go and check on them, as if I was their father, as if I was responsible. 'I wanted to come,' I said. 'I like Maggie.'

'I know.'

'Tell you what,' I said. 'Let's go to the cafe, and get a cup of tea. The kids can have ice cream. My treat.'

She sighed. I was dodging something, and we both knew that. 'Fine,' she said.

I don't know why I am remembering all this so clearly. There are other, better narratives from that time locked away in my head, rich seams of silver and anthracite, veins of gold and mica that would be so much more gratifying to unearth – but I can't get through, I can't find a way into that glittering substratum. I would much rather be woken from a dream of something else on a Sunday morning, and I would much rather tell another story – for this one is tawdry, and a little shameful – but when I look back, I am surprised to find that *this* is all I come up with. I see glimpses of another life here and there, I hear odd phrases and melodies from the prob-ably beautiful evenings of a lost time, but I can't quite locate the narrative to which those fragments belong. If my mind was a cinema, then all I could ever show of that time would be trailers and stills, short loops of fleeting, mysterious events that might have happened, at one time or another, to someone who now appears so far away and mythical that I struggle to see him as myself. As it happens, I have never found *myself* a very convincing phenomenon, anyway – it's always seemed more like a crack in the fabric of things, an ugly, damp fissure that I have spent a lifetime trying to paper over with lies and half-truths and my own brand of special effects – and to some extent, these memories of my affair with Gina should not be taken at face value. For the truth is, I was never particularly *involved* with her – I wasn't even faithful to her – and my acceptance of the situation as it deteriorated into farce is less indicative of my by now obviously masochistic personality than symptomatic of a near-clinical apathy. I had given up. The masochist may seek out pain, or humiliation, but that search is always *active*: it is always pain in a context, it is always humiliation as part of a narrative. What matters is the story. The ritual. The fact of repetition, and the choosing to repeat. In this, masochism resembles romantic love in all its usual forms: just as we fall in love with love, so we suffer for suffering's sake, and the object of our devotion is simply a character, just as we are simply characters in a story that we may well choose but cannot avoid telling, over and over again. For me, though, there were no stories in Gina's house. There was just a by now emaciated idea of normal. At other times, at some party in the woods, or lost for a moment in what Robert Lowell calls 'something with a girl in summer', I almost recovered consciousness – but I didn't think consciousness would take me anywhere other than back to the life I was trying to escape, so I let those moments pass, like gorgeous animals slipping away in the dusk, and I found my way back to Gina's house, where nothing ever happened, other than vodka and Valium and the odd half-hearted, stumbling lullaby.

Sometimes I think you love those children more than you love me.

It was the first time she had used the word *love*. She had used words like *sexy*, and *sensual*, and *lovely*, and *fond of* – but she had never said love, and as soon as she did, she realised that it was inappropriate. We both did. We also knew that what she had said was true. After the Valium episode, something had cooled in us both. There's nothing wrong with a relationship based entirely on sex, but it usually starts to fall apart once you realise that that's all it is. There has to be an illusion of something else, even if both partners know, when they're alone, that it really is just an illusion. We both tried to carry on, and sometimes we got the illusion back. Some weekends, I managed to prevail upon her not to go out by turning up with a couple of bottles of fancy wine and some sweeties for the kids, and we would just stay at hers, playing house. It wasn't going to last, though, and we both knew it. One night, I went over a little later than usual and the kids were already in bed – and though I didn't say anything, I spent the whole night wondering if they had been given their medicine that day, wondering if I would wake in the small hours to a brooding silence and go next door to find little Petra dead in her bed, the boys comatose, the dawn just breaking on their cold faces. Eventually, there were times when I couldn't face going round, so I went out to one of the Worplesdon pubs on my own and watched the Merrist Wood boys play pool – and, given my increasing unreliability, it wasn't long before Gina started making plans that didn't include me, supposedly to go for a drink with 'the girls', and I would be relieved to see the back of her. Sometimes I would even end up babysitting. One night, Rich came round to the house and found me there, on my own with *his* children. I'm not surprised he was surprised when I answered the door. The kids were asleep upstairs, which was probably just as well, but it was still awkward.

'Oh, hi,' he said. 'I was looking for Gina.'

'She's just popped out,' I said.

'Really?'

'She should be back soon –'

He didn't believe me. 'Right,' he said. 'Ri-ight. Um. Did she say where she was going?'

'Uh, not sure,' I said. 'Maggie's, I think.'

He nodded. He looked like a very wise and kindly teacher trying to figure out how to help a good-hearted, but essentially hopeless twelve-year-old. 'Look, John,' he said, 'it's none of my business, but if I were you, I'd think very carefully about what you want out of this situation.'

He waited for me to speak, but I didn't really understand what he was getting at. 'Well,' I said, 'thanks for the advice.' I hadn't meant to sound ironic, but I must have done.

He smiled sadly. 'Well, look at where you are,' he said. 'It's a Saturday night, and you're babysitting your girlfriend's kids while she's off on the town somewhere –'

'She's just popped over to Maggie's –'

'Out on the town, probably with some guy Maggie's set her up with,' he continued, patiently, with a this-is-all-for-your-own-benefit air about him. 'And you know how good Maggie is at picking out men.'

That seemed a bit below the belt, but I didn't say anything. I felt oddly repentant, to be honest. He could, quite justifiably, have been wondering aloud whether I was a fit person to be left alone with his children, and he had pretty solid grounds for such a concern, had he but known it. But he wasn't. He was trying to do right by me.

'After all,' he said, 'I do have some experience with Gina. I know what she can be like.' He gave me a man-to-man look that would have done Ted Danson proud and patted me on the arm. 'Just think about it,' he said. 'OK?'

Unscripted pain is no fun at all. Gina and I dragged on for a while longer, but it wasn't a pretty sight. All of a sudden, life had turned into an Etta James song – with me in the middle of it all, trying to pretend I wasn't noticing. It was around then that Gina's parties started, her little get-togethers of like-minded friends. Officially, she and I were still a couple, but it wasn't long before I was slipping away to the kitchen or the garden to get drunk while she danced close with some slicked Neanderthal and, eventually, the time arrived when I came back to find her gone. Another couple was on the floor, the man on top, heaving and gasping, and a lonely-looking woman whom I couldn't remember having seen before, was sitting on the floor by the TV, watching a sex film. It reminded me of the way Petra watched TV, her face about a foot away, so it was hard to imagine she could see anything other than a field of blurred colour – and the thought of Petra made me think to go upstairs and check who might be there, in her room, and when I got there, it was Gina and the Neanderthal, having sex on the floor. They didn't see me and I didn't want them to know I'd seen them. What was the point? By then, I think, Gina had come to the conclusion that I wasn't really there anyhow and she had obviously decided, as a matter of self-respect, that it wasn't hate she felt for me, it was pity. Yet, even after the Neanderthal, I kept going round to see the kids.

I knew I shouldn't, but I couldn't help myself. I missed them, especially Petra. The boys had distanced themselves gradually, as they sensed their mother's growing coolness, but Petra never wavered. She was always pleased to see me. Finally, though, even I could see that she was the only one, and it wasn't long before the last shabby scene was duly played out.

It was a Friday evening, still quite early, but Gina was already dolled up to go out when she answered the door, her lipstick beetroot red, mascara close to dripping point. She was wearing the cream-coloured dress I liked so much. 'What are *you* doing here?' she said, apparently amused to see me.

'I thought –' I looked past her into the house. Usually, when I came to the door, Petra came running. 'Where are the kids?'

She laughed. 'They're with their dad this weekend,' she said.

'Oh.' Apparently I had miscalculated. I had brought round a bag of goodies for Petra and the boys. 'I thought –'

'So there's no point you hanging around,' she said, her amusement evaporating.

'I suppose not,' I said.

She allowed herself a brief long-suffering look, then she smiled with her mouth. It was a perfect expression of grim triumph, a Pyrrhic victory over someone too pathetic to have bothered with in the first place. 'Anyway,' she said, 'I can't stop. I'm in a hurry.'

'Oh, yes?'

'Yes.'

'Got a date?'

'God,' she said. 'Who'd have thought you'd turn out to be so *needy*?'

That shook me. 'Needy?' I said. 'I'm not –'

'Oh, I'm not talking about *me*,' she said. 'Perish the bloody thought.' She waited, letting the penny drop.

'I like the kids,' I said.

'I've noticed,' she said. 'But if you like kids so much, get some of your own.'

I looked at her. I had no idea what she felt at that moment. Some contempt, obviously. Some pity. No fellow feeling, though. To her, I was a different species, and she was sorry she'd ever let me into her happy home – which was exactly what I *had* been needy for. A home. She was just incidental – which had probably made her angry for a while, though she had given up on that when I failed to even notice how angry she was. I nodded. 'I'm sorry,' I said.

She stiffened. 'Forget it,' she said. It wasn't an absolution – and I should have just turned then, and left her to it, but I couldn't let it go. 'Say goodbye to Petra for me,' I said.

Her face stayed blank. 'Fuck off,' she said. She took one last look, then closed the door.

It was a tawdry moment, but I lingered anyway, wondering exactly what had happened, and whether I had missed something. When I finally turned to go, I found myself face to face with a man in a shiny green suit that seemed familiar. The suit, I mean, not the man. The man was vast and thick and slightly damp, and there wasn't an ounce of hesitation in his entire body.

'All right, mate?' he said, a quizzical look troubling his primeval features.

'Fine,' I said. 'Wrong house.'

He nodded, then brushed past me and knocked loudly at Gina's door.

LOSING HELEN

Back in the 1970s, when my mother was still alive, she got me a job at the fruit and nut processing factory where she worked. It was a good job, clean and fairly light compared to the steel mill where I'd been employed the previous summer and, like all food-related work, it had its perks. My favourite nuts were almonds, which I would send through the fryer in illicit batches, mostly for personal consumption, and it didn't hurt, during the first few days, to hear from some of the older women that almonds were thought to enhance sexual performance. Amused and incredulous as I was, I ate them by the handful for several weeks, then noticed that I had gained eight pounds overnight and quit cold turkey. I hadn't realised a body could suffer withdrawal symptoms from giving up nuts, but I had a difficult week, towards the middle of August, when I dreamed of those pale, ridged lozenges dripping from the end of a conveyor belt in a bright slick of oil and salt.

There were other perks, too: it was easy to smuggle half-pound bags of salted peanuts out to the loading bay, then pick them up later to sell on or pass round at parties, and the company was good, the majority of the employees being older or middle-aged women. Best of all, the company operated a limited shift system, so there was no night work, just six till two and two till ten, with an hour's worth of breaks over the

111

eight hours for food and – for the handful of men who operated or maintained the larger machinery – tense and brilliant
bouts of table football in the bare, pink-and-white canteen
that overlooked the road. All the men played table football:
it was peer-pressure mandatory, like reading the *Sun*. I didn't
enjoy it particularly – I didn't enjoy real football for that matter
– but I soon developed the proficiency not to embarrass myself
in a game of doubles. After all, I was a student, in name at
least, and I couldn't appear to be lacking in any of the manly
virtues. The jury was still out on my sexual performance, but
I kept goal with the best of them and occasionally dazzled
with an explosive winning shot from my own goal line.

Women didn't play table football; for them, the canteen's
main attraction was the newly installed fruit machine. On
Fridays, some of them would break open their neat little pay
packets and pull at that machine for the entire half-hour of
a meal break, sometimes winning, mostly just standing with
their eyes glued to the display, figuring out the odds, looking
for a nudge, trying to predict the next win. This happened
mostly on the back shift, when things were quieter and nobody
made too much of it if a break got extended slightly, whether
to try to win something back, or just to empty a last handful
of change into the machine and have done with it. These
women who played the machine were older than most of the
others; sometimes their daughters would be in the room,
watching from out of the corner of one eye, embarrassed, but
joking with their friends about how much money the old girl
could save, if she would just stay home. Nobody ever tried to
intervene, though, even when one of the day-shift players
stayed on, and the best part of a week's pay disappeared into
the dim clunk and whirr of machinery. Everybody in that
canteen knew what it was like to need a win, one way or

another, and just watching somebody play with such total conviction, no matter how ill-founded, kept the possibility of winning in the air, a soft, dark presence in the room, like a tacit agreement, or a common memory.

Because the men on shift were so few, I had to play table football often to make up a four, but the rest of the time I watched the fruit-machine women. It fascinated me, that they could keep coming back after they had lost so hard, trotting back and forth to the till to get change, then jamming the money into the slot and waiting, grim-faced and strangely calm, while the wheels turned. One day, during my first week, I watched as a thin, grey woman called Wee Ellen won the jackpot, and everybody was pleased for her, for a while. At her next break, though, she came back and played away her winnings, losing with such consistency, and with such breathtaking calm, that it seemed as if money had nothing to do with what was going on. It was a ritual, a magic act: Wee Ellen could make great fistfuls of coin appear, as if from nowhere, and she could make them disappear just as easily. It had something to do with time, I thought: everybody covered for the afflicted woman for as long as her money lasted and she herself was granted, for a few intense, possibly everlasting minutes, the privilege of being off the clock in a temporal limbo, while her workmates carried on packing, or eating doughnuts. To lose a very large sum was the ultimate achievement. This usually happened on a Friday, when the wages were given out: the losing player would be talked about all weekend, then treated with an oddly detached, and not altogether kindly reverence for several days after that. Nobody ever won big and kept what they won, but if they had, they would have been envied, despised a little, and bitterly ignored. To *lose* big, however, was to be marked out as holy, at least for a while.

113

Though an outsider, I felt that holiness from the first, and I thought I understood it. I loved to watch as the women came and went, feeding money into the machine, or standing around a player, looking on in silence as she moved into the dark zones of loss. Wee Ellen, Betty G, Margaret, Agnes, Betty Turner. They were the hard core: married women in their fifties who really had nothing to lose. I loved to watch them, and though I was not alone in this, I preferred to believe that nobody else understood their games as I did. The other people in the canteen weren't really privy to the women's secret world, but I fancied I knew what they were doing and, just by watching, I got to share in their magical relationship with time. In this, I also fancied I was alone, one of life's canny observers, one of the sensitives; but I was wrong. One bright, back-shift afternoon, when all the doors and windows were flung open for the least hint of a breeze off the grass, I noticed that someone else was watching the fruit-machine women – not with the usual half-amused, half-suspenseful air, but locked in with the same reverent fascination that I felt, the same sense of privilege. She was sitting by the window at the other end of the canteen: cradling a salt-white teacup in her hands, her elbows on the table, her round, very white face reflecting the glare off the road, she looked like she was lit up from inside, and from the moment I looked up and noticed her, she was aware of me, though she didn't acknowledge the fact for the longest time. It was a test, I think: if I had looked away, if I'd pretended I hadn't seen her, she would have let it slip, but after a moment, when I didn't turn away, she lifted her chin slightly and gave me a faint but complicit smile, holding the moment just long enough before turning back to watch Betty G feed her last two coins into the machine. I didn't know who this girl was and I didn't even find her particularly

114

attractive, or not in the usual way, yet there was something about her manner that drew me in and over the next few weeks she became, as the one alternative to the absolute tedium of that particular workplace, the object of my first real and lasting infatuation. I found out later that her name was Helen Watson and that, though everyone in the factory thought of her as a student, she had dropped out of university earlier that year and was still wondering what to do next. It was a decision she never had to make, but that didn't stop her from coming to the conclusion, some time during that summer, that whatever she elected to do, it wouldn't be what she wanted.

This is a story I am telling myself, though I have no idea why. Nothing happens in this story, or nothing much: *boy meets girl*, to some extent, though not in any significant way; *boy meets girl and girl dies*, yes, but not in a way that makes for a good story, or not with the beginning, middle and end that a good story requires – by which, of course, I mean one of those stories that can be told aloud, a public event, something more than a mere dream. *Boy meets girl and girl dies*: but girl dying had nothing to do with boy and, had girl not died, boy would have forgotten her as easily as he forgot all the other girls he met and liked in passing and didn't weave stories around for the next thirty years.

I didn't see Helen again till the end of that week. It was a Friday morning; I was sliding down the ladder on the side of the building, my hands and face and the front of my white boiler suit covered in husks and dust and sticky masses of the thick, pungent grease – a heady mix of groundnut and lubricating oil – that everyone referred to as 'peanut butter'. I had been on the ladder that ran precariously up the side of the building, cleaning out the extractor fans, my body pressed hard to the wall, one arm reaching blindly into the depth of the machinery, gouging out thick, salty layers of grease and compacted husks off the huge metal rotors. It was one of the least attractive of the routine maintenance tasks I had been assigned, almost as bad as cleaning the glazing tanks – an occasional hour or so of dredging dead starlings from the depths of the slick, still pools of glazing oil in the roof, then carrying them out to the dump ground behind the loading bay for disposal. I disliked both jobs, in principle at least, though I have to admit to a certain grim satisfaction in locating every last bundle of softened bones and feathers in the glazing tanks and hauling them out, the necks flopping, the eyes stitched shut, the feathers a slick of oil and faded neon. The fan cleaning was riskier, though, and it was probably relief that made me celebrate its completion by performing an extravagant fireman's slide down the ladder, my hands barely touching the safety rail, free-falling for a few precious milliseconds before I hit the ground below, landing on my feet more often than not, though not always as gracefully as I would have liked. This was what Helen witnessed that Friday morning: a sudden rush of white overhead, then a boy in clumpy work boots tumbling like Icarus from the sky, his feet hitting the tarmac with a heavy thud before he staggered towards her, only just managing to stay upright, his hands and overalls spotted with husks and grease, a stupid grin on his similarly besmirched face. She had come outside to sneak a cigarette between official smoke breaks; the women did that sometimes, though they usually slipped out through the swing door at the far end of the packing room, while another woman kept a lookout.

She must have been miles away, thinking she'd found a quiet spot where nobody would find her for ten precious minutes, so when I dropped to the tarmac a few feet away, she was genuinely startled. I hadn't seen her either, or not till the last moment, but it felt oddly natural that she was there and, for a moment, I imagined she had intended this encounter. The notion pleased me, and I smiled. 'Sorry,' I said. 'I didn't see you there.'

She smiled back. Though she was away from the women's domain, she was very easy in herself, confident, not pretending to be shy, or hard-bitten, the way some of the unmarried girls did when they were out of their territory, though she wasn't flirting either. 'What the hell were you doing up there?' she said, apparently amused.

'Cleaning the fan,' I said.

'Ah,' she said. 'So *you're* the one.' She looked me up and down. 'Well, you're still in one piece, at least.'

The remark took me by surprise, but I had to laugh. She was referring to an incident that had happened a few weeks earlier, when the fan had come on suddenly just moments after I had pulled my arm from the rotors. This wasn't supposed to happen: according to health and safety procedures, there was only supposed to be one key to turn the fans off and on, and that was lodged securely in the pocket of my overalls while I was out on the ladder. Health and safety procedures were of no consequence, however, to the zealous chargehand who was working that shift: keen to impress the bosses with his production figures, he'd noticed that the fan was sometimes left in the off position for longer than necessary when the underling charged with its maintenance stayed out in the yard for an unscheduled cigarette break. Though I didn't smoke at that time, I'd done it myself, getting comfortable up on the ladder and gazing out over the waste ground beyond the loading bay, soaking up the touches of green along the ditches that ran behind the industrial estate, the free flight of gulls or crows over the muddy fields of willow and rushes, the high blue of the summer sky. There's nothing like factory work to make a soul appreciate the outdoors, even in its humblest forms.

Unbeknown to me, the Zealous Chargehand – over the years I forget his name, but he lives on as a type, like the Prodigal Son, or the Unfaithful Servant – had secretly cut his own copies of all the keys, including the key to the fan, so when he came along and found the fan switched off at a time of day when he thought it should be running, he'd produced the unofficial key and started the thing up. It should have cost him his job, but it didn't – mostly, according to the gossip, because his mother was having an affair with the factory manager. As for me, I had experienced a moment of strangely exhilarating shock as the fan suddenly kicked in with a great rush of noise and motion, like an aeroplane propeller, just a second after I'd extricated my thin, white arm from the tangle of blades and it had taken me a while to realise what had happened. I'd been angry for a moment, but anger doesn't last long in factories – where the practical joke is one of the few defences against an altogether crushing boredom – and by the time I learned what the Zealous Chargehand had done, I had slid down into a cold, hard resolve to get my own back. Back then, I was a keen advocate for the healing power of revenge and I was soon back at work, plotting a riposte that came a few days later and involved a Sortex machine, a loose wire and a compressed air line.

Now, with the recollection, not so much of my own close shave as of the Zealous Chargehand's ashen face and faraway eyes as he lay stunned in the dust and shadows behind Sortex No. 3, I gave her a big grin. 'Yep,' I said. 'That was me.' I was still basking in the notion that *I could have died* – a delicious idea to anyone who has ever done manual work – had the Zealous Chargehand – now universally referred to as the Idiot – found his key a moment earlier. The fan would have torn my arm out of its socket and ripped it to shreds, no doubt, but that would only have been a beginning, for the sheer power of the machine would have thrown what was left of me out and away from the side of the building, tossing me into the air like a rag doll. It had been an idea that I hadn't been able to put out of my mind for days afterwards, but it was an idea that made me feel contented and strong, not invulnerable, but oddly indifferent. Now, with a carefree smile on my face that spoke volumes about my devil-may-care personality, I was joking about it all with this smart, confident girl – and that felt good. Of course, under the circumstances – a Zealous Chargehand hovering once more by the stopped fan, a sneaked cigarette break that had gone on for far too long – we couldn't linger, but this chance meeting was the start of something, the step that came after that brief exchange of looks in the canteen a few days before, and led on to – what?

Not a romance, as it happened, and nothing like love. Not a friendship either, or not on my part. It was nothing at all really, just an accidental meeting between people detained against their will and better judgement in a place where neither of them belonged. Had they but known it, they would have seen that nobody belongs in a place like that, but they couldn't see the others, they could only see themselves: young, moderately clever, hopeful, bored. Had we not been so bored, we might never have met; had she not been transformed by death I would have forgotten her long ago. As it happens, however, I have held her in my memory for thirty years and there is no other explanation for this than the fact that, five weeks after that first encounter, she went home and died, without a word of warning, while her mother and father watched television downstairs with the sound turned down low, so their daughter, who had come home from work that day complaining of a pain in her back, could get a good, long sleep.

Every story is supposed to have a beginning, a middle and an end, and it doesn't matter what order they come in, as long as they're there. One of the things that makes a memory different from a story is that it might well come with a beginning and an end, but the middle tends to blur or even vanish altogether. The beginning and the end have more urgent claims on the attention, even in the most inauspicious of circumstances – day shift in a food-processing factory, say. Any first meeting is the occasion for a romance that might last a lifetime, a thin, subliminal stratum of scents and sounds that can be awakened years later by the faintest stimulus – even if the moment came to nothing, as mine did on this occasion. Meanwhile, any and every ending, especially if it involves a death, is easily transformed by the imagination into a defining moment, the point to which some enduring bitterness, or widescreen tragedy, or fond self-regard traces its poignant origin. The middle of this memory is much like any other: a series of snapshots, half-remembered conversations over lunch or tea breaks, fleeting glances, smiles and half-smiles, assumptions, hopes, doubts. Sometimes those conversations were intimate and private – as far as such a thing was possible in that setting – though they were more likely to be conducted on the run, with interruptions and asides from our fellow workers. Sometimes the entire exchange would take place through intermediaries, a strand of significance winding its way through an otherwise banal stream of banter or gossip, a conversation inside a conversation, an argument within an argument, private references and in-jokes bouncing across the surface of public discourse like skipping stones that the others barely noticed. Or one of us would be pinned down in the canteen by Bob, the factory's homespun philosopher, and the other would come to the rescue, jumping in on a debate about the existence of God, or the future of the Labour movement, with a smart remark or an absurdist digression. Helen was particularly good at that, perhaps because she saw herself as a contrary, the one who questioned what other people took for granted. At some point – though whether it had been months or years before, I never knew – she had decided to ignore the givens, to seek out the neglected beauties and wonders. She wanted to learn a way through to the things other people didn't appreciate, the music and books, the habits, the moments they barely noticed. I often suspected that this was a discipline she had decided to practise the way other people practise yoga or ballroom dancing. She was appalled by how readily the people around her – people who had more reason than most to question the way the social machinery was put together – were entrapped by what they had been told. At the time, she seemed smart; yet now that I am more than twice her age, I am surprised that I didn't see how naive she was, or how frightened by a life that had just moved away from her, leaving her stranded among people that she probably liked, after a fashion, even as she acknowledged that all of them, including me, were as much strangers to her as she was to them.

We *were* strangers; I see that clearly now. Nevertheless, over the next few weeks, in a rough and ready way, we became friends. By default, as much as anything, we were thrown together and there were times when we were alone in that canteen, two against the world. That wasn't enough, though – not for a boy just out of his teens in a town where young men barely talked to women, much less befriended them. I wasn't particularly attracted to her – in the way that most of us use that term, most of the time, which is to say, sexually. In that era, however, for boys of my class and background, *everything* was sexual – which meant that, sooner or later, I had to do something more than just talk. Something else – something *more* – was supposed to happen. That was the law that governed any meeting between people of our age, in that place. Something is supposed to happen and if it doesn't happen by itself, the boy has to make it happen. Part of me recognised that this law wasn't quite right, and I waited for as long as I could, but the other part of me was still convinced that I was supposed to make my move. One Friday, towards the end of my shift, we were sitting at what had become our chosen table by the window in the canteen, talking about Mexico. She had a thing about Mexico, some half-baked plan, I suppose, that involved going to Oaxaca and disappearing into the desert for a while. She was talking about that, about the desert and the Day of the Dead, while I waited for the right moment to say what I wanted to say, and she must have sensed something – my tension, the weekend coming up, some muffled trace of need or desire – because she suddenly stopped talking and gave me an odd, almost baffled look.

'You're too young for me,' she said.

'What's that?'

'You were just about to ask me out,' she said. 'And I wanted you to know that you're too young for me. Besides, the last thing I need in the world right now is a boyfriend.' She looked away, and I knew she was about to get up and go outside for a cigarette. Back then, you could smoke indoors, but she didn't like to. She preferred to stand out on the loading bay, or in the grey angle of concrete and dust under the extractor fan.

'I'm a year younger than you,' I said. 'That's all.'

She turned back and gave me a tight little smile. 'I'm not talking date of birth here,' she said.

I didn't know what to say. I was hurt, probably, but I wasn't going to admit that, not even to myself. 'OK,' I muttered, finally. 'That's fine.'

She shook her head wearily, and I had the idea that she had been through this type of conversation a few times in recent months. 'I like you,' she said. 'I like talking to you and stuff.' She studied my face, her expression cool, slightly curious. 'It passes the time,' she said.

'Gee, thanks.'

She laughed. 'You know what I mean,' she said.

'Do I?'

She shook her head slightly. 'See what I mean?' she said.

'What?'

She stacked her cup and saucer on top of her plate and stood up. For a moment, I thought how plain she looked, not at all the kind of girl I wanted to go out with, then she turned slightly and she looked different again, a strange beauty lighting up her face. She smiled. 'Too young,' she said; then she carried her crockery to the table by the serving hatch, set it down and disappeared. I knew where she was going and I could have followed her, but I didn't. In some dim corner of my mind, I understood her and it occurred to me that I hadn't really wanted to ask her out, it was just that I didn't know what else to do. It was the done thing – and to most girls of her age, in that place, at that time, to have done otherwise would have seemed insulting.

* * *

123

I didn't see her again till the following Monday. She was in the canteen when I got there, sitting with Erica, the half-German girl from quality control. When she saw me, she smiled, but I wasn't sure if the smile was for me, or just a reaction to something Erica had said. Not that I cared, at that precise moment. I was hung-over still, and desperate for fried food and a cup of sweet milky tea. I didn't know what Helen did on the weekends, but it had to be better than my nights out at the Strathclyde bar, drinking with old school friends and trying to avoid the odd flying glass. Naturally, because my evenings were so dismal, I suspected her of a complicated and exotic social life. I couldn't help but imagine her in the clothes she didn't wear to work, the dresses, the shoes, maybe a hat of some kind. I imagined her taking long walks in the countryside with her secret lover, an older man, perhaps, with a wife who didn't understand him. Sometimes I hated her for that. I didn't hate her for long, however, because two days later, on a warm, but perfectly ordinary summer's day, she left the factory at the end of the day shift and, without saying a word to any of us about how she felt, went home to bed. It was four in the afternoon by the time she got there, so some time was lost between clocking-off and arrival; when she got in, she told her mother she had a bit of a bug and, with a cup of milky tea in one hand and a book in the other, headed upstairs to sleep it off. Her parents looked in on her twice that evening, but they didn't want to disturb her. In the morning, when she didn't get up at the usual time, her dad went in and found her dead, her tea untouched on the bedside table, her book – I have often wished that I knew what she was reading, on the last evening of her life – set face down beside her on the bed, as if she had paused to think about what she had just read, and was still considering it somewhere,

124

far away, in a place where her thoughts could never again be interrupted.

Meanwhile, in the world outside, life went on. When I look back, it seems odd to think that this continuing life included me. Bored, oblivious, passing the time of a daylight that no longer included her. At the factory, we didn't hear the news until two days later – the Friday of that week, in fact, the day when the women stood in gangs around the fruit machine to throw away their pay. I'd looked for Helen on the Thursday, but I hadn't worried at not seeing her. Towards the end of the day – I was working a double, so I stayed on till ten – somebody told me that 'my girlfriend' hadn't turned up for work that morning, but that didn't worry me either. It didn't occur to me, naturally, that she might be dead. When I did learn what had happened, I felt an odd sense of having been betrayed, not only because I found it difficult to believe that someone who was so alive, day to day, could go home and die, in complete silence, while her parents did the dishes or watched television, but also because she died while I was still playing what I understood to be the accepted courtship game, which made everything that had actually happened between us – all the conversations and minor but significant exchanges of likes and dislikes, of doubts and notions – seem like the preamble to something that never occurred.

After a while, though, I could see that her death was a gift, of sorts. A bitter gift, but a gift nonetheless. With her gone, everything was simpler: our friendship was purer, clearer, more romantic, fraught with possibilities, the courtship game not entirely cancelled out. Later that night, walking over to the Strathclyde at the end of the back shift, I stopped for a bird that was singing in a tree on Corporation Street, singing for no reason, or so it seemed, beguiled by the amber street lights,

125

or maybe the soft yellow glimmer in the record shop across the square. It was always a relief to get out of the heat and walk away in the cool of the evening, but that night I experienced more than the familiar satisfaction of having a shift behind me, more, even, than the pleasure of being out in the dark, on my way to friends and alcohol and music. There was no reason why it should have been any different from any other night, but that night everything felt like a promise: the air, the tree, the bird, the spots of light here and there around the market square, all of it was more than usually *present*, like a promise or a pledge that was being kept, moment by moment, against considerable odds. I have nothing special to say about that moment, other than the commonplace factual details: for example, that it had rained for a while around seven o'clock, but was now clear, with only a faint dampness to the air, a soft, sweet dampness that was mostly green, but had this faintly silverish thread of song running through it for no reason; or I could say that there was something at the far side of the square, some cluster of shadows around a doorway, that I couldn't make out, but sensed as a vague benevolence in the night – yet as odd as it sounds, I would have to say that, though it was in part genuinely grim and in part self-consciously tragic, my mood, for this one, mildly epiphanic moment, might be best expressed in the common or garden and painfully trivialised phrase *happy to be alive.*

Much of the time, the dead are with us, more present on so many occasions than we give them credit for. At night, I get up and wander about the house, listening to their voices, seeing them as they once were, and the old religious idea that being is a gift seems more acceptable to me than it usually does in the plain light of day. I spend as much of my time

126

as I can being alone, but I never feel completely alone unless the dead are there, in their uniforms and aprons and Sunday best. I know most of them well, but why Helen should appear in their midst so often is a puzzle to me: we passed one another by so long ago and, for the boy I was, and for the man I am now, our acquaintance was a non-event, just one of those friendships that form in factories and offices, where life is so boring that any distraction is a blessing. We were never lovers, or even very close friends; we never actually touched – yet I remember her alongside my most cherished ghosts and I cannot envisage a time when I will forget her. She comes unbidden, like my mother and my infant brother and my near-mythical grandfather, still immense and graceful in his black coat, his massive, skilled hands still seen through a child's eyes. Now, compared to these, Helen is nothing to me – yet she comes, and she is not alone, for there are others who, by whatever logic memory would work in a more controlled world, should not be there. Like those others, she is not really part of my life. She is a story, nothing more – but then maybe this is why we tell ourselves stories, in order to work out why we remember some things more than others, why some events live on in the mind, why some faces and voices persist for decades, to be resurrected in the dark by an insomniac who wakes knowing he has certainly lost something on the way, but has no idea what it is. Which means, of course, that the story I am telling is not about this dead girl after all: it isn't about *her*, it's about *me*. It's not about her life or her death; it's about what I lost and how, whatever that lost thing might be, it resembles her in some way.

A week after she died, the women were back at the machines: Wee Ellen, Margaret, Agnes, the two Bettys. I see them in my mind's eye as clearly as if they were here and, although they do not come unless I summon them, I feel a warmth – a *fondness* – for these phantoms that I can't quite manage for my resident ghosts. I think, at the time, I was offended by the way they moved on after Helen walked home and died. I was irritated by the sound of the slot machine and their voices going back and forth, hushed in speculation or raised in the grim humour of the sworn loser's banter. For a couple of days after we heard the news, they had been softened with curiosity and a sense of mortality, but they had quickly moved on, at least outwardly, into that steady routine of *life goes on*. I think each of them, in her solitary moments, wondered about Helen for weeks or months after she died, but there was nothing to say when they were together, or nothing more than the usual snippets of shorthand: *it's a queer thing, who'd have thought it, the poor girl, all her life in front of her, her poor parents.* I see now that, though I mistook it for indifference at the time, the rest was tact: they didn't want to appropriate her, they wanted to let her lie. It's a tact that I wish I shared, sometimes, because whenever I look back and see a girl made beautiful by memory and regret smoking in an angle of the loading bay, or sitting on the grass, her head tipped to the sky, I know that whatever it is I am mourning, it isn't her. It never has been. If I knew what it was, maybe I could let her go, just as Betty G and Wee Ellen let her go and got on with their lives, feeding their wages into a slot machine and watching the brightly coloured wheels turn with no show of anticipation or regret, and no real concern as to what they would do with their wins and losses when they came, all things being equal, and things lost more equal than most.

CARELESS

I couldn't think of Gina as something lost and it didn't take much to put her out of my mind, though the kids weren't so easy to forget. Maybe, for a time, I felt *that* loss – but I did my best not to dwell and, as always, the distractions were numerous, if not particularly varied. One party in the Worplesdon woods is much like another and, if you don't bother with the niceties, all the one-night stands and bar-stool camaraderies merge into one seamless narrative. My flatmate was still away, working on secondment somewhere and there was no sign of her returning; work was the usual round of stale jokes and routine programming; the days dragged and the nights were either drunken or sleepless. I didn't have *normal* so much as numb, interrupted occasionally by a flurry of whispers in a wall, or some dark momentum rolling across the floor while I sat listening, waiting for what would come next, darkly fascinated by the invisible fauna around me. I look back and I am amazed to think that I went on like that for over a year. There were good days, of course – sometimes I went about my business with a theoretical cheerfulness that was almost convincing – but most of the time, I wasn't really there. I was a ghost in my own space, a phantom. I read books, I watched movies, I got drunk, I had random and short-lived affairs. I might have continued like that for decades, if I hadn't boarded the London train one Friday morning and chanced upon another ghost – a ghost from a lost kingdom, and so, for the first time in months, somebody *real*.

It wasn't Helen that I met on the mid-morning commuter circle train, but it *was* someone from my past and, in a sense, it was someone to whom *she* had led me. For, as fleeting as the contact between us had been, Helen had introduced me to a version of romantic love that I had always suspected was there, at the back of my mind, and at the back of other minds, from the very first. The original model had been sketched out when I was a child, improvising naive death and sex stories with the girl next door, but losing Helen had been the next meaningful step and, after she died, it wasn't long before I was seeking out fellow players who were as shyly aware of what they were doing as I had become. Sometimes those games involved touch, sometimes not. Some of them involved a notion of death – not actual death, of course, but an enactment, a ritual. Once, when I was staying with my parents, not long after Helen died, I revived a private game I had invented as a child, where I lay down on the floor under a white sheet and imagined myself as a corpse. I had thought I was alone in the house, but just at that moment a friend of my sister's had popped round and, since we always left the back door open in those days, she had let herself in and found me there, deathly still under the fresh clean sheet. I imagine most people would have beaten a hasty retreat at that point, but this particular girl – I'll call her Janice – decided it might be quite interesting to get under the sheet too, and lie alongside me – and for a long, delicious moment, we were partners in that improvised death, warm corpses, in the same white grave. As luck would have it, neither of us *did* anything. We simply lay dead for a while, almost but not quite touching, and totally silent. It was an intensely pleasurable experience.

Of course, they were innocent affairs, in the early days, when what mattered was an idea – a notion, an atmosphere – rather than an act of some kind. Later, though, the stories became more elaborate, the rituals more knowing. I would be lying to say that these games happened often: in those carefree days, when everybody slept with whoever they liked, my *vie sensuelle* was just as normal as the next person's, if a little frenetic. Very occasionally, however, someone would come along who was so miraculous, it was almost unbearable. Like Adele. Adele and I had almost come to grief, several years back, and I had never forgotten her, but I hardly expected to see her again on a damp Friday morning in Woking.

The first time I met her, I was looking for a place to stay. I had been in Cambridge for a few months, living in a squat in an old nursing hostel off the Granchester Road, and I'd enjoyed that, to begin with. There was no water or electricity, but my bed was in the old refectory, which I remember as a long, wood-panelled room with high windows that suited my insomnia perfectly. Nobody else slept there – the other ten or so squatters had made themselves at home in the smaller, less draughty bedrooms upstairs, but I was still enough of a child that lying alone in a wide, echoey room was an adventure. On clear nights, I'd watch a big moon sail across the high, arched windows; when it rained, I'd burrow in and listen to the sound it made against all that glass, a sound that I'd read was sacred in some eastern countries because, if you sat listening to it long enough, you could find some loophole in the ordinary run of things, a mystical sound that took you right to the core of being.

I was happy being a squatter. I didn't go about saying it

131

was only till I found something better, the way the others did. For me, it didn't matter that it was temporary, because I knew that the next place I washed up wouldn't be any more permanent. Besides, I really felt that I'd found my niche, being a squatter, and I would happily have stayed there forever.

I had a problem, however – which was that a huge, long-haired reddish-brown cat had taken up residence in the hostel and its favourite place was my refectory. I don't know if that cat had belonged to one of the previous tenants, or if it had just strayed in, but it obviously felt it had rights in this particular place. Most of my fellow residents ignored the creature, a couple would leave out food and water, which it never seemed to touch, but nobody fussed or mussed or gave it a name, nobody scratched its neck or picked it up and hugged it, nobody sat with it settled in their lap of an evening, sharing its creaturely warmth. Everybody knew at first sight that it wasn't that sort of cat. It wasn't mean-tempered either, and it didn't scratch, it simply existed in another world, a separate space to which *we* did not belong.

I didn't mind the cat – not in the daytime, at least. I didn't feed it, or pay much attention as it ghosted about the place, more or less ignoring the human inhabitants of the hostel, though showing great interest in any other life form that it happened upon: a stray butterfly, say, or the faintest rumour of a mouse in the wainscot. At night, though, it was a different story. At night, the beast wandered. Once or twice, I woke to see it busy at some chore in a far corner of the refectory, and that bothered me, mostly because I didn't know what the chore might be. Things didn't come to a head, though, until the small hours of one moonlit night, several weeks after I had moved into the squat. I was asleep and dreaming, first that I was walking across a warm meadow with my mother – a dream

132

that seemed also to be a memory, though there was no such meadow in or around the pit town where I grew up – and then, all of a sudden, that I was falling through dark water, unable to breathe, and I knew that if I didn't wake up soon I would die. It was a terrible moment, much more than a nightmare. It was blind panic, the kind of panic that goes beyond the mere fear of death to a place where, from the back of the mind, a voice comes saying, *all right, so be it, but not like this*, because death itself isn't frightening, but dying is and the real terror is of a graceless, or humiliating, or ugly last moment: death at the hands of some unworthy other, death by mob, all the possible banana-skin or public-square deaths that could be stumbled upon, death as dispatch, with a dead dog thrown after you into the darkness, like the murdered Consul in *Under the Volcano*. For a long moment, I struggled to breathe. Then, as I came gasping to the surface of the imagined flood, I flailed back into the room and came face to face with the cat – which had presumably been settled on my chest a moment before, but was now up and arching away, abandoning me with the contempt I deserved, leaving nothing behind but a faint stain of cat smell and a fleeting apparition of feline contempt – if Lewis Carroll had observed cats more closely, he would have given the Cheshire Cat a sneer, not a grin – but the fact that what had just happened *could* happen, and might happen *again*, was enough for me, and I didn't sleep another wink that night. The next morning, I packed my few possessions and, without saying goodbye to anyone, left the hostel, never to return.

If you're looking for somewhere to stay, you do better to go by luck and hearsay than by the ads in the *Cambridge Evening News*. The ads are placed by landlords, people who want deposits and a month in advance and guarantees, whereas some casual acquaintance in the Eagle, say, will tell you about an old caravan in the backyard of a pub that's going for next to nothing, or a room in a shared house down East Road where the rent is a little higher, but the guy who lives there has the best hash you've ever smoked in your life. At the time, my finances didn't allow me to consider anything above the caravan, so I took it, but it wouldn't be free until the end of the week and my interim option was either a friend's rather grubby living-room floor, or a combination of parties, early-morning rambles and the odd stolen hour or two of sleep by the banks of the river, or on Granchester Meadows, in the mid-afternoon. It being summer, I went for the latter. In the summertime, there is always a party somewhere. The first lasted all night, after which I borrowed a friend's bathroom, changed and headed out the next evening for more of the same.

I met Adele that night. I'd gone there with a girl whose name I can't remember now, though I can see her in my mind's eye: a very round face, the chin a little too pointy, her eyes exactly the same colour as the soft fondant you get in certain Swiss chocolates. She wasn't a date, and I can't quite recall how I'd run into her, or why she'd suddenly decided to take me to this house just off Mill Road, not far from the Live and Let Live, an old-style backstreet pub with pottery heads all over the walls in every possible guise – my favourite was a winsome Bedouin type with a missing tooth – but we'd not been there long when she wandered off with a wan, rather girlish boy, leaving me to drift into the garden, where I could gaze up at the stars and feel suitably remote. Which I did. I must have cut a rather silly picture, but that didn't prevent Adele from calling to me from the tree in which she was perched, somewhat in the manner of an amateur dramatics club Juliet doing a rather matter-of-fact balcony scene.

Coming up, or going down – that was what she said, or that was what I heard anyhow, and I stood a moment, puzzled by the question. Finally, I decided she wasn't enquiring about my mental state and, displaying an Errol Flynn-like agility that probably impressed her less than it did me, I climbed up on to the bough opposite the one where she was sitting.

'Up, then,' she said – which sounded unusually terse, but she didn't seem dissatisfied.

'Hello yourself,' I said.

She didn't speak, but studied my face in the half-light rising from the windows below – which meant that I could study *her* face with impunity, on a good-for-the-gander basis. I suppose it sounds excessive, given the half-light and the summer foliage, to describe her as the most beautiful human being I had ever met, but she was. In fact, even in that light, she was so beautiful it hurt. Actual dizzying pain. To describe her is to give no sense at all of that beauty, because it wasn't skin-deep – real beauty is not only *not* skin-deep, it's completely the opposite – though I suppose the attempt ought to be made.

She was dark. By this, I don't just mean that she had dark hair and dark eyes, though she did. She had rather pale skin and a very red mouth, her eyes were a deep, almost inky blue. I had never seen anyone with such dark blue eyes before. Yet even within all this darkness – a lit darkness, with her at its heart – she was nothing like those pale and mysterious girls you get in old Hammer movies: she wasn't gothic, or romantic, or sickly, she wasn't a Ligeia, or a Violetta. In fact, she wasn't like anything or anyone else at all. If I close my eyes, I can see her now – but I find that I cannot describe her. There are no points of reference.

That night, after we had sat in the tree for around half an hour, talking nonsense, flirting, trying one another out, we skipped the rest of the party and went back to her house, a short walk away. It was a strange place, that house: she shared it with three other women, but when we arrived it was still and silent and, as we passed through the downstairs rooms, I had the impression, not so much of a house as of a provincial museum of the kind found in English market towns, all bad but acceptably old paintings and cases full of pinned butterflies on the walls, every surface, every tabletop and sideboard crammed with stuffed animals, dead clocks and Victorian bric-a-brac. At the foot of the stairs, a huge grandfather clock was still ticking, a slow, suspenseful sound that rose to fill the entire stairwell and the gallery above.

'My God,' I said. 'What is this place?'

'Sh!' She took my hand and led me upstairs in the dark. I could barely see, and I had the sense that we were picking our way through a maze, rather than climbing a staircase. There was a feel of *presences* looming invisibly around us, presences that she could navigate only because she knew them by heart. It seemed to take forever, that slow climb, but I didn't care. I was giddily happy, moving through that museum of a house, hand in hand with a complete stranger, happy as a child is happy, happy as they might be in the afterlife. Finally she opened a door and switched a light on – and, with one backward glance before she led me into her room and closed the door, I saw that the maze we had just negotiated so carefully was a set of large Imari-style vases, set out all the way up the stairs, one every two or three steps, a glittering array of absurdly fragile porcelain, arranged in such a manner as to make the staircase close to impassable – and it struck me, then, how much Adele enjoyed doing this, that she ascended

136

to her room in the dark like that, not because she was afraid of disturbing her housemates, but because she liked moving through that maze of unseen vessels, all that bright colour and deep, contained space about her, and herself in the midst of it all, slow-moving, careful, alive.

It's not always possible to make out the sequence of events, or the logic, but everything ends for a reason. Didn't F. Scott Fitzgerald say somewhere that the difference between a sentimentalist and a romantic is that the sentimentalist is afraid that things won't last forever, whereas a romantic is afraid that they will? Or something to that effect? That first night, we could hear owls somewhere, right there in the middle of the town, and by the time we fell asleep, sometime after dawn, but before the others in the house were up and about, I had formed the distinct impression that the world was perfect. I was, at the very least, happy. Genuinely happy, like some pioneer of aviation, holding his breath for joy as his rickety machine soars into the ether. It was as if the afterlife had come to town – and I should have known then that it couldn't last.

If the child is father to the man, then my father was a boy who learned fear early. It's not surprising, I suppose, growing up as I did, see-sawing constantly between a child's allegedly simple need for affirmation – the simple need, that is, to love, and to be loved – and a growing dread of rejection that seemed to match me, step for step, all through my school years, till it culminated in something I can only think of now as a form of emotional power-out. The final straw was, of course, something trivial. It was the night of the school concert, and I was at the centre of everything – reciting poems, delivering soliloquies from *Wuthering Heights* and *Hamlet*, taking part in skits and excerpts from *The Importance of Being Earnest*. I knew my parents weren't going to be there, just as they hadn't been there at any of the previous concerts and prize-givings and even sports days – much as I despised the games teacher, much as I despised the whole changing-room ethic, I managed to squeeze myself on to the athletics team, running a very big-boned four hundred metres and, though I never quite won, I did manage a couple of honourable second places. I knew my father would never have dreamed of coming, and my mother would be too busy, and I always said that I didn't care, but as I stood in front of a packed house, delivering my big piece – mangling the *How all occasions do inform against me* speech from *Hamlet* – I looked out over the sea of freshly scrubbed and powdered faces and saw that not one of them was there for me. They were there for little Stewart or Andrew or Jimmy and, of course, they resented the fact that I was up there, hogging the limelight, not giving *their* bairns a chance to shine. Which I was, of course. It was all very well to say I didn't care, but I had gone out of my way to nab all the best parts and, even when I condescended to play Mercutio rather than Romeo in the school drama production (the best role anyhow, since it meant I got the Queen Mab speech and the hand on the very prick of noon to play with), even when I relegated myself to butler status for the Wilde, I shamelessly and perfidiously upstaged the other little darlings for all I was worth. And for what? There was nobody there to see any of it, or nobody that I cared about. No matter what I did, I couldn't get what I wanted, and like any other sad, bump-tious, solitary child, what I wanted was to be loved.

Trivial, of course, yet oddly decisive, in the scheme of things. Formative, even. By the time I got myself expelled from that same school, I was intelligent enough to see that most of the things that mattered were beyond my control, but not so smart

138

that I could keep from throwing away what little power I did have. I don't know if all this common or garden psychological damage did anything to exacerbate my natural tendency towards apophenia, but I see now that the child who was father to me grew up with a whole circus of exterminating angels and wilderness visions in his head, and he spent huge reserves of mental fight trying to accommodate them. Yet though it may sound perverse to say so now, the only sign of health, the only mark of a sanity that, as precarious as it might be, *still* had more going for it than normal, is that it was *accommodation* he sought, not containment, and definitely not excision. To that boy's credit, he was never in the market for an exorcism – not back then, anyhow – because, somewhere at the back of his head, he knew that, in any successful exorcism, the angels tend to get killed off with the demons.

The process of maintaining that perverse accommodation is almost impossible without an element of romanticism, however – and I think Fitzgerald was right: the defining characteristic of the romantic is the fear that something – anything – might last forever. I could look back at that first idyll with Adele and say that it was just the customary days-of-wine-and-roses gig – something I had mastered over the years – with a little sexual ambiguity thrown in for good measure. But that wouldn't be the whole truth. The truth would be more like this: I was blundering through life with a head full of voices, doing my best to act normal, but unable to stop myself from making occasional visits to the psychotic end of the spectrum, the ultraviolet zone where love and death weren't as clearly separated as they were elsewhere, the Edgar Allan Poe, *Yeux sans Visages*, you-always-hurt-the-one-you-love end – and because of this I was afraid of Adele from that first morning on: afraid of her perfection, afraid of her beauty, afraid of what we might do together. I had experienced that fear maybe twice before, in dilute form, but with her it was cask-strength, and there was no mistaking the fact that, as successful as she was in seeming as normal as the next woman, something in *her* – something at the back of her mind – echoed my own romance fantasy so precisely that, given the chance, we might carry it to some terrible conclusion. I could say, now, with the benefit of hindsight, that this was all projection, that she was just an innocent bystander who happened to stray too far into the world of a disturbed stranger she'd met at a party, but even if that were true – and our later adventures suggest that it was not – it wouldn't have made any difference. In matters of this kind, the outcome isn't affected by what is fantasy and what is not. In *Who's Afraid of Virginia Woolf?*, there's a brief exchange which goes something like this:

Martha: Truth and illusion, George. You don't know the difference.
George: No, but we must carry on as though we did.

Now, *there's* a definition of normal. An astonishing gift for pretending. The ordinary *as-if* that binds the days together. We have to pretend, Stendhal said. If we don't pretend, we're lost. And if you can't pretend, run away.

I did run away, in the end, though not soon enough. The details of what led to that flight are not particularly interesting and far from drawn out. In those days, nothing I did lasted very long and, as the mystery of fear possessed me, what began as a romance moved swiftly to a place where two people try to see how far they can go – and all the time, I was as bewildered by what I was doing as she must have been, even

140

though I was the one who was at fault. I was always the one who pushed, always the one who moved to the next square on the board and, at the end, I was the one who allowed himself to be overwhelmed by the dark tenderness that had grown between us: the first to turn away, the first to recant – and the first to wonder where it all went wrong, after our last drunken and slightly nauseating afternoon in the house of porcelain and stopped clocks.

Now, sitting in my nice jacket and tie on the Waterloo train – the laxity of Civil Service life meant that I wasn't travelling at rush hour, but mid-morning, when the usual commuter rage had abated – I was settling down with a good book, when a ghost appeared and started making its way along the carriage. I didn't believe it, to begin with. At first sight, it seemed that she had barely changed – her hair was a little shorter, her eyes weren't quite so dark and she was dressed for a business meeting in a dark blue jacket and trousers – yet I still thought that I *had* to be mistaken. I imagine she felt something similar but, even though in the final moment of actual recognition – or rather, of acceptance that what I was seeing was not an illusion or a trick of the light – I could have let her pass by. Maybe I would have done – but she chose to stop, and then to sit and then, as if we were nothing more than old friends who happened to have run into one another on the way to work, she guided us through the kind of conversation that anyone might have under such circumstances. We talked all the way to London: she was working for a consultancy company, she said, though she left the details vague, and no, she didn't live in Woking, she lived in Hampshire, in a village not far from Alton. She was married, didn't have children and what about me? She seemed amused by the idea of me in an office, but she didn't make too much of it. She didn't make too much of anything, really, other than the fact that I lived in Guildford, where she sometimes went shopping on a Saturday afternoon, and gradually I relaxed – or rather, I slid – into thinking that this meeting could go down in the record as one of those poignant but eventually forgettable mishaps that fate deals out from time to time, as a reminder of what might have been. Of course, it took all my self-restraint not to ask about her husband all the way into town, but nothing more was said about him after the brief allusion to his existence – though perhaps *he* was the simple fact that made it possible for us to travel so lightly, staying clear of dangerous memories, making ourselves out to be people we could never be, parting at Waterloo with no apparent regrets and going our separate ways, she to her next client, me to an interminable infrastructure meeting. We made no arrangements to meet again, in spite of the fact that we only lived a few stations away from one another, and though there was a noticeable tension between us at the end, we parted on good terms, like sensible people – and for something close to a month after that final moment when she turned as she was walking away and allowed herself the most fleeting of smiles, I went around in a haze of pain and dismay, thinking that was exactly what she had become. Sensible. Married. Normal.

Our next meeting happened by chance, if either of us was to be believed. It was a Saturday afternoon and I was trawling around Guildford, supposedly looking for a new toaster. As it happened, I was feeling all right that day, though I had no specific reason to be cheerful. I was on an even keel, though, and that was always good. I wasn't having bad dreams or flashbacks; I wasn't hearing voices in the middle of the night when

I lay awake in the dark, trying to sleep, or trying to work out how to divide everything I saw by the number seven. I wasn't even bored. I was shopping, and, as dull as that sounds, it's surprising how, on a good day, the smallest chore can become a pleasure. The Japanese call it *wabi-sabi*: a state of quotidian grace in which everyday objects and events become sacraments. D. T. Suzuki says, 'Wabi is to be satisfied with a little hut, a room of two or three tatami mats, like the log cabin of Thoreau, and with a dish of vegetables picked in the neighbouring fields, and perhaps to be listening to the pattering of a gentle spring rainfall.' I had been working on that notion for a while in a desultory manner and, because of that desultoriness, I was still having huge difficulties, but I had begun to suspect that it was a possible way out of the recurrent problem that, in a piece of shorthand borrowed from John Berryman, I called the *Life, friends is boring* problem – which, put briefly, was that, even if from time to time I experienced a supreme connectedness, a profound sense of *being there*, after a few minutes, or an hour, or an afternoon, there was always the fact that, with no discipline in place, no framework, and no escape from the contingencies of that old chestnut *the real world*, I eventually had to go back to the office. I suppose this banal truth was the origin of my elaborate afterlife fantasy: all the afterlife was, in the end, was a state where you didn't have to go back to the office. As Berryman's mother tells him, to say that life is boring is to admit that you have no inner resources – and I wanted to find a way to equip myself with sufficient inner resources to deal with a normal life in the Surbiton of the real world, which was proving very different from the Surbiton in my mind. The *wabi-sabi* of toasters seemed a fair enough place to begin.

It was a cool day, with a hint of damp in the air. Adele was wearing a long, navy-blue winter coat, with a blue cloche hat and a silk scarf in blue and silver. I saw her before she saw me, and I could have ducked into a shop doorway to avoid her, but I didn't. She was walking slowly, with a faraway look on her face, and I knew that I hadn't really come to town for a toaster, any more than I had gone to town every Saturday for the last three weeks to find good coffee or a pair of winter shoes or a little bag of treats from the Guildford Cheese Shop. I had been looking for *her* – and for a moment, I wondered if she in turn was looking for me, as she wandered up North Street, alone, and remote from the shoppers hurrying by, their faces blurred with nearness. She *was* remote, far away, perfect – and all I could do was stop and wait till she reached me. For a fleeting moment I wondered where the husband was – then she saw me, and I could tell that she was pleased to find me there. That day, we only had time for a brief coffee in a nearby cafe – but that was when we resumed the worrying narrative that had been interrupted years before. It was the same story, too; the only difference was that, this time, we both knew what we were doing and what had been raw and violent before was about to be transmuted into something far more tender, knowing, enquiring, solicitous and, for as long as it lasted, considerably more elegant than either of us could have hoped for.

THE HANDYMAN AND HOME
MECHANIC, OR A SUBURBANITE'S
GUIDE TO SELF-MEDICATION

There's a painting by Edward Hopper that I particularly like: *Early Sunday Morning, 1930*. It shows a row of small brick-built shops on an ordinary street, the kind of street you could find anywhere in America till not that long ago: small businesses on the ground floor, tiny apartment rooms above, a barber's pole and a fire hydrant on the kerb outside, casting long shadows in the early-morning light. Though it's impossible to make out the lettering on the windows, I like to imagine that the shop with the awning on one side of the barber's is a diner, the kind of place where the waitress calls you honey and keeps coming back to the table to refresh your coffee cup and bring you up to date on the latest gossip. On the other side, behind the brown, rather eerie facade, it's a bookshop, a narrow emporium of all the beautiful old gardening manuals and histories of the Brandywine Valley that nobody wants any more, the spines cracked, the pages edged with dust. On weekdays, this shop is tended by an elderly man whose granddaughter is always just about to arrive with a brown bag of bagels and cream cheese, but today it's empty, like the barber's and the diner, empty like the street, with that specialised, metaphysical emptiness of Sunday mornings, the streets silent and still, the shadows long and pale, the old bookseller and his neighbours asleep in their upper rooms, behind the cheap blinds and lace curtains.

Sundays at the Worplesdon end of Guildford weren't quite so clearly defined, but there were times when I would walk over to the newsagent's, two streets away, and I'd see that Hopper painting in my mind's eye: the row of shops, the long shadows, the empty pavement, that Sunday-morning emptiness when, by sheer chance, nobody else was about. It wasn't as aesthetically pleasing, perhaps: there was no red brick, no eerie brown frontage, no barber's pole outside the grey-and-beige hair salon, but there was still enough to go on, still enough to get that sense of light and space. I suppose that's what art is *for*, in every sense of the word: we make paintings and songs and stories to work these small miracles in the mind's eye, to remind us that anything can be transformed. Or this is what I supposed one particular Sunday morning, a few weeks before I met Adele again – a morning when the need for transformation seemed more than usually urgent, my best-laid plans gone totally agley, my supposedly normal life a catalogue of squalid adventures and Sunday-morning regrets. I was hung-over, aching with guilt and fatigue and the kind of thirst that doesn't just sit in the throat, but spreads through every nerve like a fever. Worse still, I was nursing a gaggle of ugly memories from the night before that worried me almost as much as the blackout that had come somewhere between the last party – where I'd been drinking vodka straight from the bottle and smoking what seemed like the same eternal joint outside a caravan at the edge of a muddy field – and the cold hallway of the flat, where I'd woken fully clothed at first light.

So even before I met Adele on that Waterloo train, I had begun to realise that I was in trouble. I told myself that I had come a long way, especially for an apophenic: I was holding down a steady job, I was living in a fairly pleasant place, I had even saved a little money – but I was bored with my excesses of a Saturday night, and with the supposed friends I chose for my escapades, bored with the Gregs and the Ginas of this world and, most of all, I was bored with the continual burden of *me*. I was frustrated and angry that I couldn't achieve what I'd set out to achieve when I moved south. I had been in the suburbs for what felt like forever, and I still had no idea of how to live a normal life. On a Sunday morning, I should have been going back to bed with a tray of toast and freshly perked coffee, a good book on the bedside table, sunlight falling golden into the room and pooling in the folds and creases of the bedspread, the radio playing Handel or Vivaldi. Instead, I was mooching about the shops, trying to find Edward Hopper in a hairdresser's window, my throat dry as sandpaper, my mind haunted by dread imaginings of what I might have done between that field and the hall carpet. I had begun to see – long after I should have seen – that it was time for another change. Or not just a change, but a transformation. A new weather, a new life. Radical surgery. That was how it seemed, that morning, in my feverish state: a soul-shift, a departure, a moment from the book of illuminations. A Sunday-morning vision, after the blackness of Saturday night and, even if I knew it was not to be trusted – because nothing a penitent comes up with is ever entirely trustworthy – I didn't have anything else to be going on with.

In short, good-resolution time had come around again – and a few weeks later, when I fell in love with Adele for the second time, *doing something* seemed all the more urgent. I had to make changes. I had to find some kind of order. Go back to meetings, maybe.

147

Hi. My name is John and –

No. I couldn't do that. It hadn't worked before, and it was hardly likely to work now. Not for me, anyhow – and I didn't want to insult that brown room full of good men who had struggled long and hard for their sobriety by merely going through the motions. Besides, it was up to *me* to sort myself out. Nobody else could do it for me. I could hear my father's voice saying as much at the back of my mind and I suppose it must have appealed to me on some level of childish irony to take heed of that voice, when all the others back there in the shadows, all the nuns and priests and kindly teachers and tough-love aunties, not to mention my dear sainted mother, were wasting their breath. And it must have been that same spirit of childish perversity that determined the three steps I decided I had to take next – I wasn't quite up to a twelve-step programme yet – because they were the three things my father never managed to do. The first was to stop drinking completely. The second was to learn how to drive. The third was to get a better job and buy a house of my own. Fairly rudimentary stuff – kind of a bottom line, in fact, for the Surbiton fantasy – but for me it was new ground. Later, perhaps, I would go on to fascinating hobbies and pre-Saga cruise travel, but for starters, these three would be enough. For the first time in my life, as sad and non-*wabi-sabi* as it sounds, I wanted to *have* something, to be something other than an itinerant phantom hiding in the suburbs because he couldn't find anywhere else to hide. I wanted to have money. I wanted to have *things*.

Shoes, for example.

Every summer, the kids in my part of the world got a new pair of light shoes – sandshoes, or plimsolls – to be worn in all conditions, wet or dry, hot or cold, for running through the long grass around the old abattoir and for wandering the streets looking for bottles so we could go to the Saturday matinee and see Stewart Grainger in *Scaramouche*. It was a sign of who and what we were: sturdy leather shoes in the winter, sandshoes in the summer, patches on the inside of the trouser leg so they would be less visible, shirt collars turned around when they frayed. For a long time, everybody I knew had one pair of summer shoes and no more. Then, one day, a boy called Daniel turned up in the middle of August with brand-new black-and-white baseball boots, instead of the white plimsolls he'd been wearing for the previous couple of months. A few weeks later, his dad bought a car – an Austin Cambridge – and we knew then that Daniel's family were *well off*. Not rich, exactly – a rich person wouldn't be living in the prefabs – but able to buy the little extras in life, and to go on holidays and Sunday outings in the car. I still remember how new those baseball boots looked, and how spacious that car seemed – and I still remember how uncomfortable they made me, those signs of wealth, those *goods*. I felt let down, to be honest. I felt betrayed and, for years after I left home, I kept my possessions to a minimum: a few clothes, a couple of books, a razor and a toothbrush. It had always been easier to stick to the one pair of shoes, the cheap seats at the pictures, the bedsit room with just a table and a chair and a single bed, simple and bare and almost empty. But now, that simplicity seemed hypocritical. It wasn't a *via negativa*, as I had tried to pretend, it wasn't *wabi-sabi*, it was something altogether more commonplace. All those shoeless years, I hadn't been living as a *wabibito*, someone who knows how to make the most of everyday, simple objects and events, I had simply been what the Japanese call *makoto no hinjin*, that is, a poor person. I hadn't been poor because I had *chosen* to live in poverty, but because I didn't know how to hold on to what I had been given and had contrived to make a virtue out of that fact. I wasn't a monk, I was a down-and-out; I wasn't poor, I was just broke.

As it turned out, finding a new job was so easy, I was surprised I hadn't got round to it earlier. I had been trained well by the Civil Service and my diverse skills were much in demand. Barely two months after that encounter with Adele on North Street, I was working for an airtime sales company based in Thames Ditton for three times what I had been paid at MAFF and I had started looking at houses on the south side of Guildford, where you could still get something decent for the kind of mortgage I was able to raise on my new salary. By that Christmas my still mostly absent flatmate and I had agreed to go halves on a run-down semi-detached in Bramley that needed everything doing to it. Neither of us could afford to go it alone, so we came to an unusual, but not unsatisfactory arrangement that gave her a base to come back to whenever she needed it, and provided me with a home. A place to do up. A hidey-hole. Most of the time, I was alone – the only other person ever to set foot in the house was Adele – and I had reached Surbiton. Or so it seemed, at least.

Now, finally, it was time for cocoa and Sunday walks and DIY. It was time for raking leaves and painting the ceiling. Soon, I had quit drinking and I was eating real food. I had established a routine and, most of the time, I was approximately sane. I bought a new suit and a Samsonite briefcase that I carried back and forth to work every day; I bought half a dozen oxford shirts and three pairs of what my mother would have called *good shoes* – and, gradually, I began to put together the semblance of a normal existence. *I went to the suburbs because I wished to live deliberately, to front only the essential facts of life, and see if I could not learn what they had to teach, and not when I came to die, discover that I had not lived.* Here, at last, I was on the threshold of the good life: here was House and Home, Home and Garden, Handyman and Home Mechanic.

And there was so much to do. The house had a long, narrow garden running down to what had once been a spur of the Basingstoke Canal, but it had been neglected for years and was hopelessly overgrown, so I bought a spade and began to dig. Inside, the kitchen ceiling was saturated with tar from the cigarettes the previous inhabitant had smoked constantly, so I stood on a stepladder for days, scrubbing the plasterwork with sugar soap, the tar dripping into my hair and running down my face. The staircase was an ugly cascade of paint and varnish, but just enough was chipped away to see the warm, golden pine wood under it all, so I got some wire wool and stripper and set to work on that. I had no DIY skills whatsoever – my father hadn't taught me any of the useful skills fathers are supposed to teach their sons – so I had to learn everything from scratch but, to my surprise, I found I was fairly good at all the corny things that people in the suburbs do. Stripping wallpaper, sanding, gardening and DIY. Planting shrubs, cooking Chinese-style, working with wood. For a while there, it felt like *wabi-sabi*, or the beginnings of something like it. I delighted in simple things – or I tried to, at least. As soon as I was settled enough for a hobby, I took up Penjing, the suitably oriental art of container gardening with trees, not quite as severe as bonsai, but similarly elegant and restful. And, once I had kicked the vices, I got healthy with a vengeance. Soon I was running five miles every morning before work and, in the evenings, I came home and read for a few hours before bed. My change of job meant I could present myself to a new set of colleagues as a clean-living, possibly slightly religious nerd who was nevertheless friendly and good at his job, a straight up-and-down guy, someone you could put in front of clients. My boss, a stocky, moustachioed guy called Ray who reminded me of a Polish actor, gave me the most interesting work I'd ever had, working with people who really knew what they were doing – no *Mastermind* candidates in sight – on a major systems spec for a large European broadcasting company. It was very strange. I'm not about to claim that office life was interesting, as such, but it wasn't too awful, either. Things could have been worse. I still had problems sleeping, but it was rare to hear women and children calling for blood or salvation through the plasterwork or the plumbing.

I couldn't believe it. Suddenly, I had worked out how to be normal and, for a while there, when I was almost entirely distracted by DIY and learning new skills like making jam and baking lemon pies in the Shaker style, *normal* was a deep and possibly abiding pleasure, especially at the weekends. I made a point of incorporating all the Surbiton clichés into my routine: Sunday-morning walks around Selbourne with Adele, say, or maybe trawling the antique fairs, handling the objects, looking for clues to the provenance, talking to the stallholders. I learned to love the village halls of Surrey, all set out with dusted bric-a-brac and the first modest items of some lifelong collection of chinoiserie or Victorian jewellery. It was all so delicately sensual, everything was steeped in *le temps perdu*, even the smallest piece a complex of patina and firing cracks and the partial narratives that might be inferred from paper or wood. A trace of some local sweetness in a turned bowl, the hint of gold at the rim of a glass, the faint handwritten note in the margin of an old book – it was all wonderfully *bourgeois* and decent and, for a long time, I thought I might stay in the suburbs forever.

Meanwhile, I was seeing Adele whenever I could – and, spurred on by the thought that I could see her more often if I had a car, I started on the driving lessons. In secret. For, as silly as it seems, I was ashamed that I couldn't drive already, ashamed that I hadn't passed my test three days after my seventeenth birthday, as all the other male suburbanites seemed to have done. Not that there had ever been any chance of that and, to be honest, motorised vehicles had never interested me that much, but all through my childhood my father had talked about how he was going to buy me A Car some day. When he was in his cups, and in a good mood, he told me that he would buy A Car for my seventeenth birthday, so I could go where I wanted and do what I liked, because A Car gives you freedom. He didn't drive himself, though he claimed that he could – he'd learned in the RAF, he said, but just hadn't bothered to get his licence. My uncle, Big John Reddington, thought different. He'd let my father drive his car one day and almost hadn't lived to regret it. For years after, he enjoyed telling the story, though I don't imagine he enjoyed it at the time, as they sputtered and clanged into action, then headed off down the brae near my grandmother's house at full tilt.

'You're sure you know what you're doing, now?' he said, made nervous by my father's erratic attempts to get going.

My father was annoyed. 'Gie us a minute,' he said. 'I'm just no used tae this model.'

'Aye,' Big John said. 'Ye're nae use, right enough.'

This would have rattled my father, but he'd got the car going eventually. It was soon obvious that he had no clear idea of how to make it go where he wanted it to go, and, being a practical man, Big John quickly began to wonder if he knew how to make it stop. The truly worrying thing, however, was that my father, who believed that a confident approach was half the battle in any enterprise, had his foot down on the accelerator and he was craning forward, his eyes fixed on the road. That was when Big John remembered that, though he was too vain to ever wear his glasses, my father was disastrously myopic. Still, he was never a man to panic, my Uncle John – and he stayed calm. 'Slow down, now, Tommy,' he said. 'You're going a wee bitty fast for the road.'

By this time, however, the old man had decided he was doing fine. He was still getting used to this model of car, but he'd begun to get the hang of it. 'Gie's peace, John,' he said. 'You're spoiling ma concentration.' And he would have needed his concentration, then, because the car was just coming up to a tight bend and Big John wasn't sure that they were going to make it.

And that, apparently, was when the struggle began. With an increased sense of urgency, my uncle – who was called *Big* John for a reason – managed to overcome my father, get a sure hold of the steering wheel and, because my dad's foot had slipped off the accelerator, and because John had managed to get a hold of the handbrake, he guided them on to a reasonably low verge, doing only the kind of damage to the vehicle that he could fix himself, and leaving the two men more or less intact. When the dust had settled, he sat back and looked about. Fortunately, there were no witnesses. And no casualties. 'My God,' he said. 'A thocht ye kent how to drive a car!'

'Aye, weel,' my father said – and I always remember the twinkle in Big John's eye when he told this, 'Ah have tae admit, Ah'm a bit rusty.'

154

My driving instructor couldn't quite manage that twinkle, but he did his best, considering. His name was – let's call him Bill. It suits his down-to-earth, gruff style a lot better than the moniker his parents saddled him with. A big man, with close-cropped hair and very clear eyes – not quite blue, but too vivid to be called grey, they seemed out of place in his head, as if he'd just stepped out of a science-fiction film – he took great delight in letting me infer how amusing it must have been for him to see someone so hopelessly ill-suited to the task – someone like me – attempting to drive. This may seem rather counterproductive in a driving *instructor*, but I found it oddly reassuring, because I also knew that the whole exercise was preposterous and I had hopes that, given the amused incredulity we were both applying to the process, things would work out fine in the end. Besides, I had a secret weapon up my sleeve that he could hardly have suspected – viz. that, if I had one of my psychotic turns and suddenly veered off the road and into a tree without warning, I would not only be going to a better place, but I'd be taking him with me.

For the majority of my early lessons, though, I sat behind the steering wheel and thought about how all this machinery went: how the clutch worked, how the fuel combustion system operated, what the effects of sudden braking might be, how the gears meshed. It was a system, after all, and we apophenic types are good with systems. In fact, once we got going, I was fairly happy, and the faster we went the more relaxed I felt. The only thing that really bothered me was when we slowed down too much and I felt the systems getting away from me, the order I had in my head either decaying or becoming too subtle and fine to comprehend. My basic theory – one that I still battle with to this day – is that I am a fairly reasonable

155

driver at anything above 40 mph, but slower than that, my mind starts to wander.

For a while, Bill put up with all this thinking. Finally, though, he made me pull into a lay-by on a back road between Guildford and Clandon. Once the handbrake was safely on and the engine switched off, he gave me a long look, then he turned his head and gazed out at the woods through the passenger-side window. It had rained earlier, but it was warm now. Steam was rising from the heaps of leaf litter along the edge of the road, giving the whole scene a distinctly unseasonal feel to it. Bill sighed. 'What are you doing?' he said finally, his voice carefully flat.

'Sorry?'

'What are you doing?' He turned to stare at me, his look at once incredulous and accusing. There was a long silence, while I tried to work out what I had done wrong. I couldn't though, because I had been doing fairly well until he interrupted me. I hadn't been going too fast in a built-up area – the usual fault – and I'd gone through all the mirror-signal-manoeuvre business, even when it wasn't strictly necessary.

'I don't know,' I said. 'Did I make a mistake?'

Bill sighed again and shook his head. From the look on his face, I could tell it was worse than that. 'You're *thinking* about something, aren't you?' he said finally.

I shrugged. 'Well, yes,' I said. 'Of *course* I'm thinking –'

'About what?'

I stared back at him now. He seemed personally offended, which was, or seemed to me at least, quite unjustified. 'Well,' I said, 'I'm thinking about the engine, I suppose.'

'The engine?'

'Yes.'

'What *about* the engine?'

'How it works,' I said. 'Well, not just the engine, obviously. The whole system. The gears. The brakes –'

I stopped talking. He was looking away again, staring out at the sunny woodland around us, and probably wishing he was out there, walking the dog in the autumnal gap between lunch at the pub and dinner with the family – and I felt for him, I really did. I felt his dismay, even though I still didn't understand what the problem was.

When he looked back, however, he was smiling. 'I hear you write books,' he said.

'Who told you that?'

'You don't write books?'

I shook my head. 'Poetry,' I said. 'Not proper books. Just poetry.'

'Ah,' he said. Then, so I would know my self-deprecation hadn't fazed him, he said, 'So what's wrong with poetry?'

I didn't have an answer to that but, as I looked out at the damp woods, I began to understand why Bill had got me to stop. He'd thought I was thinking about my latest thriller, maybe totting up the sales figures or figuring out the twist in the final chapter while I practised my emergency stop or nego-tiated the roundabout at the end of Epsom Road. For what seemed a long time, maybe a minute or more, we sat in silence, staring out of our respective side windows, communing with nature. Finally Bill turned to me. 'You know who my favourite writer is?' he said.

I shook my head. 'Barbara Cartland?' I said.

He smiled. 'No,' he said quietly. 'Try again.'

'Yevgeney Zamyatin?'

'Nathanael West,' he said, before I could go on. 'I *love* Nathanael West – as a writer.' His eyes wandered to some imaginary reading room in the trees. '*Miss Lonelyhearts. A Cool*

Million.' He considered these masterpieces of satirical fiction, ran silently through their strengths and weaknesses and their place in the oeuvre. '*The Day of the Locust.*' He gave a small shake of the head to indicate awe.

'Donald Sutherland,' I said.

He turned to me in alarm. 'I beg your pardon?'

'The film,' I said. 'Donald Sutherland is Homer Simpson in the film of *The Day of the Locust.*'

Bill looked upset. 'No,' he said, in a near-whisper.

'Yes.'

'You're getting confused with *Invasion of the Body Snatchers,*' he said.

'No,' I said. '*Day of the Locust.*'

Bill looked away again, dismayed. Evidently, he wouldn't have cast Donald Sutherland in the movie of *The Day of the Locust* if he'd had final say-so, which was odd, because the great Canadian actor had been superb, as always. I wondered who he would have chosen while I waited for him to get over the shock.

Finally, he returned from the dark place that had claimed him for all of forty seconds. 'So you know Nathanael West,' he said.

'Not personally,' I said – though to be fair, I regretted it as soon as the words were out.

Bill didn't bat an eyelid. 'Then you'll know how he died,' he said.

'Car crash,' I said. 'Somewhere near Los Angeles, I think.'

Bill nodded. 'It wasn't his first,' he said. 'He was always running off the road, ending up in irrigation ditches or whatever.' He studied my face. 'Seems his mind was always off somewhere, not paying attention to what he was doing,' he said.

I grinned. I was fairly certain that he wasn't being paid to tell me this. He was being paid to get me to do a three-point turn well enough to sneak through my driving test and get out on the open highway with all the other maniacs.

'I wouldn't mind,' Bill said. 'He was a great writer and you can't be good at everything. But he wasn't the only one who died on that fatal afternoon in El Centro, California, on the 22nd of December 1940.' He looked at me to see if I knew this part of the story. I did, sort of, but I was impressed by the fact that he could remember the date and place so clearly. 'No,' he continued, satisfied that I was in the dark. 'His wife was with him. Eileen. A beautiful woman. *Beautiful.*' He took a moment to consider the waste of this young life. 'She was pregnant, you know,' he said.

I shook my head. 'I didn't know that,' I said. I was pretty sure my hour was up by now.

Bill nodded, then he looked at me – and in his face I saw a lifetime's worth of equanimity. 'Well,' he said, 'even if she wasn't, she ought to have been. She ought to have had kids and grandkids, the whole shebang.' The corners of his mouth tightened.

I nodded. 'That would have been nice,' I said.

We sat a while then, considering Nathanael West's unborn grandchildren. His beautiful wife. Donald Sutherland. How *Invasion of the Body Snatchers* would have turned out if Nathanael West had been alive to write it. Whatever we were thinking.

By now, though, I needed to get going – and though he seemed in no rush, Bill must have sensed my impatience, because he had me start up the engine and drive back to town. It wasn't until we were in the town centre, a street away from where he usually dropped me, that he came to the real point of his sudden and uncharacteristic digression. 'I like to give my students nicknames,' he said. 'Just for me, you understand. Not to their faces.'

I nodded, but I didn't say anything. I was keeping my eye on the road, thinking about switching gears.

'I'm going to call you Nathanael,' he said. 'It seems appropriate, you being a writer and everything.'

I was looking for a place to pull in, so I could give him my full attention, but by the time I had found one, it was all over. He had been making a point, and that was probably fine, but I didn't really know what it was.

'So,' I said. 'See you next time.'

He nodded. 'Don't think so much,' he said.

Over the coming months, through a cold, snowy winter and far into the spring, I saw Adele whenever I could. In spite of Bill's reservations, I'd passed my driving test, which made it easy to meet up in secret places at odd times of day, whenever we could, which wasn't that often, but enough so we could resume where we had left off, years before, in the house of Imari. I wasn't afraid of her now, though. I wasn't afraid of what either of us might do: I was just storybook *in love* and, though to an outsider it might have seemed that we had some odd ways of expressing love, for a while there we did know *exactly* what we were doing. There was no pattern to our lives, and at times we parted with no set timetable for when we would meet again, yet I was happy, after a fashion, and I believe she was too. We had no plans, no sense of *a future* – we never once spoke about running away together, or bumping off her husband, or any of the things adulterers do in movies. We simply went from stolen afternoon to stolen afternoon, those odd mini-vacations the faithless take in

160

anonymous hotels when they are pretending to be on a course or visiting clients, and making the best of what we had – and I could see that there was a *wabi-sabi* to adultery, too, a whole Kawabata world of quiet moments and rain at hotel windows and the slow afterwards of train rides in the dark. Still, at least we weren't deluding ourselves. There was enough of the romantic in us both to know that it couldn't last forever. What we had was stolen. Illicit. People like us couldn't get married – or not, at least, to people like us – because marriage belonged to the real world. Marriage was something you had to work at and, from what she said, there were times when it was the emotional equivalent of management courses and meetings with Bob from finance. Some things we do for love – art, romance, pure science, walking to the South Pole – but marriage is more like the day job. Or so it seemed to me, at the time. Besides, we were happy with what we had and, as long as nothing happened to take it away, we imagined we might have it for a long time. Certainly until our next meeting, which was as far ahead as either of us ever chose to think.

Everything was stolen and everything was provisional – yet whenever we were together it was as if we were about to disappear. We would wake up in a white bed, sleep-warm and strange to ourselves in some market town where nobody knew us, or we would be walking in the grounds of a stately home when, all of a sudden, the path would end in thin air and vista, and it would seem that we could be gone at any moment, climbing the stairs in a provincial hotel, or toppling into some wormhole in the fabric of things, only to reappear elsewhere, not quite ourselves in a world where the usual rules had never applied. Once, I remember, we drove to a wood we'd discovered near the Pilgrim's Way, with no other plan than to walk for an hour or so, but, after we had gone a few hundred yards into the trees, it had begun to snow: big, white flakes swirling in the air around our heads, yet not quite touching us for the longest time, as if, together, we were some insubstantial thing, some atmospheric trick. Usually, on those walks, we talked back and forth, filling the gap between one meeting and the next, repairing the narrative of *us* – but that night we didn't say a word. We just walked on, as if we were there for a purpose – and, as we walked, the snow came thicker and faster, finding us at last and blanking us out as we went till, eventually, we stopped and looked at one another. Neither of us spoke, but I knew what was in her mind. On one level, we were merely deciding to go back, but there was something else, something we had never talked about and, in that moment, with not a word spoken, that other thing was rehearsed, briefly – rehearsed, allowed fleetingly to *be* and then, quietly, with the merest shiver of regret, abandoned. It was a banal story, of course, from anybody else's point of view, but from ours, it was a near-miraculous possibility and, *because* it was near-miraculous, we let it go, convinced that this was for the best. *For the best.* It sounds like a line from a movie, some *Brief Encounter* moment of renunciation or self-sacrifice, but it wasn't. It was realism, nothing more.

When we got back to the car, we were almost completely white. We were silent, still, not talking, but by some unspoken agreement, we stopped and stood a while, face to face, each of us brushing the snow from the other's shoulders and hair, before we drove away. It was late now, but there was a light off the snow, a bleary whiteness on the air, all along the dirt track from the car park to the road. People say nothing is perfect, there's always a flaw, perfection can only be found in the unheard melodies of some Keatsian other-world, but that moment was perfect. Even on the road, we drove slowly, the snow creaking under the tyres, and it was as if the weather was trying to slow us down, and so prevent us from going back to our separate worlds – and for a moment we almost stayed there, on that country road between one town and another, the snow melting on our hands and faces, our perfect, fleeting bodies silent and wounded and blessed.

This is the moment I remember, the moment that contains all the others. There is no afterwards to this moment. It has nothing to do with time or circumstance, and there are nights when I am capable of imagining that it continues somewhere, this one moment that contains all the others, travelling on and on forever, like the light from our headlamps that is still travelling through the universe, on and on and on, into infinity.

For our part, we continued for as long as we were able. We were good and careful thieves, discreet and undemanding, but we had always known it would end. For as long as it lasted, I could have guessed, but carefully declined to acknowledge, what a strain it must have been for her, being married. I also declined to entertain the idea that, once upon a time, and perhaps still, her husband probably *meant something* to her, in the way that, for reasons that Gatsby cannot comprehend, Tom Buchanan still *means something* to Daisy. Adele must have loved him, once, and she no doubt cared for him still – so it was probably with mixed feelings that she set out, on our final afternoon, eighteen months after our encounter on North Street, to give me the news that, in one form or another, I had been dreading and expecting for so long.

It was a Wednesday, in the early spring. Not warm, particularly, but clear, even a little crisp. Adele knew the road to my house well enough, and there was no reason for the accident, on that day of all days, but I suppose she wasn't paying attention. She was probably lost in herself, working out what to say to me, and what she would say to her husband, and whether she would keep the baby, and whatever else had occurred to her to worry over – and that was probably why she hit the dog. She hadn't been driving fast, she told me, but she hadn't seen the thing and at first she thought it was a person she had hit, a child who had run out into the road from one of the cottages on that stretch of road between Bramley and Cranleigh, but when she stopped the car and looked back through the rear-view mirror, there was nothing on the road, nothing on the verge, nothing anywhere. For a split second, she had been relieved – and then she saw a flash of colour flitting into the hedge on the left-hand side, a flash of black on white, she thought, like a Dalmatian, and she had left the car there in the middle of the road and run back to where she had seen it. Nothing was there. Yet she *had* seen something, she was sure of it, and if she had hit the creature at that speed, surely it couldn't have just walked away. That thought drove her back to the car in a panic because, all of a sudden, she had conceived the irrational but utterly persuasive notion that the animal was there, concealed, waiting to leap out and attack her. She had known she was panicking, and she had known that it wasn't the right thing to do, but she had started the car up and driven away, driven fast down the road that ended, a few miles further on, at my front door. When she got there, she was shaking, terrified and ashamed and disgusted with the cruelty of this happening on that day of all days – though, of course, I knew nothing about that. All I knew was that she was shaken and upset, and she needed to be looked after. I told her to come in and have some tea.

'No,' she said. 'We have to go back. We have to find it.'

164

'Find what?'

'I hit an animal,' she said. 'A dog, I think.'

'So, is it hurt?'

'I don't know,' she said. 'It was – gone. I couldn't see –'

'Well, then –'

'No,' she said. 'We have to go back.'

I took her gently by the arm and tried to guide her inside. 'There's no point,' I said. 'Whatever it was – if it was anything – it'll be gone by now.'

No,' she said. 'We have to find it.' She was desperate. 'Please.'

So it was that we spent what were almost our last few hours together wandering around on the verge of a country road, searching for an injured dog. I drove the car, though I wasn't insured. I had visions of crashing, or hitting something myself – an old lady, with my luck, or a crocodile of schoolchildren on the way to visit the local museum – which wouldn't have been easy to explain to her husband. We didn't find the dog, but then that wasn't surprising and – as I made the argument I felt like a liar, but I made it anyway – that was a good sign, because if it had been seriously injured, or killed, it would still be there. It was obviously fit enough to walk, even to run, and it was probably home by now, licking its minor wounds and putting the whole thing down to experience. Meanwhile, I had my eye on the cottages just fifty yards to the south of where we had stopped – if the dog belonged there, I didn't want some irate owner putting two and two together and upsetting Adele further. She wouldn't budge, though. Not till we had made a thorough search; not before I had clambered over a fence and plunged through a stand of hawthorn to see whether the dog was on the other side. There was nothing, of course. No corpse, no bloodstains, nothing.

Back at the house, I made tea. She sat at the dining-room

table, watching me as I moved from place to place, putting the kettle on, fetching the tea, finding cups, fetching milk from the fridge – and it was a moment before I noticed the immense sadness in her eyes, a sadness, a grief, even, that had nothing to do with what had just happened. I put the milk jug down. 'What is it?' I said.

I was afraid suddenly and I needed to know what it was right away – and she must have guessed as much, because she didn't try to break the news gently, or lead in to the big, central, devastating fact. Her eyes filled with tears. 'I'm pregnant,' she said.

I looked at her. I was shocked – it was the most banal of moments, something that happens every day to *somebody*, but I had never expected it to happen to us. 'Are you sure?' I said. It was a stupid thing to say, but it was all I had.

She gave an incredulous laugh through her tears. 'Of course I'm sure,' she said.

'Ah.' I thought for a moment. 'Is it –' She nodded. We both knew the ending to the question. I went over and kneeled down beside her. 'It's all right,' I said – probably the stupidest thing I had ever said to anybody.

She laughed again: a small desperate out-breath of laughter that felt more like blood. 'No, it's not,' she said.

The thing to do is to carry on. Go to work. Try to stay sober. Pass this time. Wait for a miracle. *How could her husband love her the way I did? He didn't even know her.* Put those thoughts out of your head. Practise *wabi-sabi*. Go to work. Pass the time. Keep busy and, most of all, stay sober for as much of the time as possible because, when you're drunk, all you can think about is that old movie *The Postman Always Rings Twice*.

But then, when you're not drinking, you feel as if your

body is being torn apart from the inside, and there are voices in the plumbing. This is when the prudent suburbanite turns to self-medication. I'd dabbled before, of course – I had been a gardener in my wandering days, and I knew a thing or two about herbal remedies. I'd even managed to poison myself with deadly nightshade and ended up in a hospital ward, having my stomach pumped, before spending several days in conversation – some would say *negotiation* – with a man in a silver cowboy suit and a strange girl with razor blades for hands. That had been a particularly bad episode in my self-medicating practice, but I had to believe I could learn from my mistakes. I couldn't continue as I was, and surely, I reasoned, anything was better than going back to booze and barbs, or worse. Besides, I was perfectly well set up. I had a garden. I also knew the location of several native British weeds that had provided succour to madmen, witches and people with toothache from time immemorial. What better way to maintain one's equilibrium than the good old native herbal, and the apothecary skills that, if they were not maintained, would soon die out altogether?

I don't want to make too much of all this or provoke a crackdown by those authorities who think spiritual experiences are only acceptable if they involve ginger biscuits and men in cassocks, but any of the ingredients for the tisanes and powders and other home-brewed medications that helped me through the next several months can be found in most well-stocked botanic or even municipal gardens, not to mention patches of wasteland or damp nooks behind old washhouses. A few had to be grown from seed in secret pots in cupboards or on windowsills, but the majority thrived in my garden for a while, nondescript shrubs and herbaceous weeds that no doubt mystified my neighbours but did me a power of good.

167

At the end of my little plot, by the canal spur, I set up a mini nursery and raised various woodland banes and desert weeds that could transform an afternoon into an episode from Coleridge's notebooks. *If a man could pass thro' Paradise in a Dream & have a flower presented to him as a pledge that his Soul had really been there & found that flower in his hand when he awoke – Aye, and what then?*

Yet, though there are people who will say otherwise, self-medication is not an exact science. Glenn Gould, one of the most skilled practitioners of recent years, came very close to making it so, keeping extremely detailed records of what he administered and when, finely calibrating the various dosages and combinations and observing the effects with the objective calm of someone whose body was a laboratory in which the one great experiment was the soul, but he only dealt with pharmaceutical drugs, whose properties are well documented and more or less consistent. Cocteau's work on opium is also a treasure trove, but he was dealing with a single drug, one that he had known for most of his adult life. The home apothecary, however, is working with a wide variety of unknowns and, in truth, the body is a random place, a maze of crossroads and underpasses and hidden currents that can amplify or dissolve the effects of a plant that must be gathered from a tract of wasteland, or from a roadside verge and, however carefully it may be handled, prepared at an ordinary table, with everyday kitchen utensils. A random science, at best, and mostly an art – which meant that I didn't always achieve the desired effects and a couple of times I got very sick indeed. Nevertheless, I found ways to soothe my mind at that kitchen table, and sometimes, half forgetting, I would find myself in a place where everything was a soft, sugared gold, like the space inside an old schoolhouse or the half-light under beech trees in the late afternoon, the sifted gold of childhood, the drowsing gold of forever. Or I would waken with a flower in my hand that, though it withered the moment I opened my eyes, was still visibly, if not a flower as such, then something that had bloomed somewhere, at one time or another.

I said that the occasion with the dog was our last meeting, but that isn't strictly true. During our Cambridge days, Adele often talked about going for a picnic on Granchester Meadows but, for some reason, we had never made it. Then, in the occasional phone conversations we'd had since she broke the news, she had mentioned it again.

'We never did go for a picnic,' she said.

'No, we didn't,' I said, but my mind wasn't on picnics at that moment.

'Remember how we always said we would?' she said. 'Some sunny day, on the Meadows?'

'Yes.'

'We ought to go,' she said. 'Just once.'

'To Granchester?'

'To somewhere.'

We'd had that conversation, or something like it, a couple of times, but we hadn't decided anything. Then, one day, I got a call. I was at home, working. Or rather, I was at home pretending to work, though really I was just sitting by the dining-room window, staring out at the garden. Everything looked very still and oddly brittle, the cup on the table, a marmalade cat on the cinder path that wandered down to the canal, the trees at the end of the path, where the neighbour woman would stand sometimes, peering at the house, a genial and not very imaginative spy who suspected, I think, that I was a very bad lot. I didn't care about her one way or another,

169

or so I thought; but after a few minutes I realised that I was looking for her, expecting to see her there, in her yellow blouse and brown skirt, her broad peasant's face ready to assume an innocent or mildly offended look if I caught her out. I was trying to think of her name, but I couldn't remember – and then I was wondering why it mattered anyhow. Why would anything matter, other than as a distraction from the ennui of a weekday in the suburbs and the brittle look everything had, as if the world was about to crack into thousands of tiny pieces?

I was working at home because the evening before, and all through the night until the early hours, I'd been having a bad spell. A lunatic night, sleepless and full of wild imaginings, the complete apophenic kitbag: noises, visions and, as the dawn broke, those terrifying transformations in the body when it seems everything is about to be ripped apart. Imagine lying in bed, at first light, with the sensation that an animal – a terrier, say, or maybe a raccoon – has taken hold of your calf muscle and is trying to tear it off. The first time that happens, you think this is the worst. Later, though, as you start to become accustomed to it, you know, with this first spasm, that the worst is yet to come: the worst, because, unlike that tearing, ripping sensation, which seems to attack from the outside, the next stage is wholly internal, a sudden tightening in the flesh that quickly accelerates to an unbearable tension, like a guitar string stretched so taut that it is on the point of snapping – and there is no way to control this. There is no possible response to it. Your own body has turned against you, it is working according to rules that you didn't even know existed. The result is agony – yes, but most pain is bearable, if it can be understood. Worse than the pain is the fear, the sheer panic as it begins: first in the right calf, then in the flesh between the bones of your feet, then in the left calf, and on, up into the thighs, sometimes, a tightening in the muscle accompanied by a seeming brittleness in the bones, a sensation that, overnight, your body has turned to glass, or blackboard chalk. Those long white, impossibly fragile chalks that teachers used in the old days, white sticks that broke right away with a bright, painful snap you could hear and feel, even in the back row.

The phone rang. It was Adele.

'Are you doing something?' she said.

'No,' I said. 'Just – sitting.'

'Want to go for a picnic?'

'What, now?'

'Yes. Now.'

'Where?'

'At the orchid place.'

It was one of our spots. We'd gone there a few times, a piece of woodland with a wide clearing that would be full of orchids and wild flowers in June. It was too early for them now, of course, but that didn't matter.

'How long?' I said.

'An hour?'

'I'll be there.' I hung up. I couldn't believe it. The miracle was happening after all. I got myself together quickly, splashed cold water on my face, changed my clothes, put on my shoes and, in the full knowledge that I was deluding myself, drove out to the woods.

It wasn't the miracle, of course, but it was far more than I had expected. In my haste to get there, I hadn't thought to bring any picnic items – obvious things like fruit and champagne and cucumber sandwiches – but Adele brought more than enough for both of us. Not that I was very interested in

171

food, anyway. I took the picnic baskets from the car and carried them into the clearing where the orchids grew. It should have been too early, but they were just beginning: spots of purple and near-brown and white amid the grass and wild flowers. We had never been here together while they were in bloom – it was a place she knew and had wanted to share with me, and now she was sharing it at exactly the right moment. She looked beautiful, pregnant. For some reason, she made me think of a swimmer, emerging from a river, or from the sea, her body brimming with a rare form of gravity, her skin salty and chastened.

'How have you been?' she asked.

'Not too bad. You?'

She started to unpack the basket. There was Veuve Clicquot, a selection of cheese, various sandwiches and sweet things, a salad. She poured us each a glass of the champagne. 'I shouldn't really,' she said. 'But just this once.'

I smiled. *Just this once.* This time, we were marking the end, instead of just walking away from one another. It was the supreme romantic gesture, the one from the songs, the moment *in* but not *of* time, the moment that nothing could take away, no matter what. Marriage. Duty, if that was what it was. Obligation, which is something else. Nothing could take away that moment, not even cliché – and for a whole afternoon we pretended that it wasn't over between us, even as we marked the end of what had been.

CALIFORNIA DREAMING (I)

After that, everything stopped. The world stalled. All the usual business continued to happen on the surface, but I couldn't help feeling that somewhere off to the side, in the *real* real world, life had come to a halt, like one of those antique clocks in the drawing room of Adele's museum house in Cambridge. Everything looked more or less the same as it had always done: the house, the street, the office, the old railway line where I sometimes walked, cut off from the rest of the world, thinking about what had happened over the last year and trying not to and, sometimes, composing lines in my head because, as Bill had somehow discovered, I *had* been writing poetry for a long time by then. Only now I was trying to find a way of making it work, of doing it seriously. The book to which Bill had referred really existed, though I had realised, almost the moment it came out, that it was little more than a collection of exercises and diversions and I knew that I wanted to make something different, something that suited the voice in my head, rather than the voice that we all learn to hear in school. I had nothing against that voice, it was just that it belonged to someone else, and not to me, and I wanted something that arose out of *my* moment, *my* experience, *my* day-to-day rhythms. All through that summer and into the following autumn, I worked on this peculiar music, reading nothing,

173

listening only to Ali Akbar Khan and Miles Davis, and finally I got an inkling of what I wanted – just a chink of light, no more – as I walked up and down that old railway line, while the brambles flowered and set, and the leaves turned, and then, at around the time Adele called to say her son had been born, in the cold grey of winter. It wasn't some big break-through, and the poems that came out of those walks were fairly basic, but I had, at least, found the method I needed – a method so simple, it was absurd, even though it made all the difference. Mandelstam called it composing 'on the lips', which meant, in essence, leaving the pencil and paper behind and making the music in your head, listening as it grew, paying attention, only holding on to what was memorable enough – musical enough – to carry home and write down, five or eight, or even a dozen lines at a time, little chunks of something that, while it might not have been a work of poetic genius, was at least organic and whole, its structure emerging from the place where it originated, not imposed from a textbook on form.

Meanwhile, I carried around a perfect whiteness, like some still, cold object at the back of my mind. Not the whiteness of a northern winter, or the white of apple blossom, not even the white of new linen on a hospital bed – though that does come close. Not Chinese white, or white lake. Not snow, or ice, or cloud, or fog. No: this was the white of a new begin-ning that hadn't happened, a clean slate that had stayed clean, the white of hiatus, the white of entropy. I could go through the days, and it was there, silent, motionless, inactive; then, in the evening, if I worked hard, I could keep it at bay, a vast space on the horizon that I couldn't forget but could still evade for hours at a time. At night, though, I dreamed it, and in those dreams, it revealed what it had always contained – which was the impossible stasis of grief. And yet, even though it should have been terrible, even though it should have felt like the brink of some limbo from which even the most stolid mind might never return, I couldn't imagine any other place that I wanted to be and, in the morning, I woke with a sense of loss, because that dream whiteness had been taken from me and put away to the back of my mind, while I negotiated, not with grief itself, but with the world that sometimes interrupted it.

Life goes on. Wonders never cease, but life goes on, plodding and unwondrous. Summer turned to winter and then to spring. I'd been fairly happy working in TV software but, after my bosses signed a deal with the South African Broadcasting Corporation, I found a sympathetic recruitment agency, who got me an interview at a knowledge-based systems company just outside Reigate, around twenty minutes along the M25 from where I lived. The company's technical division – I'll call it Knowledge UK, or KUK for short – was managed by a man called Joel, who came from New York originally, but had moved to California, partly because that was where all the interesting software developments were, and partly because he was, through some kind of family tradition, a gut-level, stats-breathing Giants fan. He was a dark, pudgy, somewhat nervy man with an odd, sudden laugh that I still found startling months later, but I liked him, even though it was obvious that he was desperate to recruit and train what he called a 'UK team' and get home to Candlestick Park as quickly as possible. I was still one of the walking wounded, in spirit at least, so I didn't take the interview too seriously – which probably made me fairly attractive as a candidate. *Never let them see that you want something* – it's the oldest rule in the book, and there I was, for once, doing exactly what I was supposed to do. Joel had me sit in a room and fill out a clever aptitude test, then we chatted about baseball for a while. I was mildly interested when he told me that I would get to work in California from time to time, if I joined, but I didn't really care one way or another if I got the job or not, because I didn't really care about anything.

The interview had been a distraction, though, and I had liked Joel. It was a pleasant drive, too, if you took the back roads and avoided the motorway – and that was what I did, driving home through the Surrey countryside and managing to pretend for a while that I hadn't lost a thing. Then halfway back, I grabbed the nearest cassette I could find from the pile that was scattered across the passenger seat and popped it into the tape deck. It was *Hejira*. The tape started at the beginning of the second song on the second side – the one about Amelia Earhart – and, as I listened to Joni Mitchell sing about the burning desert and how, *till you get there yourself you'll never really know*, I changed my mind. When I got home, I phoned the recruitment agency and asked them to negotiate the best deal they could with KUK.

It was absurd, but I had completely changed direction because of a song and, for the first time, I felt the gap in the middle of my chest close a little, and the whiteness in my head began to recede. In fact, I almost felt good. It felt right that I was entrusting my fate to chance rather than to some process of accepted reasoning. I didn't want to do the rational thing, I wanted to do something totally irrational, something wilful – because, when it's grief that you are carrying, the only way out might be to do something that makes no sense at all.

Knowledge UK offered me the job the next afternoon. At the rational level, I was taken aback, not just by the speed but also by the generosity of the package, but at every other level, I wasn't surprised at all. I had kept my side of the bargain with the radio song, after all: it wasn't that Joel had decided to hire me, in spite of my apparent indifference, it wasn't even that I had scored well on the aptitude test, the fact was, Amelia Earhart had decided the whole thing. I was going to California. That was the illogical next step. I was going to California, and the new job was nothing more than a means to that end. Later, Joel told me that I'd done pretty well on the tests, and I'd come over quite well during the interview, but the real reason he'd hired me was that I was the first person he'd met in England who knew anything about baseball. The clincher had been when I told him I loved the way Will Clark swung the bat. It had, in other words, been a meeting of two irrational minds, which was a fair indication of the craziness that was to follow.

Meanwhile, all through this time, I was still mad in myself. Not homicidal, or suicidal, or about to take off all my clothes and run naked through the streets mad, not even properly psychotic, most of the time, but I was mad nevertheless. It was madness on slow cook, just a simmer below the surface, not so much subconscious as subcutaneous, a mesh of fevers and itches under the skin of me that would sometimes erupt into the light and flood everything. There was a restaurant I went to with Adele a couple of times, a place in the country to the south of Guildford that had a stream flowing directly under the dining room. You could order your meal, then sit, entranced, watching the water through the glass floor as it flowed beneath your table, quick and dark and pure like time itself. That was what my madness felt like then – and it was just as quick and dark and pure as that stream. At least once every day, more often on most days, I would feel that flow continuing under the surface and it was a constant reminder that I was a lie, and that what I was doing was a lie, but then a lie was the only game in town, at least for the moment and, anyway, now that Amelia Earhart had chosen to get involved, I was determined not to let her down.

HOW TO FLY

I flew for the first time when I was nine years old. Nobody saw it happen, but that didn't bother me: the Wright Brothers' earliest ascent had also been conducted in the strictest secrecy and, until public pressure forced them out of hiding, any number of successful flights had gone unwitnessed. Of course, Orville and Wilbur hadn't attempted to do what I was doing: like Blériot and Santos-Dumont, they were changing the known world, but they weren't committed to flying in its purest sense. They were mechanics, not angels. What I wanted was something that they had never even considered and, though I knew that I was destined to fail, I wasn't prepared to settle for anything as mundane as a flying machine.

No: that first morning, alone on a piece of waste ground near a disused pit, I had something far more adventurous in mind – and what could be more adventurous than the impossible? Though I admired those early aviators more than anyone else in history, I knew, even then, that the people we think of as pioneers were pioneers only of machine flight – which, to my child's mind, was as different from actual flying as a conjuring trick is from natural magic. I didn't want to soar with the aid of an engine; I wanted a miracle, a triumph of the will. I wanted to fly unassisted, like a bird, or a medieval monk.

Like Elmer of Malmesury, for example. According to the legend, Elmer, dressed in his usual monk's habit, but with home-made wings fastened to his shoulders and ankles, climbed to the top of the abbey tower and threw himself off, travelling a distance of around six hundred feet before he crashed to the ground, breaking both legs. It was a windy morning in the year 1010. Apparently, Elmer had spent long hours observing the jackdaws that congregated around the abbey, and he felt sure that he had discovered their secret; according to the story, told later by William of Malmesbury, he really had flown for some distance before he suddenly lost faith in his abilities and panicked, a little like Peter who, having clambered bravely out of his boat on the Sea of Galilee to follow Jesus across the water, suddenly became afraid, and began to sink. It took some time for Elmer's legs to mend but, as soon as he was well enough, he began preparing for his next flight, convinced that his fall had resulted partly from his own lack of conviction and partly because he had forgotten to provide himself with a tail. Had it not been for his Abbot, who forbade any further experiments, Elmer would almost certainly have tried to fly again; instead, he lived a long and studious life, possibly surviving until 1066, when he was able to observe the passage of Halley's Comet, just as he had done when still a young boy, in 989. Or so William of Malmesbury tells us, and I see no good reason to doubt him.

Monks, it seems, had a particular obsession with flying: not much of an advertisement, perhaps, for the religious life. Even more interesting than the case of Elmer of Malmesbury is that of Giuseppe da Copertino who, several times during the first half of the seventeenth century, was observed to rise into the air, involuntarily it would seem, by a number of independent and more or less reliable witnesses. His Abbot was just as upset by the news of his flight as Elmer's had been, and he demanded that Giuseppe desist at once. This he could not do – it appeared to be God's will, and not his own, that made him fly – so he was obliged to become a recluse, where he presumably practised his art unobserved, until his eventual reassimilation into the fold. There he remained until he died, at the age of sixty. Those who saw him fly say he rose straight up into the air without warning, and hovered there for a time, before sinking back to earth, with a faraway look on his face, a look of ecstasy perhaps, or the expression a sleepwalker assumes on his nocturnal perambulations.

Possibly because I wasn't a monk, my own attempt at flight, on that first day, was modest by comparison. On a clear, almost windless afternoon, out on a patch of open ground near Cowdenbeath, I climbed to the top of a disused pit building and jumped off the roof. The only mechanical aids I employed were a grubby old bed sheet tied to my wrists and ankles with twine and a pair of swimming goggles to protect my eyes. I didn't travel any great distance, but I did feel a tension in the sheet at my back, and I landed further from the building than I might have expected, floating a moment, it seemed, my arms and legs splayed wide, my hands making tiny, ineffectual swimming movements, before I hit the ground, hard, and rolled sideways into a patch of broken bricks and nettles. I was lucky not to break anything, but I was also heartened by the notion that I really had flown, for two or three seconds, before I fell to earth. By the end of the week, those two seconds had been transformed in my memory to half a minute; a week after that, I was back, with more sophisticated wings, and high hopes of a genuinely *perceptible* flight. It never happened. The sheer number of my eventual failures should have been more than sufficiently convincing but, no matter what I did, and no matter how graceless and painful my falls were, I continued to believe that willed flight was possible.

Of course, I wasn't interested in air travel; what I wanted was to *fly*. My family weren't the kind of people who could afford to travel by aeroplane – in those days, holidays happened in Blackpool, or Clacton – but that didn't trouble me at all. I didn't want to go up in the air according to a schedule, piloted by a stranger, shoehorned into my seat alongside a hundred other people. I wanted to go solo. I wanted to *fly* – and, in spite of my poor record, I remained convinced that it was possible. All I lacked was the knowledge: as with so many things back then, the key to the problem was more science. What I needed, I realised, was *an instruction manual*.

I found Richard Ferris's *How to Fly* at a church jumble sale. It was published in 1910, by Thomas Nelson & Sons, one of those chunky, durable, hardbacks aimed at the more serious child, alongside *How It Is Made* and *How It Works* ('Splendid books for boys, telling them just what they want to know'). The front cover showed an aviator in a perilously fragile craft – something like a tea chest fitted with wings and the wheels from an old pram – soaring among clouds in a sky of faded cerulean. Maybe it was the colours that first drew me to the stall where the book lay, innocently priced at sixpence, between an old-fashioned bicycle pump and a tattered golliwog; more likely, though, it was the fact that the pilot, an intent, hunched figure in a flying cap and what looked like a safari jacket, was not only alone in his craft, but was barely *in* it at all. His head and his entire upper torso were completely open to the elements: flying like that, in this makeshift crate, he would have felt the cool air of the upper atmosphere on his face, he would have smelled the ozone, tasted clouds. That picture alone was probably enough: the first page, however, closed the deal, and my sixpence was duly passed over. What I read that day is with me still, like a mantra:

> The air which surrounds us, so intangible and so commonplace that it seldom arrests our attention, is in reality a vast, unexplored ocean, fraught with future possibilities. Even now, the pioneers of a countless fleet are hovering above us in the sky, while steadily, surely, these wonderful possibilities are unfolded.

This thrilled me. I had visions of a thousand souls wandering the heavens, each in his own solo craft, powered by nothing but human will. I didn't connect this vision of flight to the aeroplanes I knew about: those were nothing more than huge buses, chugging along from stop to stop. To buy a ticket and board an aeroplane wasn't *flying*; it was air travel – and air travel was what businessmen did, or rich families off on holiday to Malaga; it wasn't the stuff of adventure. When I studied the Contents page of this marvellous book, what I saw contradicted every tenet of air travel that I knew about:

THE AIR
LAWS OF FLIGHT
BALLOONS: HOW TO OPERATE
BALLOONS: HOW TO BUILD

– and, best of all, BIOGRAPHIES OF PROMINENT AERONAUTS. The men and women who jetted to and fro above my head in commercial aircraft weren't aeronauts, they were *passengers* and, from what I had seen at the pictures, they didn't do anything at all, except drink gin and tonic and look out of the window at passing clouds. They weren't exposed, they couldn't taste or smell or feel the sky, like Claude Grahame-White, 'the most famous of British aviators', or Leon Delagrange, who gave up a promising artistic career to smash the world speed record in 1909, 'travelling at the rate of 49.9 miles per hour', but was killed the following year 'by the fall of his machine'. Those men had *flown*: compared to them, the ever-increasing company of airline passengers might just as well have been on a Sunday-afternoon coach trip to the Trossachs, with flasks and sandwiches and scarves to keep them warm.

So, to my child's mind, air travel had nothing to do with flying; though it only became a lie, as such, in the late sixties and early seventies. By then, it was hopelessly accessible; by then, it had been sold too hard, it was too remote from the ether, and it was too safe. The sight of a modern plane passing overhead presented none of the beauty and awe I experienced when I studied plate 22 of *How to Fly*, a grainy photograph entitled, 'The Wellman Dirigible "America" Starting for Europe, October 15, 1910.' Here, a cigar-like airship tilted dangerously above what looked like unlimited ocean, utterly vulnerable and, apparently, just fifty feet from the cold, dark water. *This* was flying. It was easy to doubt aeroplanes, because they had been reduced to machine noise and safety features; it was easy to doubt the pilots in old war films, with their immaculate uniforms and ridiculous moustaches. It was easy to doubt the happiness of air hostesses, because they smiled so hard – and it was impossible *not* to doubt the moon land-ings, because Neil Armstrong and his colleagues were so very serious. Like everything else we saw on television, Apollo was all fifties rhetoric and odd haircuts, another outmoded and surprisingly cheapskate pantomime to divert us from the nagging sensation that something *true* was happening elsewhere. Remembering it all now, I can't tell one event from another: the badly lit, pockmarked dust of the moon's surface blurs with the badly lit face of the dead president's brother on the kitchen floor of the Ambassador Hotel, the look in his eyes betraying the ordinary realisation that history repeats itself in the most casual of ways, and the same people get away with the same crimes, time and time again. I remember a man with a golf club in his hand, but I'm not sure if that was Buzz Aldrin or some secret service guy, and I know there was a riderless horse at centre stage – though nobody wanted to acknowledge the irony of *that* image. People were flying off in all directions: to Acapulco, to the moon, to spy on the Russians, to bomb the Vietnamese. Aeroplanes were passing overhead all the time, but nobody I knew was on them. Once, flying had been an adventure, now it was merely glamorous. Once, the men and women who took to the air needed courage and skill; now all they required was money. Once upon a time, people had really flown – people like Amelia Earhart and Amy Johnson and Antoine de Saint-Exupéry; now they, and the flights they had taken, were as remote, and just as unreal, as Imperial Japan. By the time I first boarded a plane, anybody could do it and so, by definition, it wasn't worth doing. It was a chore. On my first trips by aeroplane – short hops to places in Europe, for the most part – looking out of an aeroplane window was like watching television: nothing I saw was entirely real, it was all travelogue, just a step away from cinematography. I half expected a commentary, in a well-practised Oxford-English accent, telling me what to look for in the landscape below, or naming the types of cloud that I could see on the tiny screen: *cumulus, stratus, cirrus, nimbus, mammatus, contrail, altostratus, cumulonimbus.*

*   *   *

185

I fell in love with Amy Johnson when I was fourteen. By then, I had more or less given up on the idea of flying; now, what interested me was the possibility, not of defying gravity and floating away into space, but of disappearing altogether. I still had dreams where I glided downstairs, or along an empty street, my feet just millimetres above the ground but, more often, I saw myself from the outside, walking in new snow, or in brilliant sunshine and vanishing – gradually, one step at a time – into thin air. It seemed such an obvious progression: after flying came the disappearing act and so many of the great aviators had done it. Saint-Exupéry, for example, had simply melted into the upper atmosphere, the author of my favourite book – *Wind, Sand and Stars* – becoming the very elements he most loved. I could never quite believe that any of the great aviators had crashed: I couldn't see them spiralling into the ocean, to drift for a few hours or days waiting vainly to be rescued while the sharks circled and closed in; I couldn't see them consumed by fire, or cut to pieces; I could only imagine them as lost. Which is to say: I could only imagine them in some blessed, deeply sensual state, one degree from angelhood, the air bright and sharp on their faces and in their lungs, as they slipped through some invisible barrier that only the lost can detect. By the time I was fourteen, this was what I longed for: to disappear, to be lost, to arrive at an unimaginable elsewhere. Why would I want to fly, if I could vanish? To become a Saint-Exupéry, or an Amelia Earhart, had less to do with aeronautics than with invisibility.

The most invisible aviator of all was Amy Johnson. Her story is not unique in the annals of flight, but it is perhaps the most austere, and almost certainly the most beautiful. She is best known for her solo fight, in May 1930, from Croydon to Darwin, Australia, a passage of eleven thousand miles, which she completed in nineteen days in a single-engine Gypsy Moth. The following year, with co-pilot Jack Humphreys, she flew from England to Japan; in 1932, flying solo again, she set the England to Cape Town record. Throughout the thirties, she pursued non-stop flights to the United States and India, with her husband, Jim Mollison. When war broke out, she joined the Air Transport Auxiliary, where her duties were fairly routine – and it was on one of these ordinary flights, rather than above some faraway ocean, that she disappeared, crashing into the Thames Estuary on 5 January 1941. She was the first ATA pilot to be killed: it seems she parachuted out of her stricken craft, but drowned in the icy water, silent and unseen.

Amy Johnson was the first real infatuation of my life (with the possible exception of Geraldine Anderson in Primary 4), but I wasn't very much interested in her biography. What I cared about were her solo flights. The way I saw it, it was only by flying solo that an aviator could reach the borderline between this world and the invisible, and it was only by being lost that she could *cross* that line, falling out of the sky and into forever, alone, blessed, untouchable. That was what disqualified Amelia Earhart from flight's highest echelon: she did make solo voyages, and she did disappear, during an attempt, in 1937, to be the first woman to fly around the world – but she was not alone. Her navigator, Fred Noonan, was in the aircraft with her when she went down, and presumably perished with her, somewhere near Howland Island, in the Pacific Ocean. Sometimes I dream of her solo Atlantic flight, between Harbor Grace in Canada, and the north Irish coast (she had been heading for Paris, but severe weather conditions forced her to land near Derry), and I honour her as one of the great flyers but, like so many others, she can only be numbered among the missing, not ranked with those

187

who truly disappeared. To disappear, you had to be alone. That, for me, was the fundamental rule of flying.

The missing are so many. I think of them as limbo people, stranded in some wide departure lounge of the afterlife, bluish phantoms touched with ozone and jet fuel. Otis Redding and Glenn Miller are sitting together by a window, talking about music; Thomas Selfridge, the first man to die in an aircraft accident (September 1907) is having a drink with Admiral Yamamoto and Leslie Howard; Buddy Holly is flirting with Carole Lombard. In another of the many seating areas, Dag Hammarskjöld and Yuri Gagarin are discussing history; while Patsy Cline is surprised to find that she has so much in common with Rocky Marciano. Ronnie Van Zant and Steve Gaines are forming an a cappella singing group with Jim Reeves and Ricky Nelson. It's a crowded space, and everybody here is waiting for his or her own particular flight, though whether they are going back to where they came from, to start again in a different guise, or are on the way to some other, quite unknown destination, is impossible to tell.

From those first European short hops to now, I've spent twenty-odd years of my life on aeroplanes. These journeys usually came under the heading of business travel: another step away from being an aviator, and even lower than passenger status. Yet, oddly enough, such a debased form of air travel was exactly what I needed, in order to investigate the metaphysical possibilities of flying. Who is more invisible than the business traveller? In an airport, who do we notice: the pretty girl with the rucksack, the young Indian family travelling halfway around the world to visit friends in Pittsburgh, or the man in the grey suit? If the journey of a thousand miles begins

188

with the first step, then my first step was to vanish into the crowd at the airport, the man nobody saw, the one who slipped through unnoticed, a non-first-class, unaccompanied professional type, one of those people with nothing to say, and no one to say it to. It was wonderful. I would sit by the window and gaze out as the plane prepared to touch down at Schiphol or JFK, and I would register, with infinite care, the usual details: the airport buildings; the lights; the fields around the runway; the rather pretty, oddly provincial sprawl of Long Island. Every now and then, something different would happen, or I would be overwhelmed by the strange beauty of the descent: the endless simmer of Buenos Aires, say, and the great silted mass of La Plata; the sudden apprehension of the Pacific, as the plane headed into San Francisco; the giddy sense of archipelago that came and went in an instant, just above Copenhagen. Finally, no matter where I touched down, there was always the feeling, as I recovered my bags and headed for the exit, that I was in a place where nobody knew me, a place where I could simply disappear. I could walk to the rank, get into the first taxi and go somewhere other than where I was supposed to go. There was a fictitious account running in my head, of a man more or less identical to me, who would be observed getting on to the shuttle bus, in a dark raincoat, carrying a brown leather bag, somewhat tired, perhaps, or a little preoccupied, but not looking or acting in any way out of the ordinary: just a man getting on or off the shuttle bus, never to be seen again. By now, there was more room to disappear. People took less notice; the world was less accountable. Eventually, in principle, it wouldn't matter if I disappeared or not. I could keep my appointments, I could return my rented car on time and catch the flight home, and I still wasn't entirely there – and this is why the real pioneers weren't Orville and Wilbur Wright, or Louis Blériot, or Charles Lindbergh, but Amy Johnson and Amelia Earhart and Antoine de Saint-Exupéry. Because the real accomplishment of the twentieth century wasn't, as Ferris put it, that 'Man has learned how to fly!', it was that, quietly, and with no sense of a breakthrough, people were learning how to *vanish*.

The last time I came close to actually flying, I was somewhere between Kautokeino and Lakselv, far inside the Arctic Circle, in the Norwegian province of Finnmark. It was early May, but I was still driving on snow tyres when I left the tiny, unheated *hytte* that I'd borrowed in Kautokeino and headed east towards Karasjoka; by the time I reached the hazy white turn in the road that would take me back north, to Lakselv's tiny civilian airport, the snow had almost stopped and the sun was out, glittering on the rivers and thaw streams, illuminating the land so that what had seemed like grey, monotonous scrub a few minutes before was now full of subtle colour: the rich browns and soft purples of the birch twigs; the pale yellows and greens of *Salix lapponica*; the soft oranges and blue-greys and reds of the mosses and lichens. Towards Lakselv, the land is owned by the Norwegian military: in places, it is forbidden to stop, except in cases of emergency. Normally, I pay attention to the warning signs that are posted everywhere along this route, but that day, I ignored them. I wanted to go for a last walk in this sudden theatre of light and colour: just a short hike to carry home the silent chill of the tundra in my bones and my nervous system. I pulled in and positioned the car so it couldn't easily be observed from the highway, then I struck out, heading along a reindeer track beside a wide, frozen lake, picking my way through the snow, listening to the thaw streams as they trickled down the gentle slopes, a sound I'd heard before, in the work of the Sami poet and musician, Nils-Aslak Valkeapää, long before I ever saw Finnmark.

I didn't go far. It was still cold, and I had to be back in Lakselv that night, to return my hire car; besides, I was nervous about the military. I skirted the lake for a while, letting the May sunshine warm my face, then I turned back. The great thing about the subarctic is that a few days, or an hour, or even a couple of minutes can be enough: it is a land full of signs, a land of sudden, local miracles. All you have to do is learn how to find them. That day, I thought I'd had my gift, with the sun and the colours and the sound of the thaw water; then, a few hundred yards from where I'd left the car, I disturbed a flock of ptarmigans and they flared up from the snow-covered scrub, white birds in a field of white, their wings whirring, a sound like tiny wheels turning in my flesh – and suddenly, with no sense that anything out of the ordinary was happening, and perhaps for no more than a few seconds, I was rising too, flaring up into the air, just like the birds, wing-less, dizzy, my head full of whiteness. I don't want to make of this any more than it was: it lasted less than a minute, and it was in no way mystical or even inexplicable. At the same time, though, I do want to give that moment its due, because I did take to the air, I did fly and, for a few moments, I was one of those birds, attuned to the flock, familiar with the sky. Some miracles are purely personal and may be entirely imaginary, but they are miracles, nonetheless. I'd disturbed ptarmigans like this more than once – it's difficult not to, out on the tundra – but I had never felt this sensation before. For the first time, I had come close enough, and I had been caught up, carried away, offered the gift of a moment's flight.

Later, I dropped off the car and found a place to stay for

the night. It was a quiet, rather austere guest house, the only one in town that was open. My room had a picture window, with a view of snowy birch trees and a low, dark wood beyond. The plane back to Tromsø departed around two o'clock the following afternoon; I had plenty of time, and nothing else to do but take it easy – a guarantee, if ever there was one, that I would find it impossible to sleep. When I'm away from home, I only sleep well when things are happening: in transit, say, or in busy cities, with traffic and voices all around me. That night, in a world of indelible stillness, the snow muffling any sound that might have filtered through the birch woods, the guest house itself utterly deserted, I lay awake for a long time, listening to the silence, remembering the feel of the tundra; then I got up, packed my kitbag, and went down to the kitchen, where some bits and pieces had been left out for breakfast. I had a few slices of Gjetost and some coffee and, feeling warmed and milky inside, I set out to walk the mile or so to the airport. It was six o'clock in the morning.

That far north, the nights are white in May. I walked in a cold, chalky light, the only human creature awake on the northern *vidda*, it seemed, and I took my time, stoking up my solitude rations, tuning in to the rhythm that comes off the earth in the subarctic, a rhythm like no other, a pulse that lingers for days, or weeks, in the fabric of bone and flesh: a pulse that is almost a sound, like a drumbeat, or a harmonic. I didn't want to go back to the occupied world; I wanted to stay there, to stay in tune with this land, to gaze up at this sky. The *Finnmarksvidda* is high and wide, close to the sky, a place for clearing the senses, for becoming far-sighted, and I knew that to go back was to be diminished in so many ways, to close down a little. Yet I had no choice: there were chores to do and promises to keep. By the time I reached the airport,

192

I was resigned to life as the person I seem to be, in the civilised world.

The *vidda* had one gift left for me, however. Because Lakselv is a remote, tiny airport at the very top of Europe, it is never busy and, in winter, it almost falls out of use. Once a day, it seems, a plane comes in, discharges its few passengers, then turns back and returns to Tromsø, rising from this narrow coastal town and crossing the high plateau en route, allowing its passengers a privileged glimpse of the steep, snow-covered sides of the *vidda*, one of the most beautiful landscapes I have ever seen. The rest of the time, it is quiet – though not, perhaps, as quiet as it was that morning, when I walked into the foyer and found it silent and deserted. It was darker indoors than out, which gave the place an eerie feel, and I walked through to the departure area, where I could look out at the runway. Nobody was there. The runway was covered in snow, like the land round about and, had it not been for the modern, shiny airport building, I could have been in the middle of nowhere. I sat down, facing out into the whiteness. Time had stopped. Everything was still. I was alone in the world.

People who live in the subarctic, like the inhabitants of prairies and deserts, are more gregarious than city folk: not being surrounded by strangers all day, even the most solitary among them learns to appreciate a little company. I understand that, and I understand the practical reasons for valuing one's neighbours, when they might be needed at any moment, but I prefer to be alone in almost any circumstances, and this empty place, this deserted airport, was a double gift: first because it allowed me to sit quietly and spend a last few hours with the self I am when I am far from home and, second, because it was filled with a dream of flight, a room full of sky and the group memories of aviation. All I could see was a runway and a windsock, but that was enough: the spirits of Amy Johnson and Antoine de Saint-Exupéry, of Leon Delagrange and Amelia Earhart were there all around me, suspended on the air, perfected and eternalised, in the snow and the grass under the snow, in the clouds and the ozone, in the wind that gusted across the runway and in the pulse that rose from the earth and passed like a current through my body, even here, in this modern airport lounge. The spirits of the vanished were there with me, and I was with them, alone in a cold white place, and capable of disappearing in my own right, at any moment. I sat a long time, that day, waiting for my flight – and some of me is sitting there still, enjoying the stillness, becoming the silence, learning how to vanish. Every day, in every way, I am disappearing, just a little – and it feels like flying, it feels like the kind of flight I was trying for, that first time, when I was nine years old – but it has nothing to do with the will, and it has nothing to do with *trying*. If it happens at all, it happens as a gift: and this is the one definition of grace that I can trust. The air which surrounds me, so intangible and so commonplace that it seldom arrests my attention, is in reality a vast, unexplored ocean, fraught with possibilities. Even now, the pioneers of a countless fleet are vanishing into brightness and, steadily, surely, all the wonderful possibilities continue to unfold.

CALIFORNIA DREAMING (II)

It was late in the baseball season by the time I left for Silicon Valley. I had been to the parent company's office and picked up my travel pack – the condoms and clean needles and syringes, the health notes and advice on what to do if you got arrested in a foreign country – and then, all of a sudden, I was at the airport, with *Hejira* running through my head. Hejira: a pilgrimage, the once-in-a-lifetime journey to find – what, exactly? God? Salvation? Invisibility? The fugue state of the afterlife? A few hours later, flying over the Pole, I almost believed that one or another of these was on the cards – a few hours later, for the first time in my life, I felt utterly real, as the plane crossed those massive white expanses and I stood by a window, gazing down, amazed that everybody else could be so blasé about it. Hanging in thin air over Greenland, or whatever all that whiteness below corresponded to on a map, I felt real in a way that I had never felt before, and I didn't want it to end. I wanted to stay in the air forever – flying solo into the afterlife. Because that is how it felt to me, as the plane crossed the top of the world – a few hours later, in a new world, it felt like the afterlife.

I didn't know what was about to happen, though, as I waited to embark. I didn't know I was finally about to *fly*. To begin with, waiting at Heathrow and all through take-off, it

195

wasn't even *flight* at all – it was just the usual business of air travel. The usual crowds, the usual bureaucracy, the inevitable delays. First check-in, then security. For some reason, there were armed policemen wandering the lounges, sub-machine guns cradled in their arms. All the minutiae, all the winsome, dull enquiries and advice seemed to last forever – and all the way through the process, I kept finding myself alongside a tall, very slender, grey-haired woman who seemed to drift through it all, utterly impervious to every nuisance and totally, effortlessly calm. An obvious child-of-the-sixties, she was the type of person you could imagine in a leotard, or one of those black cotton trouser suits that Chinese people wear: a meditator, a yoga teacher – no, the Chinese connection was spot on: a t'ai chi instructor. She was all balance, yin and yang, slightly amused by her surroundings, perhaps, but detached – detached, not indifferent, capable of living fully and ready to accommodate any grief or joy that the world presented, griefs and joys that she knew were both hers and not-hers. There wasn't an ounce of spare flesh on her, and no trace of self-consciousness as she passed from here to there, watching, listening, interested, unperturbed. I envied her all of these things – and maybe she saw that envy passing across my face, as we waited for security, because she smiled at me briefly, as we came through the far side and sailed on into the transit area.

I found where I had to be and sat down. I looked around. The t'ai chi woman was gone, it was just the usual business travellers and families. The invisible airport staff, cleaning, or moving softly, singly or in pairs, from one station to another. After a moment, I became aware of someone talking on the public telephone nearby: a large middle-aged American woman, all bumbag and sandals. She was talking loudly into

196

the receiver, and I couldn't help but overhear what she was saying. She talked in a slow, bemused drawl then, after waiting a while, presumably listening, she spoke again, each time more bemused, as if she had only just realised that the wonders of the world were infinite in number. All the time, talking or listening, she turned around and around, swapping the phone back and forth from one hand to the other. 'You should see the socks Ingrid bought me,' she said. 'They're *awful.*'

The other party spoke briefly. The woman turned, saw me looking up at her, and flicked her eyes away to the left before she spoke again. 'No,' she said. 'I'm *wearing* them.'

I looked at her feet: the socks were just visible through the sandals, small polygons of candyfloss pink and canary yellow. She saw me looking and twisted away, her eyes closing for a moment as she did so. 'Well, I didn't have any *choice,*' she said. 'I didn't have any clean stuff left. Still, there's one good thing. If the plane goes down in the desert someplace, I'll be easy to find.'

For some reason, this remark struck me as hilarious, and I looked away so she wouldn't see me laughing. It was a good-humoured laugh, well intentioned, full of fellow feeling, but I didn't think she would see it that way. A shaft of light was pouring into the seating area off to my right, like some special effect that had strayed from a Hollywood movie and ended up here, going to waste in a grey-and-white lounge and, ten feet away, at the end of a row of seats, the grey-haired woman was sitting with her cabin bag perched on her knees. She had been looking for something – and now she had found it: a thick notebook bound in what looked like green silk, which she extricated from the bag and opened. Then she produced a tiny pencil, made a brief note – no more than a couple of words – and put the notebook away. And at that moment I suddenly had the pleasurable sensation of *liking* this woman – or rather, of *realising* that I liked her – and it seemed to me, as I watched her close the bag, that I hadn't *liked* anyone in a very long time. She had something *to* her. Around the still point where she sat, the other passengers seemed like so much chaff, about to blow away in the first gust of wind that came along, but she was rock solid and, at the same time, utterly weightless and graceful. She was also, it would seem, something of a mind-reader because, once again, she sensed me watching and turned to face me. I suppose under normal circumstances, I would have looked away, not wanting to intrude, but on this occasion I didn't. I really did like her, in a distant, almost abstract way, she made me feel good about things, she made everything seem slower and more precise – and I think she saw *that* in my face too, because she smiled again and nodded slightly. Or had I imagined the nod? Was I looking to her for something that could only come, after a long time, from myself? Looking to her for a cure, or an absolution? I didn't know and nothing in her face provided an answer. A moment after, we got moving again, and I lost her in the crowd.

I was in California for three weeks, but most of the time I wasn't anywhere. My fellow workers were like phantoms, the offices were lighter and bigger than the offices in Surrey, but the daily round was just as dull and it was only when the working day ended and I got into my rented car that I came back to life. Not that life consisted of much more than sightseeing. I was a good tourist, heading out to Half Moon Bay to stare out at the Pacific or driving over to Yosemite on the weekend, to walk among the elk or sit out on Glacier Point while a lightning storm passed through, wandering the blue roads where there was nothing but pumpkins and wind farms or coming to a sudden halt in the ash grey of dusk, while a family of deer moved past me, unafraid and curious, on the wooded slopes at Big Basin. Some nights, I went to a ball game at Candlestick or Oakland; other times I would eat sea-eel in a Japanese restaurant, before heading off to one of the bookshops on the Camino Real, where I would spend a couple of hours browsing in the poetry section. That was the best – that, and the quotidian details of the road, the eerie light on a pumpkin field, or a slow-seeming wind blowing through the California poppies on some silty verge near Inverness or Point Reyes. I hadn't been prepared for contemporary American poetry, so much more open to the elements and free-flowing than the stuff I could read in England. Reading those poets was like arriving at a place I'd never seen before and finding that it was utterly familiar and yet strange at the same time, the way home – real home, I mean – is both familiar and strange. It began as something I recognised, something I almost knew already, then it shifted into something else, the way a room you have known all your life suddenly shifts a little, in a certain slant of light, so that everything seems a little larger and wider and the world appears less finished than it had been, a moment since. This was 1990-ish, when it was a new experience to go into a bookstore like Kepler's, or A Clean, Well-Lighted Place and sit for an hour or two in an armchair with a coffee and a pile of books to mine and I usually ended my day at one or another of those stores. They calmed me, they made me feel welcome in a world that had seemed to belong to others. I felt still there, balanced – like someone who considers himself to be happy.

It was in one of those Camino Real bookshops that I saw

the woman from Heathrow again. She had obviously been on the same plane as me, but I had missed her when we were boarding. Now, here she was, in a grey shirt and white jeans, her long grey hair tied back in a ponytail. She looked younger now, and even more graceful – and her sixth sense seemed to have deserted her, because she didn't seem to notice that I was watching. I wondered what she was looking for. What she read. What books she picked up for the title alone, or for the cover. Which books she gave as gifts, or bought for a long journey.

After a while she found a book and, to my surprise, she headed in my direction, holding the book carefully in both hands, as if it were some kind of sacred text. Perhaps it was. I glanced away then – absurdly, I didn't want her to think I was spying on her – and I thought she had passed me by, on her way to the group of seats by the coffee table, beyond the next set of shelves. There was no reason for her to remember me: our fleeting exchange had happened almost three weeks before, in a foreign country – or not even in a foreign country, in fact, but in transit. I turned back to my book – and then I sensed her, right next to me, in an easy chair just a couple of feet away. I looked up.

She smiled. 'Do you always follow strange women around?' she said.

I smiled back. I was pleased to have found her again, idiotically pleased to hear what her voice sounded like. It was totally irrational, but I was happier than I had been in months. 'All the time,' I said.

She nodded. 'I thought so.' She studied my face for a moment, and something in her own face altered. She studied me, the way a doctor might study a new patient, then she shook her head slightly. 'It seems to me that you need to let something go,' she said, the trouble passing from her eyes. 'But I guess you know that.'

I didn't say anything. I suppose I was afraid for a moment that she was about to turn into some hippie cliché, some wise-woman type, or maybe an actual, honest-to-God mind-reader. Yet as soon as the thought crossed my mind, I felt ashamed of myself. 'Yes,' I said, after a moment. 'I probably do.'

She gave a tiny nod of the head, then looked at the book in my lap. There was no reason to linger, after all. 'What are you reading?' she said. I held out the book to her and she took it. She read a few lines, then handed it back. There was a care about her, a slow quality. I remembered again how suddenly I had liked her, when our paths had crossed at Heathrow. 'It's good to see you,' she said, as if we were old friends who had bumped into one another after a long estrangement. 'I hope you enjoy the rest of your visit.' She stood up.

I moved to stand too, but she settled me back in my chair with a little wave of the hand. 'Stay,' she said. 'Read your book.' Then she turned round and began to walk away.

'Wait,' I said. I didn't think she would, but she stopped and turned. I shook my head. 'I don't know who you are,' I said. It was an odd thing to say, perhaps, but it didn't seem odd at that moment.

She pursed her lips the way my mother used to do when she was measuring out lengths of fabric. 'What does that matter?' she said, and she wandered back through the rows of books, only stopping once to take a single volume from its shelf, before moving on. She didn't look back. I watched as she paid for her books, exchanged a few words with the assistant, then left – and I wanted to go after her, maybe ask if she wanted to have a drink, or a late-night coffee, but I didn't. It wasn't what she wanted. She had found me by chance and

201

she'd taken a moment to tell me what she saw and, though this probably sounds like something out of a fairy tale, sometimes these things are true. Anyway, I stayed a while, picking up three more books of poetry and a couple of Andre Dubus short-story collections that weren't easily available at home, then I went over to pay. The assistant took my purchases; then, before she totted up the bill, she handed me another book, one that I hadn't chosen.

'This is for you, too,' she said.

I shook my head. 'I didn't –'

'Your friend bought it for you,' she said. 'She said to give it to you before you left.'

She smiled.

I took the book. It was Dante's *La Vita Nuova*. In Italian. Nothing came with it: no note, no inscription on the inside cover. I looked up. 'She didn't say anything?' I said.

The assistant – a tall, pretty woman with long dark hair and light freckles – thought for a moment, then shook her head. Outside, it was starting to get dark on the Camino Real, and the lights were on up and down that royal road, white and red and gold. The assistant passed me the bag with the books that I had chosen and I paid. She was still smiling, happy to have been caught up in this little piece of whimsy at the end of a long day. 'Have a good evening,' she said.

I nodded. 'You too,' I said.

Later that night, I drove out and sat for hours on a dirt road near the ocean, watching a huge Monterey cypress as it filled with the wind and then emptied under an immense darkness barely lit by the stars and the wet slit of a moon. It was beautiful, that motion, like something breathing. There was nothing else for miles, other than the darkness and a stony road to

202

nowhere special, but that was what I had driven out there for in the first place – for the American night, for the smell of it and the wideness and the feeling that whatever happens is part of this story with no beginning, no middle, no end, just an infinity of tiny, improbable details of light and shadow, of colour and shape, of gravity and time. Though it didn't really exist, I wanted to drive away and stay in that American night forever, in the width and the darkness and the sweet smell of it, a mixed bouquet of cypress and poppies and wild deer. America smells so sweet, once you get away from the cities. It doesn't matter where you are, that smell is there, under all the other smells: a rich, sugary scent that you never find in Europe, a sweetness so deep you think you will never finish breathing it in. As a child, I had dreamed of being in America – not New York, or Chicago, not Hollywood or Disneyland, but the America of this scent – a scent I had never known, but inferred from films and books and anecdotes. Nicholas Ray. John Steinbeck. Alfred Hitchcock. The American Night. The lonely American fantasia of the wind and the darkness and everything secretly connected to everything else. Not the cities, not even the small towns, but the roads in between, the roads, and the places just off the roads, all that God-in-the-details of the land: the sway of cottonwood in the wind, the black of a secluded lake, the monumental quiet of a Monterey cypress near a roadside motel on the way from nothing to nowhere. That was the place I had dreamed about all my life, a place to be lost in, a place where I might disappear, once and for all.

I don't know to this day what changed during that California trip, but when I got back to Surrey, I felt better than I had in a long time. I seemed to myself, not healed exactly, but capable of being mended. Of beginning again, beginning from scratch. Clean, this time, sober, in control, wise to the damage that I was capable of inflicting on myself and others. It didn't last, of course. For six months, I practised *wabi-sabi* and wrote poems that approximated the poems I wanted. Then, for sins I didn't even know I had committed, the powers that be sent me to the Enormous Room.

THE ENORMOUS ROOM

It was just another IT department, but I knew I'd seen it before, if not in real life, then at least in my mind's eye – though it wasn't until a few days later, as I sat at my desk with all the ambient drivel of such places slopping around me, that I recalled the original of this grey hangar, a bland version of hell that, as a teenager, I had constructed from e.e. cummings' memoir of the detention centre at La Ferté-Macé, that Enormous Room full of undesirables and ne'er-do-wells where the young poet was interned as a potentially hostile alien in1917. By contrast, my new home-from-home was populated with computer programmers and insurance busybods rather than the more usual varieties of con men and thieves, but it was also the Enormous Room: a long, wide, low-ceilinged dinginess on the upper floor of a nondescript office building, a ghastly hybrid of attic space and warehouse, divided evenly by four-foot-high screens into a maze of smaller spaces called *pods* in which designated teams of programmers, analysts and underwriters – four to each pod – worked together to find the least interesting solutions to the problems at hand. This Enormous Room was of the style described as semi-open-plan, and it was probably intended to foster a sense of teamwork and shared goals: a work space in which everyone played his or her part, and every role was important to the overall aims and objectives of the corporation.

The Enormous Room: that name was descriptive, as far as it went, but this was neither as interesting nor as vital a place as cummings' slop-scented corner of hell. Cummings' Enormous Room may have been a gaol, a place from which there was no escape, yet he claimed to have had the time of his life there and he came to see his fellow detainees and their warders as characters in a modern-day Pilgrim's Progress. My Enormous Room was just a semi-open-plan office, like semi-open-plan offices anywhere; my fellow detainees barely registered as discrete individuals; there were no Delectable Mountains to be discovered, and I was no Christian. In fact, for as long as its detainees exercised the necessary cognitive dissonance to make their daily routine seem worthwhile, this Enormous Room was a near-democratic space, not merely a place for the congenitally mediocre to earn a decent living, but safe haven for a whole host of white-collar lads with a modicum of savvy and resilient girls who drank Boddies by the pint, a laminated, air-conditioned echoland of good-humour and industry.

To foster this sense of near-democracy, none of the computing staff had his own office; instead they – and 'consultants' like me – lived and played and had their being in the aforementioned pods, like whales, or locusts. Mine was at the farthest end from the main door, next to the fire exits and, like the other consulting staff, I had been placed among the general population, presumably in order to facilitate knowledge transfer. If you wanted to think, you came in early; if you wanted to stop for a break and make coffee, you had to at least offer to make it for the entire pod, or risk being seen as *not-a-team-player*. The only exception to this rule was the Project Manager, who had a roomy, all-glass, open-door-policy cubicle in one corner (this cubicle was almost invariably empty, however, because the manager was always either i) at a meeting or ii) on a training course). Cummings called his room 'the finest place on earth'. It might have been a detention centre, but during his stone-walls-do-not-a-prison-make internment, he appears to have discovered what he was later to call *effortless spontaneity*, a notion my grey-haired woman on the Camino Real might have recognised – though she probably wouldn't have called it that. She wouldn't have said anything about the Enormous Room either. She would have just looked at me, the moment I arrived in that place, and willed me to turn around and walk straight out again, because from that moment on, I was falling again.

Unlike cummings, though, I got to leave my particular detention centre in the evenings. To begin with, this meant going back to a hotel room to listen to breathless middle-aged people shagging in the next room, or to while away the night in the so-called Cocktail Bar drinking Northern beer and chatting to a barwoman called Kate. Of course, Kate knew I wasn't chatting, I was trying to get in her pants, which is what all men do when they're bored and far from home. Meanwhile, the couple in the next room were bound to win a prize: three mercifully short but strenuous bouts in one hour before the other noises began: shower, hacking cough, nose clearing, loud piss, flush of toilet, glassy laughter. The next day, they did it all again, at exactly the same time, and the day after that too – and then they moved out and I started to miss them: all that assiduous coupling and the sweet collapse when the bubble burst after about seven minutes, each of them sighing, though perhaps for different reasons.

That was Lytham St Anne's by night. Sex through the wall and creamy beer. No surprise, then, that Blackpool started to look like an actual seaside resort, despite all the odds. Twice a week, sometimes more often, I went over by taxi and wandered up and down the front looking for the heart of Wednesday night or, failing that, some decent speed – and it was here that I met a girl who said her name was Crystal, though it might just as easily have been Little Orphan Annie, or Katie-Morag. There was definitely something Scottish about her, though she said she was Blackpool born and bred: a sweet-faced red-eyed girl with white skin and lightly etched teeth, Crystal was more fun to get drunk with than anybody else I'd ever met, and when we went back to hers in another taxi we arrived in the 1950s, on a street that was pure seaside surreal, a long row of faded wedding cakes made from icing and dust, cats wandering from window ledge to window ledge, the occasional half-starved clematis struggling up from a concrete basement and, behind each painted and peeling front door, a hallway, a staircase, *odour*. You find these districts in every seaside town: soft ruins of Victorian comfort or Georgian grandeur converted now into bedsits and flats, singles and couples and shifting boho communes all piled up one on top of another, the apartments wide and airy on the ground floor, but progressively smaller as you ascend till, at the very top, under a wave of rain and birdlime, you come to the dusty, triangular attics where, back in the old days, the servants or the children were stored until they were needed, like tin soldiers or playing cards. This was where Crystal lived, right under the roof – and from that night on, once or twice a week, this was where I went to forget the Enormous Room. To begin with, we began the evening in the proper fashion, which meant going out on a date, but it wasn't long before I was skipping the formalities and simply turning up at the door of her far from enormous attic with vast quantities of assorted bottles. Sometimes, if the opportunity arose,

208

Crystal supplemented these with hash or speed, obtained from an old boyfriend with whom she had stayed friends, but mostly we just surrounded the bed with bottles and glasses and rolled around till the roseate hues of early dawn came peeping in at the window. *Cheap thrills*, Crystal called it once – and that was more or less accurate, though perhaps not the whole story. We had both been blessed with addictive personalities, that seemed obvious enough, but I had spent my entire life in the sometimes weary, occasionally desperate pursuit of cheap thrills, and this was something else. There were times, I suspect, when I could have loved Crystal like a sister, and there were times when I thought that one or both of us would die up there under that roof. As far as I was concerned, either one would have been fine.

This routine continued for the next several weeks, during which time I moved out of the hotel and into a company flat near St Anne's pier. Days, I sat in the Enormous Room and tried to pretend I cared about the tedious machinery of it all; nights, I got wrecked in Blackpool – an easy place to get wrecked in – or wandered about on the backstreets or the sands with strange noises in my head and faint, sweet flutterings, like butterfly kisses at my cheeks and neck. Sometimes I sat in the flat and watched old movies, or lay on the floor in the dark listening to Arvo Pärt through headphones, but nothing seemed to work and I would rush off to see Crystal again, arriving each time with a bigger bag of booze, breathless and feverish with anticipation, though I wasn't quite sure of what. And every now and then, halfway through the afternoon, or in the small hours under Crystal's crusty duvet, I promised myself that soon – very, very soon – I was going to get in my car and drive away.

* * *

209

I suppose I might have driven away sooner, if I hadn't met Esmé. It surprises me to this day that I was still in Lytham on that cool, bird-haunted morning a couple of months later, when our paths crossed on my morning walk to the office. I was on the seafront, gazing out over the sands, delaying for as long as I could the inevitable downturn of the day, and suddenly she was next to me, talking about the birds, a surprisingly grown-up teenager – fifteen, in fact, as I later discovered – who quietly incorporated me into her world, treating me like some fellow traveller she'd known all her life: a soul-friend, a *companion*. At the time, what was most striking about that world was how very well, even perfectly defined it was, an indelible map of colours and shadows and the lineaments of magic, each item individually marked in a clear and confident hand. I'd not seen her on the front before, but that was probably because I'd set off later than usual that morning, and I'd dawdled along the way, stopping to gaze out over the wide sands between St Anne's and Lytham, a stretch of coastline that brought to mind the sea paintings of Philip Wilson Steer and P. S. Krøyer, all light and shimmer with a hint of something unseen in the distance, some huge flock of geese or godwits, or just the vast quiet of the sea, waiting to be heard. That morning, I had gone out a little later than usual and I was taking it easy, lingering at the promenade rail to watch the birds out on the sands and trying to fill my lungs with enough air and my head with enough light to get me through another day in the Enormous Room – and then I heard her voice, somewhere off to my right.

'The people round here used to eat wading birds,' she said. I turned and saw a girl in a black, or maybe a dark grey blazer, leaning on the promenade railing a couple of feet away. 'They particularly liked godwit. In fact, time was when godwit was more prized than any other fowl.'

She was petite, even for her age, with short, dark brown hair cut in something that resembled but wasn't quite a bob. The fringe was just a little too long, which only drew attention to her eyes, eyes that seemed so aware, so bright, they suggested a perpetual, amused curiosity. She smiled – and I realised then who it was that she reminded me of. It was Anna Karina, from the old Godard movies. Anna Karina in *Alphaville*, say, or *Made in USA*. 'Better than swan,' she said – and, in a single, uncalled-for moment, everything changed forever – though, to be fair, that wasn't *her* fault.

I have to call her something other than the name her parents gave her, so I think it only right to call her Esmé – after the girl in Salinger's story *For Esmé – with Love and Squalor*. Names are changed to protect the innocent and – though I am sure she would disagree, being at the time one of those people who confuse innocence with unknowing – Esmé was the most innocent person I had ever met. That morning, we talked for a while, then she headed off to school and I to work, thinking, or trying to think, that it had just been one of the pleasant interludes the real world sometimes offers, more or less for free – though every pleasant interlude in the real world is touched, necessarily, with poignancy – but the next morning, I was there again, and Esmé was too, and though we pretended we had met by accident, each of us knew that we had both been hoping for another brief encounter. Though not so brief this time, perhaps because, at the point when I tried to play the responsible grown-up and suggested it might be time for her to trot off to Double Geography or something of that sort, she smiled and enquired – knowingly and in all innocence – whether it might not be time for me to hurry along to the office.

211

'Oh, I'm in no hurry,' I said. 'But I wouldn't want you to miss the river systems of Argentina.'

'We did that last week,' she said.

'Alluvial fans?'

'Yep.'

'Oxbow lake formation?'

'Got the T-shirt.'

I laughed. 'So you're not going, then?' I said.

She shook her head. 'You look a bit lost,' she said. 'I think I'll hang around and make sure you don't get into any *real* trouble.'

And so it began – and whether or not Esmé was the knowing innocent that I thought her to be, surely I was the more innocent for being so unknowing. Or rather, for knowing and refusing to know what I knew – which was that this would end in tears, one way or another. The very fact that I was now about to skip work should have been enough of a warning that things were already on the way to getting out of hand – and the fact that my companion in truancy was dressed in a high school uniform should have been the clincher. Not that I had any intention of luring her back to my shoebox of a flat for nefarious purposes – or not consciously at least. I was only deciding that I liked her. She made me smile. She made me laugh. These phenomena were unlikely to occur in the Enormous Room.

'My car's just there,' I said. 'Do you want to go somewhere?'

She laughed. It *was* a preposterous thing to have said. 'Why not?' she said.

'Where shall we go?'

'Let's go walking on Morecambe Sands,' she said.

'Isn't that dangerous?'

She smiled. 'Not if you know what you're doing,' she said. 'Do you know what you're doing?'

212

I shook my head.

'I didn't think so,' she said.

If this was a movie I would have to show a montage at this point. A montage of happy, likeable people – because happy people are likeable, on the whole. I could show us on Morecambe Sands, or walking along the seafront between Lytham and St Anne's, I could show us out on the beach, or sitting on our favourite bench in the park. I didn't see her as often as I would have liked, and sometimes we only met for half an hour before school. For the most part, it was rather a chaste romance, considering. Certainly no crimes were committed. Yet it was *amour fou*, nevertheless – and in all that time, it never once occurred to me to ask myself what the hell I thought I was doing. Not once. We didn't talk about it either. You'd have thought we might have talked about it – but the closest we came was a brief exchange while we were out skiving on the sands. It was a grey day, and I was starting to wonder – not for the first time – what we were doing out there when I had a flat, coffee, music, a bed. It would have taken no more than ten minutes to get there – but we kept on walking and looking out to the sea and to the birds in the late-Victorian distance. Finally, Esmé stopped and turned to me. 'Sometimes I think that you think I'm a fictional character,' she said.

I laughed, but I didn't answer. I thought she was just teasing.

'Or maybe it's *you*,' she continued, and something in her voice stopped me dead, so I had to look at her and see that she wasn't joking after all. She was serious. 'Maybe *you're* the one who's fictional,' she said. It wasn't serious as in sad, or upset, it was simply an observation that she was making. She had been thinking about what was happening between us, and she had worked something out – and now she was telling me what she had concluded.

'You're not fictional,' I said.

'So it's you, then,' she said.

'No,' I said.

She shook her head and waited a moment to show that she wasn't going to be satisfied in the least by a simple no.

I laughed. 'Well,' I said, 'what do you want me to say?'

She looked out across the sands. Rain was coming in. 'I don't want you to say anything,' she said. 'I just don't want to be treated like a child.' She turned her back to me.

I understood what she was saying. If I really liked her, I had to do something about it. But how could I? She was just a girl, and she was an innocent, whether she liked it or not. I didn't want her to look back someday and see me as the creep who took advantage of her when she was too young to know any better. But I didn't say anything. I couldn't even give her that much serious consideration – because the only thing I could think of, at that moment, was that I didn't just like her, I was in love with her, and I should have just told her so, but I was afraid to say it, so I said nothing. I *loved* her. *Amour fou.* I was an idiot.

She shook her head and smiled sadly. 'Well,' she said, 'you certainly know how to make a girl feel wanted.'

The vagaries of *amour fou*. How certain pieces of music, from a chart song to a Britten quartet, can restore me now to the condition of terrible joy that I thought I had put behind me forever. How, for years afterwards, I enjoyed the lingering sense that nothing really mattered, because the real drama had been played out: a walk on a beach in the early morning; a conversation in a car with the radio playing, a moment when

214

everything stopped and Ketty Lester started singing 'Love Letters'; all that corny stuff that isn't corny at all when it's happening, because it's the everyday *wabi* of falling in love, which is never a good idea, though it cannot be avoided. *No se puede vivir sin amor*, and all that. It's a bad idea, falling in love, but it's a sin to jump out of the way when you see it coming. Bad karma. Somebody possessed of good luck and preternatural skill and judgement can find a way to live alone, I mean *truly* alone, someone armed with a vocation, a lifetime discipline can do it too, but that doesn't mean he has escaped the cycle. Not until the last cut. Not until the very last breath.

Still, that said, the truth remains: it's never a good idea to fall in love. Falling in love reveals things about ourselves that we'd much prefer not to know. Falling in love is an abandonment of order. All that madman, poet and lover stuff you hear about is wrong because, no matter how odd or perverse his actions might seem, the madman is striving towards order with whatever raw materials he has at his disposal, like somebody trying to make a cake out of sand, rose petals and a scale model of the Tower of London. The visible product may be a disaster, but his intention was honourable, and if somebody had let him have some flour and eggs and butter, he would have used those. But they weren't available – surely we can see *that* by now, after all the theorising and late-night chit-chat on the subject? Surely we can see that madness is a symptom of a wider disorder, a general deprivation? Apophenia is usually talked about in a context of excess sensitivity, which would make the apophenic symptomatic of some wider malaise, just as the loss of an indicator species like a filmy fern or a long-eared bat serves as an early warning that the wider environment is being degraded. The mad are symptomatic of a societal failure, not random episodes of perversity

215

or bad luck and, most often, what they want is *order*. Much the same goes for the poet – but falling in love, *falling in love*, is abandonment, falling in love is a total and unquestioning assent to the inevitable, wherever it might take us. For years, I made myself believe that falling in love was an imaginative act, an investment in some chosen object. But that wasn't love – that was just making movies in your head, in order to avoid a more random and dangerous event. An event that is, in essence, as destructive and as eventually regenerative as any natural disaster.

I had thought I would never feel the same way about anyone as I did about Adele – and it was true, I never did. Nothing I felt about Esmé changed or diminished my memory of Adele. The true romantic may well believe in that old cliché, the single lifelong, definitive love, but that isn't how *amour fou* works. With *amour fou*, we go on loving the first true love in everything the real world throws at us: happiness, pain, banality, desire, lust, temptation, forgetting. That first afternoon, as we drove back from Morecambe, I knew that I was about to get lost – but I also knew that I was about to be lost in the same territory where I had once been lost with Adele, and as illogical as it may sound, being with Esmé wasn't a way of leaving Adele behind, it was a perverse, possibly twisted – and certainly unfair – way of finding her again. All I knew then was that I wanted to be lost again – for who couldn't love being lost? Who couldn't love reaching out for something that is slipping away even as his fingertips graze the impossible surface? Who wants to keep anything forever? Who would willingly accept the sheer tedium of the imperishable?

Who wants to be safe? Who wants to be sane? Who wants to be *normal*?

* * *

216

I suppose the big slide began at around this point. By day, I would see Esmé whenever I could – which meant most mornings, at least – but I was also seeing Crystal two or three times a week, driving over with half a supermarket's worth of booze, then driving back hung-over and half asleep the next morning. At first this provoked nothing more than the odd leg-pull at the office – boys being boys – but after a while, I imagine at least some of the other denizens of the Enormous Room started to worry about me. Not that I wasn't doing my job. As boring as it was, I carried out my role in an exemplary manner for a long time – only running into trouble, ironically, when I wrote an honest and very detailed analysis of the next phase of project development, warning that the plans a couple of the in-house people had drawn up were wildly optimistic and almost certainly doomed to failure. One of these in-house people was a tall, rather handsome, boyish-looking guy called George, who had quickly worked his way up from programmer to lead an entire team – something he had managed by combining technical ability with a gift for only ever saying what his bosses wanted to hear. He knew that, whatever else you might do, you *never* brought the higher-ups bad news.

I liked George. Of all the people I met in the Enormous Room, he was the one I had the most time for. So when he asked me into the end office to discuss my analysis, I expected him to be reasonable about the estimates and, since the report was entirely realistic, I even expected him to come round to that realistic position. I was, of course, completely wrong. It was blood on the carpet time.

'Shut the door,' he said, sitting down on the other side of the desk. I could tell right away from his tone of voice that this wasn't going to be fun for either of us, so I closed the door and stayed where I was, rather than taking a seat in the obvious place opposite him. I didn't want to make this meeting any longer than it had to be. 'So,' he said, looking up at me. 'What the hell is this?' He waved a sheaf of papers that I guessed was my report. It had been copied to four people, three from the Enormous Room, and one back at my home office.

'It's as accurate an analysis of the project as I can give at this time,' I said.

He glared at me. 'It's fucking bullshit,' he said. 'That's what it is.'

I shook my head. 'It's as accurate an analysis of the project —'

'Aw, fuck off,' he said. 'Stop stonewalling me.' He was much angrier than I had expected — and I remembered that he had some kind of sporting background — rugby, or football, or some other crypto-sexual pursuit — and I wondered if anger management had ever been covered on one of the scores of courses he would have had to attend during his rapid ascent.

'I'm not,' I said. 'I have to reflect things as they are. You don't have enough trained staff for —'

'Ah,' he said. 'So that's it. You want us to buy in some more consultancy —'

'Hell, no,' I said. '*We* don't have the resources —'

'Don't interrupt me,' he said. 'And will you fucking well sit down!' Reluctantly, I sat. It seemed diplomatic to let him vent, but of course, now, he changed tack. He got sad. Quiet. Rueful. He'd thought I was on his side. We'd been out drinking together — an evening I obviously didn't recall — and we'd laughed and sang the company song and done gymnastics on the front lawn — or something like that. 'I didn't expect you, of all people, to stab us in the back,' he said.

'It wasn't my intention to stab anybody in the back,' I said — and then I stopped, and thought about what I was saying. *It wasn't my intention to stab anybody in the back?* What kind

218

of crap was that? And what did he mean by *us*? Was this one of those quaint Northern expressions – *give us a pint, lass,* that kind of thing? Or did he mean his team? Or maybe the whole company? 'I was asked to write a report,' I said. 'I wrote an accurate report.'

He lifted his chin. 'Fair enough,' he said. 'As of now, you'll not be asked to write any more reports. We've done our own reassessment of the project, and yours doesn't tally at all.' He leaned on the desk, chin jutting now. 'Look at those lads out there,' he said. 'They've worked bloody hard to get to this stage. Now you're saying they're not good enough –'

'I'm not saying they're not good enough,' I said. I was trying very hard to stay calm. 'I'm saying –'

'You've *insulted* those lads,' he said. 'They've put their heart and soul into this, which is totally new ground for them, and they've done a bloody good job.' He stared at me for a long, hard moment, the disappointment visible in his face, then he tossed my report into the waste-paper basket and turned away. 'Get out of my sight,' he said, without looking at me. 'I've said what I needed to say.'

I stood up. 'Fair enough,' I said. I turned around and opened the door. Outside, those lads were all looking at me, some with the resentment of the insulted, some with what appeared to be compassion.

'Oh, by the way,' George said, his voice loud, but drained of rage. 'Is it true you're tupping some girl from't high school?'

I turned around slowly and looked at him. 'What did you say?' I said.

He smiled – a sweet, nasty smile. 'I heard you were going about with some kid from't high school,' he said, in his best broad-Lancastrian accent. Playing to the gallery, of course. 'Is that right?'

I didn't reply. Everybody in this half of the Enormous Room was listening now and they were waiting to see how I would react – and I managed, just, to smile and shake my head as I walked away, though I suddenly felt sick to my stomach with it all.

'You can get arrested for that,' George called after me. Which was perfectly true, of course – and it hadn't even occurred to me. Not once.

I expected our next meeting to be stony, or ugly, or both, but it wasn't. Give George his due, now that he had said his piece, he was ready to move on. Or maybe he just felt good because he had something over on me. Whatever the truth of the matter, the one thing I did know was that he would be keeping an eye on me. Under the terms of our service contract, clients could ask for an on-site consultant to be shipped home whenever they wanted, and they didn't even have to give a reason – so the Enormous Room could easily have sent me packing that very day. I rather suspected, however, that George wanted to keep me close, maybe to make me suffer and maybe to have the satisfaction of proving me wrong. He really *did* love his lads, and he really *had* seen my report as an insult to them. And he was confident that those lads wouldn't let him down. So the next time he saw me, he was all big-hearted equanimity and water under the bridge, though the accusatory, *dirty-old-man* grin was still there, an inch below the surface. He thought he had something over on me – and he liked that.

And it was true: he *did* have something over on me. They all did. Someone had seen me with Esmé, walking on the promenade, or sitting in the park; somebody driving by on the way to work, somebody looking out of a window, it could have been anyone in the office, and now the whisper was doing the rounds, sly innuendoes in the pub, parleys around the coffee machine, ugly laughter and curious stares over the hotpot in the canteen. By the time it got right round and back again, the girl from the high school would have shed a few years and we'd have been caught in flagrante in the bushes by Fairhaven Lake, and there was nothing I could do about it. I spent the next few days trying to figure out who it was, I went on fishing expeditions with the guys in my pod, but I soon realised there was no point. Nobody was going to talk. Besides, I think some of the guys – the Red Hot Dutch crowd, say, or the ones who passed around videotapes of *Salon Kitty* – didn't think I was doing anything wrong. Old enough to bleed, etc. They would probably have despised me if they knew the truth.

Chaste. That was what I had thought. Though, of course, neither of us was really chaste, or we wouldn't have been seeing each another – a simple cold fact that emerged on the very next occasion I saw Esmé.

It was right after school on a warm, slightly overcast day. I had gone in early that morning and fixed a couple of outstanding problems; then, after a cool and courteous consultation with George, I had taken some personal time to keep an appointment. He'd been moderate in his enjoyment of that – a little smile that wasn't even levelled at me, but was pointed down at the desk, while he refilled his fountain pen. He always wrote with a fountain pen, did George. Real old school. A bit rough around the edges, but still a diamond. I miss him, sometimes.

I met Esmé in the usual place, on the front. My car was parked nearby, on Clifton Drive, and I wanted to get away quickly, before anybody saw us. 'Come on,' I said. 'Let's go for a drive.'

'OK. Where are we going?'

'I don't mind,' I said. I could feel a hundred pairs of binoculars trained on me. Andy from systems support was hiding in the bushes with a telephoto lens and a high-powered microphone. The vice squad were patrolling the front in unmarked cars. I felt a sudden rush of indignation at the whole hypocritical, porn-loving crew but, since none of *them* were in evidence at that moment, my anger got displaced on to Esmé. 'Let's just go,' I said.

'My, you're in a hurry,' she said.

'Bad day at the office,' I said, immediately feeling guilty. 'I just want to go somewhere far away and breathe.' It was a fair effort, I suppose. Certainly it got her moving in the right direction, though she wasn't in any hurry.

'All right,' she said. 'But I think it's going to rain.'

'It's not going to rain,' I said.

'Yes, it is,' she said, her voice sing-songy. 'We'll get drenched and then I'll have to explain how I got all wet during trumpet practice.'

'You don't play the trumpet,' I said. I had slowed now. There was no point trying to hurry her – and besides, if someone saw us getting into a car together, that would only make things worse.

'I do now,' she said.

'Really?'

'Well, where do *you* think my *mother* thinks I *go* after lessons?' she said. She was doing somebody, but I couldn't have said who. If anything, she sounded like Elizabeth Taylor in *Cat On a Hot Tin Roof.*

'No,' I said. 'You mean you lied to her –'

222

She laughed. 'Don't worry,' she said. 'She's not going to find out. After a while I'll drop out of trumpet and take up archery or something. It's not as if she'd booked the Albert Hall or anything.'

I had to smile at that. She really was a resourceful little madam. 'Fine,' I said. 'But let's get out of here, OK?'

'We could go to your place,' she said suddenly.

'What?'

'I said, we could go to your place,' she said.

I stopped walking and turned to face her. She was, at that moment, painfully beautiful – and I could barely stand it. That old, dark tenderness I had felt for Adele was there again: a weight in my body and, at the same time, something outside and around me. Something *beyond* me. It was *present*, I could feel it in my blood, but I could no more lay claim to it than I could lay claim to the weather – and I suddenly knew I had to get away from her. I don't know, now, what harm I could have done her, but at that moment, I felt I was a danger to her – by which I mean that I was, or felt myself to be, an actual threat, a threat that was more metaphysical than physical, perhaps, but still a threat. That's not quite the right word, but it's close. Esmé wasn't even sixteen yet and, in spite of her extraordinary intelligence, she had no idea what she was dealing with. 'No,' I said.

She looked sad. 'No?'

'No.'

'I see.'

'We can't,' I said. 'You know we can't –'

'So you *don't* fancy me,' she said. 'I thought you did.'

I looked at her. 'You *know* I fancy you,' I said. 'Though I wouldn't –'

'Then why not go to yours?' she said. It was a simple question.

223

'Because, we can't,' I said. 'And we have to stop talking about it –'

'What,' she said, 'are you scared?'

I laughed. 'No,' I said, 'I'm not *scared*. It's just that – it wouldn't be right –'

It was her turn to laugh. 'Oh,' she said, 'it wouldn't be *right*.'

'Yes,' I said.

'Yes what?'

'That's enough,' I said. 'End of conversation –'

'Oh no it's not,' she said.

'I can't,' I said. Everything was getting hazy, the world was slipping away from me and I wanted to run as far away from her as I could. 'It's not right. You know I want – you know I love –' My eyes brimmed. I looked at her. 'You have to promise me –' I said – and then I couldn't say anything else.

She put her hand on my arm. 'What are you talking about?' she said. She was trying to stay calm, and she was managing – just. Though maybe she was on the point of tears. I couldn't tell. I could barely see her now. 'Come on,' she said. 'Don't get upset.'

I nodded. 'It's OK,' I said. 'Let's just get in the car and drive somewhere.'

She smiled. 'Let's do that,' she said.

We drove up the coast road. I wanted to drive forever, past Blackpool, past Lancaster, going north and away, past Carlisle, past Glasgow, not stopping till we came to some village on the shore of a loch somewhere in Argyll, or Sutherland. I wanted to drive into a desert somewhere and go on driving for days, never stopping, like the couple on the run in an old movie. Farley Granger and Cathy O'Donnell, in *They Live By*

224

Night. Henry Fonda and Sylvia Sidney in *You Only Live Once.*
That world. I wanted to drive to the border and disappear. It
wasn't a healthy state to be in, not for me. It's usually a warning
sign when your interior landscape turns into a film-noir tribute
reel from a *That's Entertainment* special. Suddenly, Esmé started
to cry. Her head sank and big tears started falling on her hands
like raindrops. I pulled over. We were close to the South Shore,
not that far from where Crystal lived.

'I'm sorry,' she said.

'No,' I said. 'It's – I shouldn't have started this –'

She looked up at me in alarm. 'Don't say that,' she said.

I shook my head. 'No,' I said. 'I'm sorry.'

She was silent for a moment. I waited, then I asked her if
she wanted to go back. She shook her head. 'I don't understand,' she said.

'I know.'

She looked at me. She had stopped crying, just as suddenly
as she had started. '*Do* you love me?' she said.

'Yes,' I said.

She laughed, a surprised gasp of a laugh, as if I had said
something unexpected. Perhaps I had. 'Then I don't understand,' she said, after a moment.

'No,' I said.

'No, what?'

'No, me,' I said. 'I mean, you're right. I can't –' I looked
at her, then I started the car. 'Come on,' I said.

'Come on, what?'

'I'll take you back,' I said.

'Back where?'

'I'll take you home,' I said.

'No.'

'We need time,' I said. 'We need time to think –'

'*I* don't,' she said.

I looked at her. 'I'm sorry,' I said.

She turned away. 'Sounds like you've already made up your mind,' she said.

I didn't say anything. There was nothing *to* say. When we got back to St Anne's she told me to stop.

'Drop me here,' she said. Her voice was hard. I had hurt her.

'Don't be silly. I'll take you –'

'No,' she said. 'Just drop me here.'

I saw that she was right, of course. I could hardly drive up to her front door and let her out with all the neighbours peeking out their curtains and her mother at the door, taking down my registration number. It was only much later, looking back, that I realised that *that* wasn't what she meant at all.

That night I picked up the usual box of goodies from the supermarket, but instead of taking them over to Crystal's, I went back to the flat and drank it all myself. The next day, I went to work and, when I left, I did the same thing again. I'd brought all my favourite videos up from Surrey, and I drank vodka straights while I watched *Double Indemnity*, then *Invasion of the Body Snatchers*, after which things got a little hazy. When I woke up, at four the next morning, the TV was on, and there was a video in the machine that I didn't even remember putting on. A home-made copy of *Ordinary People* that I didn't even know I had. The writing on the case wasn't mine, it was the wrong make of video and for one unsettling moment, I thought somebody else had been there, in my flat, watching Mary Tyler Moore go to pieces while I lay sleeping on the floor. That day I didn't go to work. I managed to haul

226

myself to the supermarket for more supplies, then I sat all day drinking and watching movies till I lost consciousness. Then, some time later, when I woke in a bluish gloaming that I couldn't explain, I began again.

So it went on, for how long I'm not sure now. More than a week. Maybe ten days. I didn't go to Crystal's, and I didn't go to the seafront. I suppose, if I *had* done something right away, Esmé would have taken me back, and maybe we could have worked something out. But I didn't. When I finally dragged myself back to work, I went through the days on automatic. Then, in the evening, I got drunk and watched more movies. I could have gone on like that forever, or until the first heart attack, at least. Then, late one afternoon, a programmer in my section came to my desk and put a note on my table.

'This came for you,' he said. His name was Dave. He had a soft, slightly wet smile that would draw office bullies to him for years to come.

I didn't look up. 'Thanks,' I said – but he didn't go. He loitered. I looked at him. 'What is it, Dave?' I didn't want to sound impatient, because I liked him and he bruised easily, but I didn't want company either.

'Nothing,' he said. 'I was just wondering if you were going to Angela's party.'

I looked back to my workstation. 'Angela's party?'

'Yes.'

He was talking about Angela's party, but that wasn't why he was there. I looked back to him and sighed. 'When is it?' I said.

'Tonight.'

'Oh.' He was so deliberately ignoring the note on my desk that I had to look. Then I had to pick it up, because I could

227

see from the writing that it was from Crystal. I looked back to Dave. 'I don't know,' I said.

'You're invited.'

'Am I?'

'Yes.' He looked bewildered, and I remembered that Angela was the very attractive woman who worked in Systems Support whom I had spent an evening flirting with when I'd first arrived in the Enormous Room. An enterprise that had been witnessed by everyone and, as they would all happily tell you, there were no secrets in that office. It occurred to me, then, that this undue interest in whether or not I was going to the party was a test of some kind. I could prove that I was normal and liked real, grown-up women. 'She *specifically* invited you,' he said. 'In the canteen.'

I nodded. 'So she did,' I said and decided that the best policy was to play along. '*When* is it again?'

He grinned. 'To*night*,' he said.

'Where?'

'Christ, John, she told you. You wrote it down. Don't you remember?'

I shook my head. 'No,' I said. 'Write it down for me.'

He wrote down the address. 'Me and Phil are going for a drink beforehand,' he said. 'You want to come?'

'Maybe.'

'OK,' he said. He grinned some more. He liked to grin. Somebody should have told him that he looked like a chimpanzee when he grinned, but it wasn't my job. He made to go, then, as if on an afterthought, he glanced back. 'Who's the note from?' he said. The grin was gone. 'Lady friend?'

I shot him a dangerous glance, then looked at the note. It wasn't in an envelope; it was just a sheet of letter paper folded in half, with my name written on the outside in purple ink.

228

I wondered if Dave had taken a peek on the way to my desk. I didn't think so. If he had, I would probably have seen it in his face. He might even have blushed. That was the thing about Dave: you had to like him, but you could see his working life stretching ahead for the next forty years and it didn't look too hopeful. But then, who was I to talk? I unfolded the note and pretended to read. 'It's a begging letter,' I said. 'From my mother. She's always after me for money.' I looked at him, and he didn't blush. He just shook his head and went back to his own desk.

As it happens, Crystal's note *was* a begging letter, of sorts. She hadn't seen me and she was worried, she wanted me to go over that night, as soon as possible, because she had to see me urgently, but she didn't say why. Usually when a woman sends a note like that, it can only mean one thing – but I didn't think it was that. It was the logical conclusion, but it barely passed through my mind before I dismissed it. This was something else. I read the note again, to see if I'd missed any clues, then I tore it into small pieces and threw it in the bin. An hour later, Dave reappeared. He was wearing a raincoat, which was ridiculous, because it was sweltering.

'You coming?' he said.

I looked at him. 'Angela lives with somebody, doesn't she?' I said.

He grinned happily. 'Used to,' he said. It was odd, that grin of his. Like the cat that got the cream. Only he wasn't the cat and, most of the time, the cream was imaginary.

And that was the problem with the kind of social life you had in offices: every exchange seemed either glib and slightly insulting or clumsy and slightly bewildering. I didn't dislike Dave or Phil or Colin or the others. In spite of everything

229

that had gone on between us, I actively liked George, even if he was in the process of graduating from young blood to all-out company man and openly enjoying the experience. There was no real harm in any of them and, in the abstract at least, I liked them – but conversations were a form of mild torture.

That night we spent more time in the pub than was probably healthy, and the talk was inane, but eventually we moved on to Angela's. By the time we got there, though, I was worn down by sexual innuendo and football predictions, and I was starting to feel guilty for not going over to see Crystal. Then, almost the moment we arrived, I wished I *had* gone to Blackpool. There were people everywhere, and Angela was somewhere in the middle of it all, incommunicado amid all the conversation and crush. Though the music wasn't overly loud, it was of that Blandulike, osteoporosis-inducing variety of recent charts and driving rock classics that you get on those compilation albums they advertise on late-night TV. I would probably still have tried to get to her, but the gang I had arrived with surged straight through the hall and into the kitchen in their search for more beer, and I was carried with them. Ten minutes later, drink in hand, I was in the back garden, out in the cool air, alone.

The garden wasn't much more than an elongated courtyard at the back of the house, with high brick walls around a patio and a tinier patch of lawn beyond that quickly petered out into a mass of paling and rubble. The light from the kitchen reached almost to the edge of the patio, but the far end of the garden was dark, so I crossed the lawn and went to stand out in the shadows where nobody could see me – and, as I did so, I realised that it had started to rain: that sweet, slow rain that only seems to happen in the west, in small towns and suburbs, not as sooty as city rain, not as hard or as cold as the rain on an open field or a hillside. It was beautiful, and I stood a long time, letting it settle on my face and hair, then I ducked in under the cover of a big conifer, half in, half out of the greenery, looking back towards the house.

The music was louder now, but not raucous. I didn't know what it was, but the lead singer sounded a bit like Michael Stipe. I could picture Angela as an R.E.M. fan, one of those souls who get a little drunk when they are down, or tired, sitting with a bottle of white wine in the front room listening to 'Losing My Religion' or 'Nightswimming' over and over again. Or maybe not. Maybe I wasn't thinking of her at all, because I had no idea who she was. Maybe I was thinking of someone else. The doors to the patio burst open and one of the guys from the office – a tall, thin, blondish man called Barry – tumbled out on to the patio. He was waving his arms and staggering a bit, but he wasn't really *that* drunk. He was putting it on – it was *that* kind of a party. He regained his balance and stood a moment, gazing up into the rain, then he started to sing.

'*Regrets, I've had a few . . .*' He stopped singing and thought for a moment and I could see that he was wondering what came next. He didn't know, so he started over. '*Regrets, I've had a few . . .*'

Another man appeared – it was George – followed by several new bodies who wanted to see what was going on. George had been drinking too, but he was in complete control of himself. He took Barry by the arm. 'All right,' he said. He turned to the others. 'Barry regrets to say that he's had a few,' he said. He got control of Barry, and started leading him back into the house. 'Come on, Bazza,' he said. 'Come in out of the wet.'

It was then that I sensed it. It wasn't a person, but it had

231

the same bulk as a man, and it was next to me, maybe an arm's length away, deeper into the shadows. I couldn't see it – I couldn't see anything – but I felt it, and there was a smell, the kind of smell you mean when you say *clove-scented*, only it wasn't cloves, it was more like carnations, cooler and darker and less spicy. I felt the hairs rise on the back of my neck: whatever it was, it was able to stand that close and yet remain unseen, and that unsettled me. No, it *scared* me – because it wasn't something that was just there, in that garden. It was *my* companion. It was there because I was there and all at once I knew that, when I went elsewhere, *it* would be coming too.

As soon as the coast was clear, I walked off down the road, found a phone box and called a cab. Forty minutes later, I was climbing the stairs to Crystal's flat. I knocked for a long time before she answered but I went on knocking because I knew she would be there. Her note had said. Eventually, I heard a soft, scurrying noise.

'Who is it?' she said.

'It's me,' I said.

She opened the door. She was naked. 'Where have you been?' she said.

'I'm sorry,' I said. 'I've been a bit –'

'Never mind.' She grabbed me by the sleeve and pulled me inside. 'Let's go to bed,' she said.

I woke up: it was already morning. I could hear rain, heavy and insistent at the window. Crystal was sitting on the edge of the bed, her eyes fixed on my face; it was obvious she had been watching me for some time. I didn't see the knife at first, it was only when her hand moved – very slightly, more of a

232

nervous flutter than anything else – that I caught a glimpse of silver, and I realised that she was holding the big pointed carving knife that she kept on the kitchen counter. She'd told me once that she kept it by her for safety, and sometimes she even left it on the bedside table, so it would be there if she needed it in the night, and I'd thought that was fairly crazy, but I'd not said anything. To be honest, I quite liked the idea of being in bed with her, and that eight-inch blade there all the time, it added something to the proceedings, a frisson, a potentiality. I still had warm memories of Caroline, who'd taken a knife to me once in the kitchen of her London flat, and I hadn't forgotten Adele's fondness for razor blades and needles, but I was pretty certain Crystal didn't like to play that game and, for the moment, I was trying to seem casual and not in the least threatened, as if I hadn't seen what was in her hand, so I kept my eyes on her face.

She smiled. 'You're awake,' she said.

'Yes,' I said. 'I'm sorry. I didn't mean –'

'It's OK,' she said. 'I don't mind. I like watching you sleep.' From the way she said it, it was obvious she had watched me sleep before, and I wondered if the knife had come into the equation then, too. 'You look peaceful, when you're asleep,' she said.

She got up slowly and stood over me, an odd, possibly wistful smile on her face, then she walked over to the kitchen counter and laid the knife down carefully in its usual place. 'Look,' she said. 'Last night was good.' She stood by the counter, looking out the window. She looked pretty, with the rain light on her face. 'And I really like you,' she continued, almost, but not quite dreamily. 'Maybe I like you too much. Which is why I don't think we should see each other any more.'

233

I was taken aback. This sudden pronouncement was the last thing I had been expecting and I couldn't think of anything to say.

'I really *do* like you,' she said, turning back to me. 'Don't get me wrong.'

I shook my head. 'So – why –'

She smiled the sad smile again. 'I like you,' she said. 'And I think you like me too, in your way. But you have to admit it. You're not really here. Except when we're fucking. Otherwise, your mind is – somewhere else.' She stopped to ponder where this somewhere else might be, then looked me in the eyes. 'You're in your own little world,' she said after a moment.

I understood I was supposed to explain myself. But how could I? The only explanation I could have come up with was an insult, at best. 'I'm sorry,' I said. 'I didn't mean –'

She smiled and waved her hand vaguely, as if brushing something away. She really did look very pretty, saying goodbye in the rainy light. 'Don't be sorry,' she said. 'It's been *good*.'

I nodded. 'Yes,' I said. 'It has.' I think I even believed that for a moment, though I'd long ago forgotten what *good* meant, in a cheap-thrills context.

She nodded back, but she wasn't sure. She studied my face for a long moment, to see what I was thinking; then, when she was satisfied that I was all right, she went over to the sink and filled the kettle. 'I'll make you a cup of tea,' she said. 'Before you go.'

I arrived late at the Enormous Room, but at least I arrived. I had raced back to the flat in a taxi, showered and shaved, and put on a clean suit, and now I looked more or less normal. I couldn't think straight – but, after my run-in with George, I had been left to my own devices, programming and testing, so it hardly mattered if I was under par. I didn't have to go to meetings now, and nobody expected any original ideas from me, just reliable code and test results. If my breath smelled like the floor of the Student Union at six o'clock on a Sunday morning, then it couldn't be helped. At least I was wearing the suit and the shiny black shoes; at least my hair was combed.

I had to pass George's office on my way in, and I didn't want him to know how late I was. He would have had to say something – because that was how it worked. He probably didn't want to – I think, by then, he was tired of me – and I certainly didn't need the hassle, but he had to go by the book and, had he been there, he would have been obliged to go through the motions. His office was empty, however. No George, and a strange quiet to the place. Relieved, I proceeded to my workstation and sat down. Nobody else was in my pod, and I reasoned that they were all in the same place, at a critical meeting, a meeting at which my presence was no longer required. If it ran true to form, that meeting wouldn't end before lunchtime, so I had time to catch up, time to settle and get my head down. I sat down at my desk, switched on my workstation and watched the screen come to life.

I didn't see the note to begin with. It was an A4 sheet, folded neatly in two, and tucked under my keyboard: a clean, crisp page that looked like it had never been touched by human hand. Nothing to say who had left it there, or to indicate for sure that it was meant for me – though as soon as I unfolded it and read the words printed in small caps in the middle of the paper, I knew it was. It said:

JESUS LOVES YOU
BUT EVERYONE ELSE THINKS YOU'RE AN ARSEHOLE

I read the words, then I read them again. At first, I thought it was funny – the kind of thing a computer geek would enjoy, and I let myself think someone had left it there for my amusement, the way people circulated daft snippets from local papers or badly translated instruction manuals in the internal mail. After a moment, however, I realised that this wasn't meant for general circulation – it was meant for me. I stood up and looked around. The Enormous Room was empty, or empty as far as I could see, the printers silent, the workstations displaying their slogans and starbursts to empty chairs. It reminded me of the day of the bomb scare, when everybody else evacuated the building and I was left on my own, not wanting to abandon the interesting little problem I'd just discovered. Some of the suit-and-tie boys had been annoyed about that, but we'd managed to laugh it off. I picked up the sheet of paper and read it through again:

JESUS LOVES YOU
BUT EVERYONE ELSE THINKS YOU'RE AN ARSEHOLE

I had to laugh. Really. It was the best put-down I'd seen in a while. Part of me was insulted, and part of me was curious about who had written this note, but deep down, hung-over and half mad and secretly grubby under my shirt and tie, I just thought it was funny. I looked up at the clock on the wall: it was almost noon. I could stay at my desk and wait to face the music, or I could give it all up now and take myself off somewhere so the farce I had embarked upon could run its course. Not much of a dilemma. I folded the paper up and tucked it into the breast pocket of my jacket, then I turned and walked the length of the Enormous Room for the last time – and all the while the conviction was beginning to form

236

that none of this was real. The room, the stage set of desks and computer terminals and empty chairs, that apology for daylight at the windows – none of it was real and, for the moment, this conviction made me want to laugh out loud.

I drifted around Lytham till seven that evening, then I took a taxi over to Blackpool, heading for a pub called the Galleon, where they opened till late and had live music. The music was sometimes provided by an ancient couple who played jazz, and I liked them, because they were inept and loving and they cared about what they were doing. They weren't there that night, though, so I had a couple of drinks and wandered away, needing to be on the move, restless, searching for something. I had a couple of drinks in another place I knew, then I headed out again. Halfway along the road to the next place, I saw Crystal. She was standing against a wall, and a man was with her. He seemed to be holding her, or maybe pushing her into the wall and it looked to me that something bad was happening. The man was moving her about in an odd way, like she was a doll, or a puppet, and I needed him to stop doing that.

'*Hey!*'

I ran over to where they were standing and grabbed the man by the arm, pulling him away from Crystal, who flopped back against the wall like she was really hurt. I pushed the guy against the wall. He was tall and thin, with stringy black hair and a pencil moustache, around thirty maybe, his eyes big and wet and dark brown, like a deer's. 'What the fuck do you think you're doing?' I said.

He was amazed. He didn't try to fight or get away, he just stood there pinned against the wall staring at me, like I was a ghost.

'I said what the fuck are you doing?' I said again.

237

He shook his head. 'No, man,' he said. 'It's what the fuck are *you* doing?'

'What?'

He was stoned. I could see that now. He stared. 'I mean, who *are* you, anyway?'

'I'm a friend of *hers*,' I said.

'No you're not,' he said. He seemed utterly convinced of this.

'Yes, I am.' I banged him against the wall, and he blinked wildly, but it was no use. He was fairly gone.

'What the fuck do you think you're doing,' he said, his voice coming as if from far away.

I let him go and he stood, dazed, looking off to one side. Then I hunkered down and grabbed Crystal by the arms. 'Come on,' I said. 'I'll get you home.'

She looked up at me, but she was pretty far gone too. And now I realised that the guy hadn't been attacking her, or beating her, or whatever I first thought. He was *with* her. They had probably got high together and then she'd fallen over or something and he was just trying to help. He was looking after her. He was trying to *help*.

Crystal looked up at me and her eyes cleared. 'What's wrong with you?' she said.

'What's wrong with *me*?'

'Yeah.' She laughed softly. 'You look different,' she said.

The guy hit me then, from behind. It wasn't very hard, but it was hard enough. He couldn't have known what he was doing; if he had he would have followed through, but he didn't, he just hit me then flopped away and, a moment later, I had him back against the wall and I was punching him in the face, once, three times, more, so the blood came. That was when Crystal started screaming.

'Leave him alone,' she screamed. 'Leave him alone, you fucker.' Then *she* was hitting me, and the whole thing went pear-shaped. Somebody came to a door and shouted that they were calling the police, then the guy broke free while I was trying to fend off Crystal and he started away, staggering off down the road, blood dripping from his nose and mouth. After a moment, Crystal started after him.

'Crystal!' I shouted.

She turned round. 'Fuck off!' she screamed, then she caught up with the guy and together, more or less holding one another up, they tottered into the darkness. A man's voice came from off to one side. It was an old voice, old and indignant. 'The police are on their way,' it said. I wasn't sure I believed that, but I hurried back along the street and ducked into the first pub I could find.

When I recovered my senses, I wasn't where I expected to be. I could hear music and I sensed someone standing over me, but it was too dark, or I was still too hazy, to tell who this person was before she spoke. At first I couldn't hear what she was saying, but I knew she was talking to me, because she was very close, a matter of inches away. So close, in fact, that all I could really see were the eyes, which looked kind, though they were at an odd angle, and one was much larger than the other, which was what I noticed, and focused on, if you can talk about focus in a situation like this, till I began to make out what she was saying, something she had said before, perhaps more than once, and was now beginning to tire of repeating, or rephrasing, as if a different set of words, or the same words in a slightly different order could get through to me. I could tell this, without thinking about it: she was a good Samaritan type, but only up to a point, and that point had already been reached.

'You need to wake up now,' she was saying. 'You don't want any trouble.'

I nodded. I was trying to pull off that much practised trick – much practised, and always unconvincing – of seeming to know exactly what she was talking about. 'I wasn't sleeping,' I said, trying to sense where I was without obviously looking around in dismay. 'I was just resting my eyes.' I could hear music, and there were voices. The woman's face pulled back and I saw her friends, an entire hen party of them packed in around a nearby table, watching this exchange with varying degrees of curiosity and amused disapproval. They were dressed in the kind of clothes people from *Coronation Street* might wear on a big night out, all glitter and sequin, barmaid-chic. All except the one who'd talked to me, who was much plainer. A sober brown jacket and brown skirt. Spare make-up. No earrings.

'Come on,' she said. 'Just get up and walk to the door. You'll be fine.'

Glitter balls. Real disco mirrorballs. Disco music. Women in shiny dresses and big hooped earrings. Where the hell was I?

'Where is this?' I hadn't meant to say this out loud. It was supposed to be a thought, one of those inner double takes the mind performs when there's nowhere else to go. I had to have been blind drunk when I blew into a place like this. She said something that I didn't catch – and now, for the first time, I became aware of men. There were men everywhere, and some of them were watching us a little too closely.

I shook my head. 'I mean – *where* is this?' She gave me a confused look, and I could see that she was wishing she hadn't bothered. 'What town?' I said.

She shook her head in despair. 'Blackpool,' she said.

240

'Ah.'

I struggled to my feet and started walking towards the door. The woman didn't come with me, she just stood where she was, watching – and the closer I got to the exit, the more aware I was of the men, till it seemed that the whole room was populated by that species of masculinity familiar to all drunks and druggies: new middle-class, smart-casual in dress, sporty, with a job in distribution or sales, he is almost professionally Northern. He knows his way around, but he never flies solo and, towards the end of the evening, he waits for a last little bit of fun in places like the one I was at that moment trying to exit gracefully, him and his mates gathered around the bar, eyeing the women and sinking pints of Grolsch, or whatever passes locally for real ale. He isn't a traditional hard man, but he does tend to get vicious when excited. There are dive pubs where a man can drink himself into the carpet, and nobody bats an eyelid, pubs where my current spectators wouldn't last three minutes, and where I would have been safe to go on my merry way. This wasn't one of those, though. This place smelled, suddenly, of offended respectability. And of that other thing: the tyranny of the group. Not for the first time, the only thing that stood between me and that tyranny was a woman who, asked to do it all again, probably wouldn't bother.

Outside, it took me a while to get my bearings. I'd never been to this place before – I didn't remember having arrived there, and I had no idea why I would have chosen it – and I wasn't altogether sure of where I was. One of those seedy backstreets far from the promenade, where the Illuminations went unnoticed and the whole year was one dull coppery glimmer around the optics of self-designated nightclubs. A street with late-night takeaways and bad hotels and, at this, the ugliest end, a series of places where you could drink for a couple of hours beyond time if you were ready to pay. I had no idea what time it was. I looked at my wristwatch – or rather, I looked at my wrist, where my watch used to be. Now it was gone. I had no memory of losing it, or even of taking it off, and for a moment I considered retracing my steps to see if I could find it. It was a nice watch. A thought that simple can defeat you, though, when it's after midnight and you are on a street you don't know in a town you've mostly seen through the bottom of a glass and, besides, I knew I had to get walking before the lads in the bar decided to come out and see me off. So I walked away, trying to pass for someone who might know what he was about. Up ahead, about fifty yards away, a wider, well-lit street was just visible between the buildings, so I made for that. That was a nice watch, I thought. I didn't mind if it was lost, though, as long as it didn't fall into the wrong hands. Maybe I had taken it off somewhere then forgotten it, and some kid would find it next day, some kid on holiday with his parents, like the kid I had been, almost thirty years before, a lonely and slightly weird kid who was pretending to be neither of those things, the kind of kid who talks to himself all the time inside his head, and thinks his troubles will end when he grows up and can decide things for himself.

I woke up in the flat. I had no memory of getting there, but there I was, large as life, sprawled diagonally across the bed, in the clothes I had worn to go out. I looked at the clock on the dressing table. It was five fifty. I got up, walked through to the kitchen and put the kettle on; then I turned on my heel and went into the bathroom. A shower, a shave, a cup of coffee. The three basics to starting a day. If you can get through those, in the condition I was in that morning, you can go on to just about anything. At least I wasn't having hallucinations, or hearing things.

I ran some hot water and lathered up. I didn't feel that bad, all things considered. I took a fresh razor from the bathroom cupboard, looked at myself in the mirror. When I was a child, my eyes were extraordinarily blue. According to my mother, people would stop her in the street and remark on how blue my eyes were. Nobody could understand where it came from: my mother had pale blue eyes, my father's were grey, but they all agreed, these aunts and cousins and neighbours: I had the most beautiful blue eyes they had ever seen in a baby. And now they were a faraway, washed grey. I peered at myself in the mirror and studied these grey, washed-out eyes – and at that moment I had a sudden, stinging memory of my father. My father as a younger man, before he began to slide. My father when there was still some gravity to him.

In those days, he always made a big performance about getting ready to go out. He would insist on having neatly pressed trousers and a clean white or navy-blue shirt, with which he would wear one of his many ties and a black or dark blue blazer with a PER ARDUA AD ASTRA RAF badge stitched to the breast pocket. He would always shave before leaving the house for the evening, even if he had shaved already that morning, and his hair would be freshly Brylcreemed, in true RAF-style. I would observe this process with something approaching awe – *this* was how a man was supposed to be, *this* was self-respect. Dignity. He really did have an air about him at such times, and I remember wishing him well, hoping he would be able to hold on to this dignity until he got back home – and, at the same time, I also remember feeling an odd distaste, a sense that it was all for nothing because, by

243

the end of the evening, it would be gone. By the end of the evening, he would have thrown all this away. He would roll home drunk with his so-called friends and sit till all hours, talking about nothing and spilling whisky and ashes over my mother's half-decent sofa. It would seem a long time, then, since he had gone out looking like somebody.

Now, as I stood in front of the mirror, razor in hand, I saw that I was performing a long-familiar ritual. I saw *his* face in the glass, *his* predicament in mine, *his* ability to deceive himself in my ridiculous attempt to put on a normal face. I saw myself and I saw *him*. The one thing I had always wanted, growing up, was to be different from him and here I was, faking normal in an empty bathroom, his mirror image. Faking normal, telling myself the kind of absurd, convoluted story that he told all the time. For much of his life, my father had a strong constitution, which made it all the harder to drink himself into an early grave, but he carried on undaunted and, all the way to the end, he was telling stories, making things up – and I am sure that, at the beginning of his last worthless evening, as the kids went in from their games and the first cool settled on the streets, he stepped out of his front door in his blazer and neatly pressed flannels and made his way to the Silver Band Club with the same dignity he could summon for the start of anything – and everyone, even the neighbours who knew exactly what he was, even the kids in the little square outside his Corporation house, would have seen a proud man who wasn't going down without a fight.

Of course, this wasn't exactly what *I* saw in the mirror, as I finished shaving then proceeded to get dressed in my office clothes. Mine was a much softer carapace, and the clothes were of a slightly better quality. But I knew what I was and, even if I was a less convincing version of the beast, I was,

244

when all was said and done, the same kind of liar and, if I had any sense at all, I told myself, I would give up and begin again, at exactly that moment – give up pretending, give up poisoning myself, give up being an idiot. This I saw and I saw it all as clear as any normal person might. Then I put on my jacket and went out into the morning sunlight, to get back on the carousel. It was only six thirty – the whole sorry performance had only taken forty minutes – but I thought I needed to go for a drive before work – up the coast, maybe – to straighten myself out.

A good idea; but by the time I got behind the wheel of the car, I had decided that I needed to go and find Esmé one last time, before she went to school. I would catch her when she left home and I would explain that I'd made a mistake, that I hadn't been thinking straight when I had said all those things I'd said – *when was that?* I had to think for a moment before I remembered how long it had been – which I should have realised was a sign that I wasn't really as much in my right mind as my clean shave and fresh clothes might have suggested.

My first problem, as I saw it, was that I didn't actually know where Esmé lived. I knew it was somewhere off the road that ran between Lytham and St Anne's, but I didn't know specifically which house was hers – so it should have been a clear warning that I thought I could just drive up a street and catch her as she left for school, maybe pulling up alongside her a few doors away from home, so her parents couldn't see, then swinging the passenger door open, the way they do in American movies. Then she would throw her books into the back seat and we would drive away. It was an image so clichéd that I found it completely persuasive.

I loved those seaside streets, first thing in the morning. In the city, it was all a matter of scent: warm bread, newsprint, diesel, hops, that sooty rain you only get where there are early-morning buses or, depending on which city it was, the dark, sweet scent of carthorses. All along the avenues and water-fronts, there would be that aroma of freshly ground coffee, the most beautiful and, strangely, the most poignant smell of all. In the suburbs, though, it was different: the residential streets were slower to wake and, in the gap between night and day, between true dark and light, the people would still be asleep as I wandered from road to road, reading the ordinary narratives that had been suspended the previous evening, the toys and implements scattered across a lawn or a patio, the child's bicycle abandoned in a driveway, cars full of inconse-quential yet telling evidence: tapes and half-eaten chocolate bars on a passenger seat, discarded clothes in the back, out-of-date parking vouchers for the next town or some distant city. The seafront was all hotels and flats and businesses, but further down, off the inland road between St Anne's and Lytham, it was entirely residential. White bungalows in tidy squared-off gardens, family homes with porch lights and makeshift playgrounds in the yard, corner shops that could still remember the 1960s, cosy churches that looked more like glorified villas than the official residence of the Lord.

This was where Esmé lived – somewhere on those streets, in one of those houses. The problem was, I didn't know which one. It was odd to think that I was familiar with them all from my insomniac rambles in the small hours – the blossom-pink or primrose facades, the eerie doorways fringed with shadows and flowering quince, the portals to some forgotten dynasty of pastry cooks or French polishers, crumbling around the ears of the last in a long line while he sat reading news-papers from thirty years ago. Ever since I'd come to St Anne's, I had divided my time between old movies and these streets, just a couple of hundred yards from the sea – but it wasn't really a division because much of the time I couldn't see the two as separate worlds. On the TV screen, in black and white, or in soft, slightly fuzzed fifties Technicolor, a woman came to the window of a house and looked out; then, an hour later, on the street that ran parallel to the coast road, a woman came to the window of a whitewashed bungalow and watched me cross the street – *and it was all the same.* It was all continuous. Or it was for me, because I couldn't tell one from another. On the street, I was always waiting for the killer to step from the shadows, or a beautiful woman might suddenly appear in a pool of street light twenty feet away and call me over, her voice soft, urgent, dangerously appealing. Every night, I slipped back and forth between real world and story, between monochrome and colour, not the plain colours of daytime, but the fuzzed blues and wet crimsons of a sixties night-time, and sometimes it came as a shock, when I strayed out of the story I had been living in and found that I wasn't in a movie, that nothing was just about to happen, that I wasn't waiting for someone or, if I was, they weren't real.

Now, however, as I wandered through this zone of painted house fronts and remembered plot lines, I was looking for something specific. I was looking for Esmé's house – and I felt sure that I should know it. I thought, if I really loved her, I should be able to guess which it was – and I wandered for an hour or more while the darkness turned to a summer-morning dusk, searching for the telltale sign that would restore me to the unfinished narrative I had so carelessly abandoned on the South Shore. It was the purest form of logic: I would find Esmé and, as if by magic, everything would work out. Order would be restored, the darkness would lift and my cracked mind would be mended, at least for a time.

247

Only, I couldn't do it. I couldn't guess which house was Esmé's. The main trouble was that this zone was much bigger and denser than I had realised and eventually, after I had been driving around for a while, I simply came to a halt on a wide street lined with detached, single-storey thirties houses in seaside colours, not because I thought Esmé's house was there, but because I couldn't drive any further. I was starting to hear things again – soft auditory hallucinations flaring out of the engine noise and dying away before I could make out what they were, staccato pops and whines, like distant guns, voices calling from two streets away, brutish, snuffling yet oddly inti- mate animal noises so close to the back of my neck that I could almost feel the breathing. And all the time my mind was playing tricks on me as the lucid, normal, hopeful man in a suit from an hour before collapsed into a pathetic array of guesses and second-guesses. There was one house – a pretty, yellow-and-cream villa that looked terribly familiar, and I suddenly had an image of Esmé walking to the door of that villa and going inside. I hadn't *seen* this, as such, but I saw it in my mind's eye and it seemed right: I remembered the porch, part timber, part glass, I remembered the begonias and trailing geraniums in the hanging baskets. I remembered that particular yellow on the windows and around the door. I remembered everything – and then, just as surely, I knew that I was wrong. This couldn't be Esmé's house, it was further on, it was the one with the privet hedge and the lamp above the front door, or maybe it was the one with the Japanese- temple-style gravel at the front. Yes, that would be it. And then, just as I was beginning to think it was this house, I realised that it didn't matter, because I suddenly knew that Esmé had gone to the park to see if I was there, in our usual spot. In the park. Why had I been such an idiot? She was

248

bound to be in the park, because that was where we always met. In the park, at our usual place, facing the sea. All of a sudden, I was certain of it.

And she was. She was right where I had thought she would be. When she saw me, though, she looked away. She wanted me to know that she hadn't been waiting for me, that this had been her favourite spot long before I ever showed up. I walked over, and said hello. I felt shy.

'What happened?' she said. 'You look terrible.'

'I didn't sleep very well,' I said.

'Looks like you didn't sleep at all,' she said.

'I'm fine. I was just – I was thinking. About you –'

'Oh no,' she said. 'Don't do that.'

'No,' I said. 'Let me explain. I know I made a mistake –'

'No,' she said. 'You don't get to do this. You can't just change your mind.'

'But –'

'No –'

'I'm not asking –'

'No!' She was angry now. Hurt, still, but angry as well. 'You were right,' she said. 'There's nothing between us anyway – how could there be. You're –' She looked at me, almost curiously, then she thought better of what she had been about to say.

'I'm not saying there has to be anything between us,' I said. 'I just want –'

'That's enough.'

'No. Let me explain –'

'That's enough. Don't say anything else.'

'But –'

'No. I've got to go. I'm late –'

'All right,' I said. 'I understand. I'll come back later – we can meet later and talk.'

'Stop it!' She was staring at me. I will never forget that look – the way she stopped everything and made me stop too, with a single word – and then, the way she took me in, every last detail of me, as if she wanted to memorise me before abandoning me forever. And she did stop me. For a moment, in fact, everything stopped. The whole world stopped, like a carousel when the ride is over. Then it started again and when it did, she was already walking away.

I DREAMED I SAW ST AUGUSTINE

After that, things get very hazy. I remember being in a kitchen, drinking instant coffee. I remember being in a car, but I don't recall getting in or out. There was a woman with dark eyes who seemed to know me from somewhere, but I couldn't understand what she was saying. I remember someone giving me water in a little waxed paper cup. I don't remember how I got there, but I remember waking up in what looked like a library. It was night-time, but the room was bathed in a cool, silvery light that I knew was coming from outside and when I lifted my head I could see a street lamp and a wide expanse of neatly clipped lawn reaching away towards some trees at the edge of the darkness. I looked around: the room was large, with book-lined shelves all along one wall, and there was a desk next to the window, but it wasn't a library after all. It was a child's room – a child's, or a teenager's – and for one terrible moment I thought I had woken up in Esmé's house. But that was impossible. Her house would be a modern semi, or a villa surrounded by other houses and gardens and this was – what? A country house? An institution of some kind?

A psych hospital? But then, if I was in a psych hospital why wasn't I in one of those isolation rooms they have for when you're first brought in, and why did I feel so clear in my mind when they would have hit me for six with a double dose of Largactil or something like it the moment I came through the door? Because, really, I felt very clear. I felt exceptionally good, in fact, better than I had felt in weeks. I was totally lucid: I could see every detail of light and shadow around me. I could hear the owls hunting in the trees and further off, across the fields that lay beyond. I couldn't see those fields, but I felt them. I had a sense of huge space around me, open sky and trees, wet after rain, at the edge of a wide meadow, and I could feel a great mass of roosting birds, hanging invisibly in the branches like one vast web of flesh and bone and plumage, heavy and dark and resonant as a bell. I felt wonderful, but I had to find out what was happening. I had to find out where I was. I tried to get up but, as soon as I made the effort, my legs felt heavy and, at the same time, impossibly weak – and I realised that I couldn't move. I was paralysed from the waist down. At any moment, a nurse would come in and tell me there had been an accident, but that I shouldn't be afraid – but there was no nurse, and this wasn't a hospital. So where was I? I kept my head up for as long as I could, trying to see out into the grounds and so find some clue – but all I saw was a bat flickering past the window, a solitary bat, hunting for moths in the silvery light.

I woke up. I was lying on the floor of the flat in St Anne's, fully dressed, my clothes soaked with rain or dew. It was dark. Next to my ear, a voice was whispering the same word over and over, but I couldn't make it out at first. Then I heard

pulverised pulverised pulverised pulverised pulverised pulverised

over and over and over. I turned my head to see, but I didn't try to get up, because I thought for a moment that I was still paralysed. There was nobody. Nothing. Only the voice, hurried and high-pitched

pulverised pulverised pulverised pulverised pulverised pulverised

Pulverised. I remembered, then, that this had been my favourite word when I was about seven or so. I'd seen it in the *Beano* and I had sounded it out, not knowing what it meant the first time, but as soon as I looked it up, I knew it was one of *my* words. *Pulverised*. I had seen it all so clearly: dust on the wind, dust in the wake of the bomb, pollen and ash and chalk rising into the sky and mingling, in clouds that I knew were full of tiny, invisible particles, or drifting for miles through oat fields and summer grass before they settled, imperceptibly, into the earth. A comic-book word, to begin with: a threat, a warning. Then the etymology worked on me slowly, as I forgot Desperate Dan and the Bash Street Kids and grew into the childlike logic of Latin, till at last I was charmed, not by a threat, but a promise, when the priest stood over a coffin and repeated the formula

> *Remember man that thou art dust*
> *And unto dust you shall return*

which meant that everybody was born into a future where what was separate and incommunicable now would be united for a time, before it was sifted out again from the earth or the rain into new combinations, separate once again, separate bodies, separate lives. The afterlife, in other words: the place where we are now.

Finally, it came to me that I could, in fact, move, and I managed to struggle to my feet. I was sodden. The voice was still talking and, as I rose, it rose with me, repeating the same word several more times, then mutating slowly into something else, till it began to sound like the Walter de la Mare poem, 'The Listeners'. I listened:

> *'Is there anybody there?' said the Traveller,*
> *Knocking on the moonlit door –*

I walked through to the sitting room and it was as if the voice was guiding me, leading me into this space warmed with sunlight and much larger than it usually seemed, larger and touched here and there with movement, like birds fluttering at the edges of my vision. For a minute or more, I was sure they were inside the room. Everything was so bright. I followed the voice to the middle of the room, to where the light was strongest, then I stopped. The voice was gone and, in the quiet that ensued, I heard a sound. The sound of a cup being set carefully on a table, perhaps. A cup, or a bowl. A sound that would normally go unnoticed.

I looked towards the sound and I saw, then, that there was someone in the kitchen. He was standing at the kitchen window, looking out over the roofs and chimneys towards the sea: a man of around forty, in a baggy charcoal-grey cardigan and a black shirt. He looked like a priest. He wasn't an apparition, or a ghost, I knew that. He was a solid presence, yet it seemed to me that he was only just present and that it was costing him an immense effort just to be there – and then he turned and I could see that the face was sliding, coming apart and losing form, because he couldn't maintain that effort, and it was almost a scream that was forming, only it wasn't even that, because a scream would have taken more energy than he had left. A moment later, he came to pieces utterly, a man decaying in mid-air – yet even as he decayed, he was beginning again, a few feet away, a solid presence and, as he did, I came to the realisation – not in some logical way, not verbally, as it were, but in the hollow of my chest and the marrow of my bones – that my phantoms, or demons, or hauntings, or whatever they might be, those voices and shadows and shifting presences that had heretofore been fleeting and elusive, were now moving into a new phase, a phase, one might say, of *permanent residence* –

– and that was when I ran. I grabbed my bags and ran about the flat throwing clothes and books and videos into them more or less at random, while that screaming man evaporated and reappeared and evaporated again. Finally, when the bag was full, I hurried out and found my car. It was late in the afternoon and the sun was already going down, which seemed odd, because it had been so sunny, just a few minutes before, but I didn't stop to think about it. I got into the car and started the engine, still fairly far gone in my head, but more or less able to function: a man in a car, driving in the evening light, and then in darkness, on a rainy motorway, passing through zones of light and dark, woodland and flatland and office malls suspended in pools of gorgeous light strung along the road all the way to Surrey, music on the tape deck, music in my head, every detail printed on my retina as it flashed by, printed then replaced as it all flowed on, replaced but not lost, laid down in folds of cell and nerve, for as long as this flesh and this mind persisted. I was by no means sane, or normal, but for the time being I was able to cope with being neither of those things, and that was enough. The term for what I had just begun to experience is usually breakdown, but that wasn't how it felt then, and it's not how I think of it now. A breakdown is all negatives, a systems failure, a blown fuse, a torn gasket – but the nights I had just endured, along with every other wild night that I ever vanished into, strike me now as clumsy and unschooled attempts to go on living as a real person – by which I mean, to retain the hope and the privilege of a life that might be my own, and not something foisted on me by circumstances and the expectations of others. To be whole – or rather, to continue in the pursuit of wholeness. To be not-normal after all. As I drove I put an Ali Akbar Khan tape on the cassette player and went gliding down the M6, new rain fuzzing the windscreen, the lights of the world all around me, beautiful, because every light is beautiful in the dark: silver, gold, cherry red, far greens, splashes of crimson and blue in the night. I was probably the most dangerous driver on the roads that night, but it didn't feel like that as the music drove me along, all energy and the sense that I was about to call time on a lie.

Hearing voices. Seeing things. It's not like it is in the movies – or it wasn't for me, anyway. What you hear is definitely a voice, but it doesn't tell you what to do, Son of Sam style – on the contrary, it's usually elliptical, even secretive, and though it can be anything from a whisper to a howl, it's almost never conversational. It's not privileged information, so to speak. Nothing is shared. The same goes for things seen. They happen most often at the corners of vision, or in the field but not quite of it, there's always something other about it, always that *certain slant of light* sensation. Or almost always. That night was different, though. That night, I could feel the world around me being unpicked and remade as I drove. Everything was changing, the world I knew was decaying and at the same instant, exactly at the moment it was fading away, it was being brought back into being, the same but different, lit by a new

256

logic, told by a different voice. Yet, all the time, even as this total *dérèglement* was unfolding around me, I recall that I wasn't so much afraid as totally and unbearably *fascinated* by it all. Fascinated in the old and most powerful sense. The desperate fascination of *amour fou,* or religious ecstasy. Not something you want to be dealing with on the M6, in traffic.

It took me a long time to get home. I kept stopping off at services just to get out and breathe the night air. I think I was hoping the journey would never end and I would go on driving forever. When I finally reached Bramley, it was almost dawn, but no one was about. I could have been the last person in the world, or the first, as I pulled into my own street and switched off the music. I knew this street, and this was the time of day when I knew it best, the only time I really felt that I belonged there, alone before first light, just me and the cats and the birdsong, but it didn't feel like home at all now and, when I reached the door of my own house, I couldn't go in. I stood for a long time with the key in my hand, but it felt wrong, as if I were about to commit a burglary, or maybe a confidence trick, passing myself off as the rightful occupant of a place in which I was now a stranger. After driving for hours, driving and stopping and starting again, thinking I was on my way home, I couldn't go into my own house, because I wasn't home after all, and I eventually put the key back in my pocket and went around to the back, where the garden furniture was set out in the usual places on the patio: a green cast-iron table and chairs, damp from the night, surrounded by scruffy Penjing trees in the pots I had chosen so carefully to set them off, Southern beech and Japanese larch and hornbeams. I sat down, my back to the house, looking out across the garden towards the canal spur at the far end. Light was seeping in through the plum trees and the ivy, the shadows were turning from black to charcoal, the colours were returning, one by one, yellow, green, blue, red. There's an old haiku poem about standing in the garden at evening, watching the colours fade one by one, first the blues and reds, then the greens and finally the yellows and whites – and this was the opposite process, everything returning from the dark, renewed, freshened, like the blocks of pigment in a child's paintbox, coming to life with the merest touch of a wet brush. That was how it felt: new, strange, not mine, something I had still to see for itself – and I was strange too, suddenly aware of how dull my habitat had become, and how colourless I was in my grave routine, trying to blend in. How, in spite of my good intentions, the dullness and the routine hadn't saved me. I had told myself, when I first landed in the suburbs, that I wanted to start a new life but, as I sat on that damp garden chair in the first light of morning, a neighbour stirring here, an upstairs light coming on elsewhere, I realised that I'd never intended to change – that, in fact, I'd always believed that a person can't change in any meaningful way, because what he is – *what*, not *who* – is a question of the soul, and the soul is murky and deep-rooted and wet, not some ethereal, winged thing, but the dank mud where the lotus is anchored, the mud and the silty water and the spreading of the leaves and, yes, the flower opening into the light, but all of it together, and not one good thing, not the higher thing, not the thing that can be cleansed or perfected. A banal thought, perhaps, and it is banal *as a thought*, but as an experience it isn't banal at all, it's just the simplicity of recognition. *Normal* had never held any real attraction for me – and I couldn't see how it would hold any real attraction for anybody. Certainly, as an alternative to *mad*, it barely passed muster.

It was light now. A soft grey, then blue across the meadow

at the end of the garden, and people were up and about all around me, getting ready for work or school, having breakfast, talking, thinking about what the day would bring or discarding the husk of the night's dreaming, while the radio delivered the usual schedule of voices and jingles. Soon, my neighbours would be emerging, with satchels and briefcases, off to work or school. I stood up quickly and walked to the end of the garden where a flight of railway sleepers led down to the edge of the canal spur. I didn't want to be seen. I felt too exposed, a body so raw that the lining showed, the gristle and nerve and tatters of soul peeking through – but I was ashamed too, now that I was back, because I had been lying for years and I hadn't even had the courtesy to admit as much. I had pretended for all that time that I was other than I was, going among these people like a stranger who turns up at a funeral and passes himself off as an old friend of the deceased. I was ashamed, not embarrassed – which meant that, even now, I was still on my own. I could acknowledge the disrespect for these neighbours in my sham existence, but I didn't really feel guilty, and I didn't feel embarrassed, I felt ashamed. I wanted to be invisible, not because I felt I had shown my neighbours a rarefied and subtle form of contempt, but because I was ashamed, and I didn't want anybody else intruding upon what was essentially a private moment. I wasn't having a change of heart, and I wasn't beginning the long journey back to community and acceptance and maturity that I might have travelled had I been a character in a novel. On the contrary: on that first morning of the remainder of my life, and on the days that followed, I was more alone than I had ever been, more alone, more separate, and – now, finally – indifferent enough that I wouldn't even bother to pretend any more. It was the end of my time in the suburbs. I had tried to be normal, and I had failed – not because I hadn't tried hard enough, but because, unlike madness, *normal* was a lie.

Over the next few weeks, while I slowly detached myself from my surroundings and began to move away, first in spirit, then physically, I was like a man who wakes up in a hologram and gradually realises that, though the figures moving around him might be real somewhere, they are phantoms in the space he occupies. Everyone I met seemed monochrome and remote, like people I recognised from somewhere, but didn't actually know: the other guests at a party I hadn't wanted to attend, say, or a group of tourists in some provincial art gallery, following an umbrella from the minor Utrillo to the Atkinson Grimshaw. They were spectres, phantoms – and no matter what they did, I was never entirely convinced that they were actually there. Yet, at the same time, even I could see that my neighbours and colleagues hadn't changed. I could see that they were as real as they had always been, and even though it appeared to my eyes that the normal life they were leading was just an elaborate pretence, I could also see that, whenever two or three were gathered together, whether for business or pleasure, *I* was the only phantom in the room.

THE EPILOGUE

Three in the morning. In Norwegian: *ulvetimen*; in Swedish, *vargtimen*. The hour of the wolf. This is the hour when people are most likely to die, the hour when the mad go all the way down to hell, the hour when the body is at its weakest and most vulnerable. It's winter, the cold as hard as a knife, the snow perfect and unmarked on the fields around this house where I now live, almost perfectly sane, with a road into the after-life running right past my front door. This is my favourite time of the day and of the year: on any winter's night, I can sit up till this wolf hour, when the walls are mercifully silent and everyone else is asleep, and I feel utterly connected to the world – to the land, to the stars over my roof, to the wind that blows the snow off the fields and powders it across the road – and sometimes, often, I turn off all the lights and sit listening to the silence, waiting to hear what else might come. I really am quite sane now, but I have to do this from time to time, to flirt with the night, or maybe to test myself – and still, no matter how dark it is, no matter how far away I am from the others sleeping around me, nothing arrives from the darkness that doesn't belong there. The wind. A night bird. Some jitter or creak in the plumbing. Everything is just as it should be, everything is just so, founded in the solid matter-of-fact – and yet, even though it's all quite explicable, it still

261

feels miraculous. It still feels unlikely. The mystery isn't how things are in the world, Wittgenstein says, it's the fact that there is a world at all. Words to that effect. And perhaps, for all those years, that was the real cause of my supposed madness. In the days when I was crazy, on the days when I was clinically insane, I just couldn't take that given world for granted. I couldn't filter enough of it out, it was just too much to take in. It flooded me: an intolerable contradiction, like flight.

It's a long time since I wanted to be normal. I've been there, and they wouldn't even sell me the T-shirt. Now, I have no desire to be sane, partly because it's not in my nature but, mostly, because the generally accepted definition of sane is hideously inadequate. If Surbiton – real or imaginary – is sanity, then I have no desire to be sane. I have no desire to be mad either, but I don't regret having *been* mad, once upon a time. The world is not too much for me, these days, but it's more than enough – and *these days*, after long consideration, I have begun to think that there might be an alternative to the twin poles of mad and sane, a discipline somewhat like flying, or vanishing. On any night of the year, but especially in the deep midwinter, when the land is silent and still, I can sit up alone, listening, watching, aware of the road to the afterlife running past the window, and occasionally, for a minute or two and sometimes longer, I can feel like some old-time aviator, rising high in a bright thermal, floating in thin air, guided by the crudest and least trustworthy of navigation systems, but touched with the holy and unexpected blessing of the flyer, which is to be and not be at exactly the same moment, to be always there, in the eye of gravity's needle and, at the same time, to be always on the point of vanishing. Moment by moment, breath by breath, into the afterlife.

Incipit vita nova.